An

An Introduction to
Philosophy

Jon Nuttall

polity

First published in 2002 by Polity Press in association with Blackwell Publishing Ltd

Reprinted 2003

Editorial office:
Polity Press
65 Bridge Street
Cambridge CB2 1UR, UK

Marketing and production:
Blackwell Publishing Ltd
108 Cowley Road
Oxford OX4 1JF, UK

Published in the USA by
Blackwell Publishing Inc.
350 Main Street
Malden, MA 02148, USA

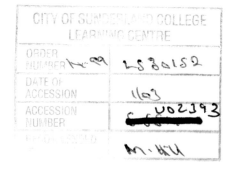

A catalogue record for this book is available from the British Library.

Library of Congress Cataloging-in-Publication Data
Nuttall, Jon.
  An introduction to philosophy / by Jon Nuttall.
    p. cm.
  Includes bibliographical references (p. 000) and index.
  ISBN 0-7456-1662-3 — ISBN 0-7456-1663-1 (pbk.)
  1. Philosophy—Introductions. I. Title.
  BD21 .N88 2002
  100—dc21
                                    2001007564

Typeset in 10.5 on 12.5pt Times
by Graphicraft Limited, Hong Kong
Printed in Great Britain by MPG Books Ltd, Bodmin, Cornwall

This book is printed on acid-free paper.

For information on polity, please visit our website: http://www.polity.co.uk

Contents

Detailed Chapter Contents

1 The Nature of Philosophy

2 The Start of Modern Philosophy: Descartes' *Meditations*

3   Perception and Reality

4 Knowledge, Belief and Logic

5   Space, Time, Causality and Substance

6   The Mind

7 God

8 Morality

9   Political Issues

Philosophers Past and Present

The following philosophers, in chronological order (with dates) are mentioned in the body of the text.

Ancient

Socrates (470–399 BC), Zeno (*c*.470 BC), Plato (428–347 BC), Aristotle (384–322 BC)

Medieval

St Anselm (1033–1109), Roger Bacon (1220–1292), St Aquinas (1224–1274), William of Ockham (1285–1347)

Modern

Seventeenth century

Thomas Hobbes (1588–1679), René Descartes (1596–1650), Robert Boyle (1627–1691), John Locke (1632–1704), Isaac Newton (1642–1727), Gottfried Wilhelm Leibniz (1646–1716), George Berkeley (1685–1753), François-Marie Arouet de Voltaire (1694–1778)

Eighteenth century

David Hume (1711–1776), Jean-Jacques Rousseau (1712–1778), Immanuel Kant (1724–1802), Jeremy Bentham (1748–1832), Pierre Simon Laplace (1749–1827), Arthur Schopenhauer (1788–1860)

Nineteenth century

John Stuart Mill (1806–1873), Gottlob Frege (1848–1925), Bertrand Russell (1872–1970), Albert Einstein (1879–1955), Ludwig Wittgenstein (1889–1951)

Twentieth century (authors in alphabetical order)

Alfred Ayer (1910–1989), Donald Davidson (1917–), Daniel Dennett (1942–), Peter Geach (1919–), Nelson Goodman (1906–1998), Carl Hempel (1905–1997), Saul Kripke (1940–), Thomas Kuhn (1922–1996), John Mackie (1917–1981), Robert Nozick (1938–2002), Karl Popper (1902–1994), Willard Quine (1908–2000), John Rawls (1921–), Richard Rorty (1931–), John Searle (1932–), Richard Swinburne (1934–), Alan Turing (1912–1954).

Acknowledgements

I would like to thank Andrea Christofidou and Bob Frazier for helpful suggestions on drafts of the earlier chapters. I would also like to thank an anonymous reader for his/her efforts with earlier drafts of the manuscript, supplying numerous and detailed comments, criticisms and helpful suggestions, which ensured that at least some errors were avoided. I am grateful to Rebecca Harkin, who provided support and encouragement.

1 The Nature of Philosophy

- What is philosophy?
- Some philosophical questions
- What sort of knowledge can philosophy yield?
- Three main areas of philosophy
- An explanation of the term 'metaphysics'
- About the rest of this book
- Summary

What is philosophy?

Two answers are frequently given to the question 'What is philosophy?' One is that philosophy is an activity rather than a subject – in other words, you *do* philosophy rather than learn about it. The other is that philosophy is largely a matter of conceptual analysis – it is thinking about thinking. Both these suggestions contain more than a germ of truth but are unsatisfactory, giving little or no idea of the content of philosophy. It is all very well to say 'Philosophize' or 'Analyse concepts', but philosophize about what and in what sorts of ways; analyse what concepts and how? The most direct way of seeing what philosophy is about is to look at the sorts of questions that philosophers think are important and how they go about answering them.

What is common to all such questions is that they are questions that can be answered only by reasoning. In other disciplines, there are various ways of finding out answers to questions – such as by studying nature or ancient manuscripts, by conducting experiments or surveys, by building a piece of apparatus or a model or by running a simulation on a computer. By and large, these are what can be termed 'empirical investigations'. The outcomes of these investigations – new discoveries, new data – will often be relevant to philosophy, but empirical invest-igations cannot provide the answers to philosophical questions.

Some philosophical questions

Let us first look at the sorts of questions philosophers have considered and then see how they have tried to answer them:

- Do our senses, of sight, touch, hearing, taste and smell, present us with a true picture of the world around us?
- Does every event have a cause2? If every event does have a cause, is this incompatible with being able to make free choices?
- We each have a body of flesh and bones, and we also have a mind; are minds separable from bodies (could we have minds without bodies)?; do minds and bodies interact and, if so, how?
- We observe certain patterns and regularities in the world around us. On the basis of such, essentially limited, experiences we propose laws of nature. These laws we take to be universal, applying to the totality of objects existing in the infinity of space and the eternity of time. Indeed, perhaps we take it that our laws apply beyond this, to possible objects in parallel universes. What can justify such claims?
- When we judge that someone has done something morally good (or bad), are we doing any more than expressing our own personal views? Can morality be anything other than subjective?
- Is it the duty of government to try to redress the imbalance of wealth within society or does any government lack the legitimacy to do this, so such attempts at redistribution are morally equival-ent to slave labour?

Some initial thoughts on these questions

The reason we cannot answer these questions by making observa-tions or doing experiments differs in each case. For example, if we doubt our senses, what are we going to check them against? We have developed all sorts of instruments capable of making more precise and more sensitive measurements than our senses, but we rely on our senses to read these instruments. In any case, if we doubt whether our senses give sufficient evidence that objects really exist, then we must doubt the existence of the instruments themselves. When we ask whether all events have causes, we can produce examples of events that do have a cause (although philosophers have questioned even this) but we cannot observe that *every* event has a cause. And if it really is the case that every event has a cause, what experiments could be conducted to show this to be compatible with free will? Our actions may appear to be free, but if this feeling of freedom were an illusion, how would we ever find out?

So far, I have suggested ways in which the questions cannot be answered. Yet, what may be worrying those new to philosophy is how we are going to make a start at producing answers. First, and this is why philosophy has been described as conceptual analysis, we can try to clarify what we mean by the terms used. When we say that one event causes another, do we mean that the cause has some sort of power over the effect? What about 'an act of free will'? Is this an act that is not affected by the events that precede it?

One of the first things we discover in philosophy is the way in which questions that at first sight look quite separate have a bearing on each other. For example, think how we might explore what is meant by 'cause'. Perhaps we will begin by considering what looks like a straightforward example, such as the sequence of events when one billiard ball collides with another. What do we actually observe in such cases? Do we literally see one event causing the next or do we see nothing more than a succession of events? This takes us back to the question with which we started: what can the senses tell us about the world? As well as seeing billiard balls, do we also see causes? If we do not literally *see* a cause, how do we know about it? Do we infer it? If it is a matter of inference, is such an inference justified?

Consider the question about thoughts and bodies. The scientific theories of Newton encouraged a picture of the universe as a system of particles in constant motion, in which the idea that every event has a cause was a natural one. But where do minds fit into such a universe? Are minds also part of the pattern of cause and effect? Do mental events have causes and effects? And, if so, are these causes and effects restricted to other mental events or can they extend to physical events? If mental interactions cannot be the same as physical interactions, what sort of interactions are they?

It may be less obvious that questions about moral judgements or political duties relate to questions about causation or the reliability of our senses, but there are connections. If every action is caused, and if this is incompatible with free will, where does this leave moral judgements? If we treat human actions as events, like any other sort of event, do they become inappropriate objects of moral judgement? Further, making a moral judgement is itself an event, caused by preceding events; does this mean that a moral judgement is simply another fact? Even if moral judgements are evaluations, the ability to make correct evaluations depends upon knowing some facts. But how do we find out the facts? Is our knowledge based on what we see, hear, touch, etc.? If so, then anything which casts doubt on the ability of our senses to give us knowledge of the world is liable to throw doubt on our ability to make moral, and political, judgements.

The last two of our original set of questions also give rise to further questions. If moral judgements are not simply the expression of personal opinion, then what are they and what are they based upon? How do we discover what is good or what our duty is? Do we discover these things through some sort of moral sense (analogous to the way in which we find out about objects in the world by using our senses of sight, hearing, etc.), through a process of reasoning, or in some other way?

Asking a philosophical question invariably leads to other philosophical questions. To add to the difficulties, there is no solid foundation on which to start building answers. Philosophy commonly questions beliefs that we usually take for granted. Philosophy may even try to question the process of reasoning itself. It is hard to begin to answer a question when nothing can be taken for granted. Perhaps this also adds to the excitement of philosophy!

What sort of knowledge can philosophy yield?

If philosophical questions can be answered only by reasoning, can philosophy be pursued independently of a study of the world? Historically, this has not been the case – many of the philosophers of the past were not engaged purely, or even in some cases primarily, in philosophy. Scientific discoveries trigger philosophical speculation, while theoretical confusion in science creates the demand for philosophical analyses.

That such a relationship exists between science and philosophy is a contingent matter. This observation might provoke a deeper question: is it possible to arrive at knowledge without relying on our senses? The knowledge we gain from experience is called 'empirical knowledge'. Knowledge that is independent of sense experience is termed '*a priori* knowledge'. The knowledge that black is black is *a priori* knowledge; it can be had independently of our senses telling us what things are black or even of the experience of anything black. Our senses tell us that grass is green, but we do not have to observe anything to know that black is black. (Whether we could understand the sentence that expresses the truth that black is black without experience of the world is a separate matter.) Are other sorts of *a priori* knowledge possible? If the answer is 'yes', we would look to philosophy to provide this knowledge.

Three main areas of philosophy

There are many ways of dividing up the subject areas of philosophy. None of them is entirely satisfactory, since there will always be topics that cut across or fail to fit neatly into the divisions. None the less, we begin to get a better idea of the scope of philosophy by considering the following three broad areas.

First, metaphysics. This area of philosophy deals with the ultimate nature of reality. Is the everyday world real? If not, what is the nature of the reality that lies beneath the world of appearances? What is the nature of the space–time framework within which we and the objects around us appear to exist? Given that something exists, why that and not something else? Why that and not nothing? Why is there change? How can there also be permanence through change? Do the things that exist fall into different types, such as minds and bodies? If there are minds, are there disembodied minds? Is there a God?

Second, epistemology. Here the concern is with whether and how knowledge of reality is possible. What are the limits to our knowledge? Can we rely upon sense perception to tell us what the world is really like? Is there an unknowable reality lying behind appearances? Does science give us knowledge of a deeper reality? Does science give us knowledge at all? Can our powers of reasoning give us knowledge? Can our powers of reasoning at least correct errors that might arise from the senses? Are there other sources of knowledge, for example, ones that would enable us to perceive values or know the true nature of God?

Third, the areas of moral and political philosophy. These areas deal with how we conduct ourselves within the world. What is there, if anything, to guide our conduct? Should we follow our feelings? Can our reason tell us what is right and wrong? Can reason tell us what political institutions to set up? Do we have obligations to the political institutions that exist in the society in which we find ourselves? Are the only values the ones that we, as individuals, create for ourselves?

There are, of course, other ways of dividing up the subject. (The above scheme is based on one suggested by Anthony Quinton in the *Oxford Companion to Philosophy*.) As we shall see in a moment, some schemes include epistemology as a part of metaphysics. Some separate out moral and political philosophy. Logic will often appear as a separate branch of philosophy. A more detailed analysis would produce many more branches of philosophy, some of which are highly specialized. The above is not intended to define philosophy but simply to give a broad picture that can be refined at a later date.

The order in which the three areas have been set out above might suggest an order of priority: what there is, what we can know about it and what we do about it. A moment's reflection will show this to be too simple. For example, how can we tackle the questions as to what there is without first investigating the limits of our knowledge? Are we not in danger of making grandiose claims about ultimate reality only to discover that we have no way of knowing such ultimate reality, not even whether it exists? Coming from the other direction, we may feel that moral and political questions are the ones that should be tackled first since they are the most urgent. We can postpone consideration of the ultimate reality, whereas we cannot postpone a decision about someone with a terminal illness pleading to be released from suffering. Even so, we might feel that our answers to such questions can be no more than provisional. They would have to be revised if we were convinced by arguments showing that values are subjective or that there is a God (when previously we thought values were objective or that God did not exist). The best we can say is that the three areas are interdependent and the answers we obtain to questions in one area will affect answers to questions in the other areas.

An explanation of the term 'metaphysics'

'Meta'-activities

A little more needs to be said about the term 'metaphysics'. The prefix 'meta' has the meaning of 'after' or 'behind' and is often used in philosophy to indicate what is referred to as a second-order activity

– an activity which, in general terms, looks at the framework within which a first-order activity takes place. Mathematics, for example, involves proofs of one sort or another; meta-mathematics, on the other hand, involves the study of formalized logical systems that underpin any proof. Similarly, while ethics deals with what is right and wrong, meta-ethics deals with what is meant by 'right' and 'wrong'. A 'meta' subject operates at a higher level of abstraction and generality than the subject itself.

From these considerations, the term 'metaphysics' seems an appropriate one. Whereas physics (along with the other sciences) deals with the interactions between objects in the world around us, metaphysics deals with more general questions, such as why there is something rather than nothing, whether causation is a necessary connection, and so on. The term 'metaphysical' has also been used for very general, all-encompassing systems that purport to describe a reality that is beyond or that transcends everyday experience. Such transcendental (or, more accurately, transcendent) systems have been criticized for making claims to knowledge when, according to the critics, no such knowledge is possible.

There is a much more mundane account of the meaning of 'metaphysics'. 'Metaphysics' was the title given in the Middle Ages to a set of lecture notes by Aristotle. Aristotle divided Science (or knowledge) into two branches, Theoretical and Practical. Theoretical Science was further subdivided into Mathematics, Physics, and what Aristotle termed the First Philosophy. A later editor of these notes placed the section on the First Philosophy after the section on Physics, and this section became known as the 'Metaphysics' simply because it came after Physics. This name then became transferred to the subject matter of the lecture notes.

In Aristotle, metaphysics encompassed the two broad areas of ontology and epistemology. Ontology deals with general issues relating to existence, including the existence of God, and to the processes of change, causation, etc. Epistemology is concerned with knowledge: the structure of knowledge, its origins, the attainability of knowledge and the limitations placed on it. Epistemology has already been described as one of the three main branches of philosophy, standing alongside and distinct from metaphysics. What is left, when epistemology is removed from metaphysics, is a number of different topics, often connected only tenuously. Thus, while the area of epistemology is clearly defined, metaphysics is much more of a ragbag of topics.

When a greater emphasis came to be placed on epistemological issues, metaphysical discussions seemed to some philosophers to be too divorced from a knowable reality. Thus the term 'metaphysical' acquired derogatory connotations. Hume, for example, suggests that we commit works of metaphysics to the flames. More recently, metaphysical claims have been taken to be nonsense – because they are not verifiable, they were thought to lack meaning altogether. Wittgenstein, in the *Philosophical Investigations*, argues that philosophers are misled into thinking that they have asked meaningful questions and produced meaningful answers when they have used words outside their normal context, where they become meaningless. He saw his task as removing this source of philosophical confusion by bringing 'words back from their metaphysical to their everyday use' (paragraph 116). Despite these criticisms, both Hume and Wittgenstein dealt with metaphysical questions, and some of the topics within metaphysics are among the most interesting and most profound in philosophy.

About the rest of this book

The following eight chapters attempt to cover some of the main themes in the above three areas. Philosophy has a long history, and philosophers of the past are still read for the contributions they make in identifying, formulating and attempting to answer philosophical questions. Any introduction to philosophy should try to give the reader a feel for this historical dimension. This is not an exercise in the history of ideas, since philosophers of the past are contributors to contemporary debates.

The history of philosophy goes back at least two and a half thousand years (although philosophizing surely goes back much further) and, since it would be impossible to do justice to even the main figures in this history, coverage of this kind has not been attempted. Although earlier philosophers do get a mention, the next chapter looks at the work of a particular philosopher of the seventeenth century. In a relatively short work, Descartes introduces many of the themes that were to be central to philosophy for the next three and a half centuries.

The historical emphasis continues in chapters 3 and 4, which develop the epistemological issues raised by Descartes. Chapter 3 deals with perception and what it can tell us about the world. Chapter 4 broadens the discussion to look at knowledge. Descartes raises the problem of scepticism in an acute form and thinks that he solves it. The prevailing view is that he has not, and Descartes' successors respond in various ways to the challenge of scepticism.

Chapters 5, 6 and 7 introduce various metaphysical issues: space, time, substance and causality; minds and mental attributes; and finally the nature and existence of God. Although the questions considered are metaphysical ones, they serve as introductions to a number of other subdivisions in philosophy. These include the philosophy of science (also encountered in chapter 4) and in particular the philosophy of physics; the philosophy of mind; philosophical logic (again, also encountered in previous chapters); and the philosophy of religion.

The final two chapters, chapters 8 and 9, deal with those branches of philosophy relating to the conduct of life, in particular moral philosophy and political philosophy.

Each chapter has a short introduction, to put the topics covered into context, a summary of the main results and some of the questions raised or suggested, which you might like to think about further. There is also a guide to further reading at the end of the book, with entries for each chapter. This guide does not pretend to be complete or even extensive. The problem for the beginner in philosophy is not that of finding material on a particular subject but of trying to limit this material to something that is manageable. The recommendations made should be accessible in terms of content and they should be easy to get hold of (even without ready access to a university library); in many cases, I have found them interesting and thought-provoking. Most will have their own bibliographies to suggest further reading.

Chapters 2 to 9 appear here in the order in which they were written, although this is not the order in which they have to be read. For those with little or no prior knowledge of philosophy, it is probably a good idea to begin with chapter 2. To the extent that it is possible to deal with philosophical issues in isolation, the chapters are self-contained, but there are invariably cross-references between topics. Whatever the order in which chapters are tackled, learning about philosophy is like putting together the pieces of a jigsaw puzzle. There is no best order in which the pieces should be fitted together, but the more pieces that are joined together, the clearer the picture becomes – always assuming that they have been put together correctly.

Summary

- There are two short answers to the question 'what is philosophy?':
  it is an activity and it is conceptual analysis or thinking about
  thinking. A look at a range of philosophical questions shows the
  nature of the subject more clearly.
- Philosophy can be divided into three main areas: metaphysics,
  dealing with the nature of the world at the most abstract level;
  epistemology, dealing with whether or not we can have knowledge
  of this world; and moral and political philosophy, dealing with the
  questions of conduct within the world.

2 The Start of Modern Philosophy: Descartes' *Meditations*

Introduction

The beginnings of modern philosophy can be found in the work of the French philosopher René Descartes (1596–1650). This chapter embarks on an exposition of the claims he makes and the arguments he puts forward in support of them.

It is fair to say that the questions Descartes raised and the particular form he gave them are as important as his answers. He treated seriously the problem of scepticism, which casts doubt on our ability to acquire knowledge, and tried to devise a method by which knowledge may be attained and the sceptic foiled. He considered the nature of perception and the role it plays in the acquisition of knowledge. He gave an account of the nature of the self and, in doing so, raised questions about personal identity, freedom of the will, the nature of mind and matter and the interactions between them. He also considered the nature of God and attempted to prove his existence.

Many of these different concerns have given rise to distinct branches of philosophy. Thus, as well as providing an introduction to a key figure in philosophy, the aim of this chapter is to introduce some of the themes that will be developed in succeeding chapters. An examination of Descartes' masterpiece, *Meditations on First Philosophy*, should not, however, be thought of simply as an exercise in the history of philosophy. Descartes' *Meditations* should be read for the clarity and conciseness with which he introduces philosophical problems. An understanding gained here will provide the context for much of what follows.

Background to Descartes' *Meditations*

Contemporary philosophical problems have their roots in the works of the great philosophers of the past, going back to the Greek philosophers Plato (*c.*428–347 BC) and Aristotle (384–322 BC), in the fourth century BC, and beyond. Although in some ways an over-simplification, modern philosophy can be seen as starting with René Descartes, born in 1596, who published *Meditations on First Philo-sophy* in 1641. A study of this short but influential masterpiece will introduce many, although by no means all, of the issues explored in subsequent chapters. Before embarking on the *Meditations*, it will be helpful to place Descartes' work in context.

The context was scholasticism, which had developed in Europe during the latter period of the Middle Ages, fired by the rediscovery of the works of Aristotle. Scholastic philosophy was the object of increasing criticism from many of Descartes' contemporaries. The criticism of scholasticism went hand in hand with attempts to lay down the founda-tions of what we now refer to as science. It involved a rejection of the scholastic belief that knowledge rested on the authority of the ancient philosophers, primarily Aristotle. Much earlier, Bacon (1220–1292), although deeply influenced by Aristotle, had claimed that the way to find out about the world is through observation and experiment. Knowledge obtained in this way, that is, 'empirical knowledge', thus rests on evidence from the senses. While recognizing the importance of observation in the pursuit of knowledge, for Descartes knowledge could be obtained only through reason; the senses could not provide the foundation for knowledge since they were too vulnerable to sceptical doubt. Descartes' aim was to establish methods for obtaining knowledge and, as part of this, to set out a clear criterion for knowledge.

From our early twenty-first-century perspective, the sceptical question 'How can we know what the world is really like?' might seem spurious. Who can now seriously doubt whether scientific knowledge is possible when surrounded by the fruits of such knowledge? Descartes, however, was writing at a time when modern science was in its infancy. The familiar school science subjects of physics, chemistry and biology did not even exist as separate areas of enquiries having distinctive methodologies; the significant discoveries within these disciplines still lay in the future. For Descartes, and others of his time, the question as to the possibility of scientific knowledge was still an open one. Descartes' philosophical and mathematical work was to make an important contribution to the answer.

Although we may feel that the possibility of scientific knowledge is firmly established, Descartes is generally considered to have failed in his attempt to answer the sceptic. One of the reasons he fails is that he sets a very exacting criterion for knowledge. Rather than silencing the sceptic he makes the sceptic's position appear unassailable. It might seem a mark of singular incompetence that Descartes managed to achieve the opposite of what he was attempting, and hence difficult to see why he is still studied. However, this misunderstands both the nature of philosophy and Descartes' immense contribution to it. In order to silence the sceptic it is not enough that Descartes is able to better those of his contemporaries who maintain a sceptical position. What Descartes has to do is to show that, no matter how well the sceptic argues the case, the arguments against scepticism are stronger. Thus Descartes' first task is to assess the threat posed by scepticism by making the case for scepticism as strong as possible. If this case can be overcome then the sceptical threat to knowledge has been removed.

It is a mark of Descartes' greatness that the problem he failed to solve has exercised many philosophers over the intervening centuries.

Descartes not only posed the problem in a particularly clear form. With his test for true knowledge, he also set restrictions on the form that an answer should take. Despite the spectacular progress of scientific knowledge over the last 350 years and the technological spin-offs that have transformed our lives, we still face the possibility that our scientific knowledge may be no more than a set of fortuitous beliefs. Unless, that is, we can complete the work that Descartes started.

Although Descartes' project is directed at the attainment of knowledge, he raises other questions that also continue to stimulate debate. For example, what do our senses tell us? What is the relationship between the appearances presented by our senses and the objects as they really are? What, in essence, are we? What is the relation between the mental and the physical? How do mind and body interact?

The above helps explain the importance of Descartes' enquiries but does not show why his works are of more than historical interest. That contemporary philosophical questions were first raised by Descartes is not enough – we do not think it necessary for someone interested in physics to study the works of Newton. Contemporary textbooks that give an account of Newton's theories do not quote from Newton's works. Why then are the 'undigested' works of the great philosophers of the past part of the contemporary debate? The answer must be that it is not only Descartes' ideas that are important but also the way he expresses these ideas. Although the concerns of each age colour a philosophical discussion and add new twists to it, a historical perspective on a philosophical problem helps one to appreciate the ramifications and nuances of the contemporary debate. Much philosophical discussion is conducted using words rich with meaning, and a historical perspective will start to flesh out these meanings.

An overview of the *Meditations*

If one expects a philosophical masterpiece to be long and complex, then Descartes' *Meditations* (published when he was forty-five years old) does not fit this image. It is short and easy to read, being relatively free of jargon and technical terms! Leaving out the preface and synopsis, it is under sixty pages, with around 30,000 words. Even so, those not used to reading philosophy may initially find the going quite hard. It may also come as a surprise to see, for example, the word 'God' appearing among the titles of the meditations. It may even be off-putting. Descartes thinks that he needs to prove the existence of God in order to refute the sceptic – which is one of the aspects of Descartes' argument philosophers have found unsatisfactory. However, Descartes is not trying to instil a religious belief in his readers. Descartes succeeds only if he manages to *prove* that God exists, and it is possible to decide this irrespective of whether or not one has faith or believes in God. It is reasonable to assume Descartes, like most people of the time, did believe in God, but belief in God is not the issue here, and the reader should not let his or her own religious beliefs prejudice a consideration of Descartes' argument. We need also to see what Descartes means by the term 'God' as well as whether he proves that such an entity exists.

Another term that needs to be explained is 'material thing'. Nowadays we are inclined to think of material things as possessions, and the term may even have pejorative moral or religious connotations. However, Descartes uses it here simply to mean a physical object or a physical body. Examples he gives of material things include the parts of his body (head, hands, feet, etc.) but also the sky, the earth, the sea. Not included are minds and God.

As with 'material thing', the problem with the term 'essence' is not so much its meaning as its philosophical significance. Within scholasticism, 'essence' is a technical term: to specify the essence of something is to specify the characteristics it must retain in order to stay the same thing. If, as Descartes argues, his own essence is self-awareness, then he ceases to be when unconscious. If the essence of being a physical object is to occupy space (and thus exclude other physical objects from occupying the same space) then anything that does not occupy space is not a physical object.

Outdoing the sceptic

Descartes resolved to consider his beliefs and reject any that were open to doubt. By doing this, he hoped to arrive eventually at a belief that was absolutely certain and so could be used as the foundation for his edifice of scientific knowledge. Descartes' conception of a body of knowledge would be familiar to anyone who was exposed to Euclidean geometry in their school mathematics classes (unfortunately, a decreasing number these days). Here, from a small number of 'obvious' geometric facts, theorems are deduced which are not at all obvious. (I have put scare quotes around 'obvious' because in philosophy this is a dangerous assumption. According to the theory of relativity, some of the geometric claims that have seemed obvious for 2000 years are false as descriptions of the world.)

Doubting the senses

What is the first thing that Descartes doubts? Perhaps surprisingly, it is the evidence of his senses – surprisingly because we tend to place a great deal of reliance on our senses: seeing, we say, is believing. Descartes acknowledges this: 'Whatever I have up till now accepted as most true, I have acquired either from the senses or through the senses' (*Meditations*, 12). He then adds: 'But from time to time I have found that the senses deceive, and it is prudent never to trust completely those who have deceived us even once.' The sort of example he gives here is of an object in the distance, say a tower, appearing to be round but turning out to be square, or a landscape looking bluer in the distance than it does when closer. These cases, however, do not seem to warrant the wholesale rejection of the evidence of his senses.

Dreaming

A further point occurs to him: in dreams we are convinced we are doing all sorts of things when, in fact, we are not. We may even be convinced we are awake and proving to ourselves we are not dreaming. This raises the possibility that all our conscious experience could be like or even part of a dream. Then all the things that seem to exist would no more exist than objects in a dream. Yet even in dreams there are some things which we should not doubt: 'arithmetic, geometry and other subjects of this kind, which deal only with the simplest and most general things, regardless of whether they really exist in nature or not, contain something certain and indubitable' (*Meditations*, 14).

The malicious demon

Descartes, however, has only begun to develop the sceptic's position. 'May I not simply go wrong every time I add two and three or count the sides of a square, or in some even simpler matter, if that is imaginable?' (*Meditations*, 14). Perhaps God has brought it about that mathematical statements appear to me to be true when they are not.

Descartes considers the argument that God (if he exists) is supremely good and so would not deceive Descartes, but rejects it because it claims too much. If God's goodness were to prevent Descartes being deceived, how does this square with the fact that Descartes is deceived on some occasions? On the other hand, if there is no God, Descartes has even less assurance that he can avoid error, since a less powerful creator makes imperfections in his creatures more rather than less likely.

At this stage in his argument, Descartes considers he has no rational justification for any of his beliefs. Until such time as he does, he resolves to suspend his beliefs by withholding assent from the propositions that express them. To assist him in this, Descartes supposes that he is constantly deceived by a malicious demon. We need to be clear that the supposition of a malicious demon is simply a device used by Descartes to break himself of the habit of thinking that the familiar objects which surround him really do exist. For as long as his beliefs, even though highly probable, remain open to doubt, Descartes is determined to treat them as false.

The basis of knowledge

The *cogito*

Descartes ends the first meditation resolving to doubt everything. Can there be no certainty? Does the possibility of an evil demon, out to deceive Descartes, leave him in the state of being certain of, and hence of knowing, nothing? In the second meditation, having, in the previous meditation, rejected a number of plausible candidates, Descartes finally arrives at something that is certain: that he exists. For if he tries to doubt that he exists, he must exist in order to doubt. Let the malignant spirit 'deceive me as much as he can, he will never bring it about that I am nothing so long as I think that I am something. So after considering everything very thoroughly, I must finally conclude that this proposition, *I am, I exist*, is necessarily true whenever it is put forward by me or conceived in my mind' (*Meditations*, 17). With this,

Descartes has reached bedrock. But how does Descartes move from this starting point, the knowledge that he himself exists, to knowledge of other things?

Clear and distinct perceptions

At the beginning of meditation III, Descartes reviews what it is that he knows. By now this includes not only that he exists but also that he is a conscious being who believes, doubts, etc. He then considers what distinguishes the beliefs about which he is certain from his other beliefs: 'In this first item of knowledge there is simply a clear and distinct perception of what I am asserting' (*Meditations*, 24). In order for this to count as knowledge it can never be the case that 'something which I perceived with such clarity and distinctness was false.' This suggests to him a general rule, 'whatever I perceive very clearly and distinctly is true', that gives him a way of deciding whether his perceptions are true. First, though, he wants to distinguish between different types of perceptions, by which he means thoughts that are present to his mind.

Ideas

Some of his thoughts are images of things, and these Descartes terms 'ideas'. Ideas can be considered as they are in themselves and, as long as Descartes does not think they represent anything outside himself, they cannot be false. He is liable to fall into error only if he thinks these ideas are actually taken from external things. The following example might clarify this. One can consider a photograph in two different ways. If one sees it as colours and shapes on a flat surface, there is nothing to be wrong about. It is when one sees this photograph as a photograph *of* something that error becomes possible. The possibility of error arises through making inferences about what is depicted by the colours and shapes.

In the case of ideas, Descartes suggests, it is very difficult to avoid making such inferences or judgements. We do not see shapes and colours, we see trees and houses and people. Moreover, we have no control over whether or not we have ideas, and this, or so it seems to Descartes, makes it natural to assume that they have come from something outside.

The fact that I have no control over whether I have certain ideas may *explain* why I believe they come from something outside but it does not *justify* the belief. There 'may be some other faculty not yet fully known to me, which produces these ideas without any assistance from external things; this is, after all, just how I have always thought ideas are produced in me when I am dreaming' (*Meditations*, 27). The belief that ideas have some external source seems to be the result of a natural impulse, and natural impulses have frequently led him into error. Thus, receiving ideas from the senses does not demonstrate that there are external objects; still less do these ideas tell him what objects are like if they do exist.

The idea of God

One of Descartes' ideas stands out as being different from the others, and that is his idea of God. As every idea must have a cause, so his idea of God must also have a cause. Descartes argues that the only possible cause is God himself. In other words, the idea of God shows that God exists. Later we will consider whether the argument holds up; for the moment suppose it does. If Descartes has succeeded in proving that God exists, how does this help him? We have already seen that the existence of a God who is good does not support the conclusion that he, Descartes, cannot fall into error. The conclusion that Descartes thinks he can draw is that God will allow him to fall into error only if he has provided him, that is Descartes, with a means for discovering this error. Descartes is sometimes deceived by his senses, for example, when perceiving distant objects, but he has the faculty for correcting this. Descartes may be deceived into thinking he is sitting in his chair when he is in fact lying in bed dreaming, but again God has provided Descartes with a way of discovering this. For Descartes, the existence of God does not provide the assurance that he cannot fall into error, but it does assure him that he has the ability to discover and correct those errors to which he is liable.

Chief among Descartes' faculties for correcting the errors of his natural impulses is his power of reason. His faculty of reason provides him with clear and distinct ideas. Memory is also important. If Descartes remembers having had a clear and distinct perception, then he can use the result of this without having to check it out each time. By attending to the ideas of two and three, Descartes can see clearly and distinctly that these combine to give five; by remembering this, the result can be used without having to be checked.

The existence of physical objects

Descartes' argument for the existence of physical objects is a little more complicated, but it also depends on knowing that God exists. There are three possible sources for Descartes' ideas: objects (which is what he spontaneously believes), some other being (able to implant ideas in him), or God. If anything other than the bodies themselves caused the ideas, then God would have provided Descartes with the means to discover his error. Since God has provided no such faculty, Descartes' natural impulses must, after all, be correct. Hence physical objects exist.

Descartes has not quite finished, for, although he has proved to his satisfaction that objects exist, he cannot claim to know what they are like. He may be misled as to the true nature of an object by his senses and by the natural impulse to believe an object appears to him as it really is. As we shall see shortly, the use of reason will provide him with a way to correct his mistakes. Thus Descartes ends the *Meditations* claiming that he has answered the sceptic and created the foundations for scientific knowledge.

Objections

Is the *cogito* justified?

It would be possible to devote the rest of this book to the arguments presented in the *Meditations*. Subsequent chapters will develop some of the issues raised there, although often without direct reference to the *Meditations*. The purpose of the present section is to note some of the particular criticisms of Descartes' attempt to refute the sceptic, if only to lend support to the claim that Descartes was not successful. First, Descartes' argument for his own existence – an argument usually referred to as the *cogito*. Can Descartes conclude he exists from his awareness that he thinks? It is certainly true that if Descartes is thinking then Descartes exists – things that do not exist cannot think. But Descartes' starting point is not the statement 'Descartes is thinking', it is the awareness of a thought. The awareness of a thought does not entitle Descartes to say 'I am thinking' but only 'There is some thinking going on'. He then has to justify the step from 'There is some thinking' to 'There is a thinker'.

Thinking is considered by Descartes to be a property, and so there must be something, a substance, which has that property. In the same way that we cannot have yellowness without having some substance that is yellow, so we cannot have thinking without having some substance doing the thinking. In the case of yellowness, the substance is a material object; in the case of thinking, the substance is a mind. 'I' serves simply to pick out that substance. Whether this move from thinking to thinker is justified will turn on whether the substance/ property distinction is a sound one and whether thinking is a property. We will return to this later.

Criterion for knowledge

Descartes' criterion for knowledge (certainty) is a clear and distinct perception; but is it not possible to make a mistake as to whether a perception is clear and distinct? Descartes himself admits: 'I previously accepted as wholly certain and evident many things which I afterwards realised were doubtful' (*Meditations*, 24) and that 'through habitual belief I thought I perceived clearly, although I did not in fact do so' (*Meditations*, 25). Could he not find the same again? What extra guarantees does he have now? His answer is that, in those instances where he was mistaken in the past, his perceptions, although clear, were not distinct. He claims to perceive the truth of the *cogito* both clearly and distinctly. A clear perception, he explains, occurs when a perception is present to the mind and the mind is attentive to it. A distinct perception, however, is a perception that is clear and that contains only what is clear. It is this distinctness that is supposed to provide the guarantee of truth, and not clarity alone.

If we accept Descartes' terminology, that it is the clearness and distinctness of the *cogito* that provides the assurance Descartes seeks, we can still question whether Descartes has correctly identified what clarity and distinctness consist in. Descartes appears to think that it consists in having a certain sort of experience. However, it is difficult to see how the nature of an experience could be a guarantee of truth. If we recognize the truth of the *cogito*, it is not because we have a certain sort of experience when attending to it but because it is a proposition with a certain form. Now, if what Descartes means when he perceives an idea clearly and distinctly is that the idea is expressed by a proposition that has a certain form, then there is a further problem. Some of the other propositions Descartes claims to perceive clearly and distinctly do not have this form, and so the guarantee that comes with the *cogito* does not come with these other propositions.

Proving that God exists

Should we accept Descartes' proof of God's existence? Later we shall be looking a little more closely at Descartes' conception of God and at the second proof of God's existence (to be found in the fifth meditation), but it is the proof in meditation III that is crucial if he is to refute scepticism. Descartes assumes there are different degrees of reality and accepts, as self-evident, a principle which states that a cause must contain as much reality as the effect. He goes on to distinguish between the reality an idea has as an idea (what he calls its formal reality) and the reality an idea has through representing something (its objective reality). If I have the idea of a horse and the idea of a unicorn then the two ideas (considered solely as my ideas) have the same formal reality. However, I have seen horses but I have not seen a unicorn. Hence my idea of a horse and my idea of a unicorn have different objective realities. This means, or so Descartes would claim, that the cause of my idea of a horse must have greater reality than the cause of my idea of a unicorn. This claim seems to be correct. Horses exist in reality whereas unicorns occur only in fiction and so, whereas the cause of my idea of a horse is likely to have been a real horse, the cause of my idea of a unicorn will not have been a real unicorn. What is not clear is how Descartes can use this. Whatever credibility is vested in the previous example of horses and unicorns relies on the fact that I have seen and felt horses but not unicorns. The difference, in other words, is supplied by the senses. In the case of someone who has not encountered actual horses but has only read about them, perhaps in a fantasy in which both horses and unicorns appear, there seem to be no grounds for saying that the two ideas have different degrees of objective reality.

When Descartes turns to his idea of God, the cause of this idea must have as much reality as what is represented by the idea. Since what is represented by his idea of God is an infinite, omnipotent, omniscient being, the cause of this idea must also be an infinite, omnipotent, omniscient being. This is, at best, a dubious piece of reasoning. Even if we can make sense of it, it is not the clear and distinct perception that Descartes demanded.

Proving that material things exist

Finally, in this section, let us look at Descartes' attempt to prove that material things exist. If we accept that God exists and has created us, the key questions are 'What would show that God was a deceiver?' and 'Does God's nature preclude him from being a deceiver?' The fact that we make mistakes using faculties provided by God does not make God into a deceiver. But, Descartes claims, if God has not also given us the faculty to correct these mistakes, this would make him a deceiver. Does this follow? Even if we were so constructed that we invariably made mistakes, would this mean that whoever made us was a deceiver? For someone to be a deceiver does there also have to be the intention to deceive? In the case of God, perhaps his omnipotence and omniscience makes this further condition unnecessary. After all, God is not able to make our faculties defective inadvertently and nor would he be ignorant of the use to which they were going to be put.

Descartes seems to have in mind something like the following. God has given us both a concept of truth and the natural impulse to believe that what we perceive with our senses is truly there. If there were no outside world corresponding to these perceptions then there is a sense in which we could not help but be deceived. If we accept that this makes God a deceiver, the question now becomes: does God cease to be a deceiver if he also provides us with the faculty for discovering our mistakes? Alternatively, we might ask, has God acted in a way consistent with the attribute of being perfectly benevolent? May it not be that we are better off being mistaken about some things? Clearly these are difficult questions to answer, and, at the very least, someone trying to defend Descartes has some work to do. However, we must move on to look at other issues raised by the *Meditations*.

Perception

At the beginning of the *Meditations*, Descartes notes that most of what he took to be knowledge came from the senses, but he counters this with the fact that they have, in the past, deceived him. What reliance, finally, does Descartes think we can place on the senses?

The senses provide us with sensations. It is through the organs of sense that 'I am now seeing a light, hearing a noise, feeling heat' (*Meditations*, 19). Yet since these sensations could occur in dreams, all I can claim for certain is that I '*seem* to see, to hear, and to be warmed. This cannot be false; what is called "having a sensory perception" is strictly just this, and in this restricted sense of the term it is simply thinking.' Sensory perceptions or ideas can come from different sources. Some of Descartes' ideas appear to him to be innate, that is, they derive simply from his nature. His idea of God is an example of this. Other ideas are what Descartes calls 'adventitious'. These are the ideas he receives from his senses, and he has a natural impulse to believe they come from external objects. Finally there are ideas which he has invented himself, which he calls 'factitious' ideas. The idea of a unicorn would be a factitious idea. It is with adventitious ideas that we are concerned. Do these ideas tell us anything about what the world is like?

The nature of objects

Descartes does not think that the ideas we receive from our senses give us a true picture of what objects are really like. For example, the idea of the sun that I get from looking at it is quite different from the idea of the sun that I get from science: the senses present the sun as being very small; science tells me it is much larger than the earth. Both ideas cannot be correct, 'and reason persuades me that the idea which seems to have emanated most directly from the sun itself has in fact no resemblance to it at all' (*Meditations*, 27).

The idea of the sun which I get from the senses is an adventitious idea. What of the idea that I get from science? Is this also an adventitious idea? Descartes suggests that the idea of the sun 'based on astronomical reasoning' is 'derived from certain notions which are innate in me' (*Meditations*, 27). This will seem puzzling so long as we think of the sciences as being based on observation and experiment. For Descartes, however, astronomy (and indeed, science in general) is based on mathematics, which in turn is based on reason. We see the truths of mathematics by the natural light; hence they are truths about which we can be certain. Science, in Descartes' view, is concerned not with the changing world of appearances presented by the senses but with the reality lying behind these appearances. Science provides knowledge of the essence of material objects.

Appearance and reality

There are two important points to grasp here. The first is that Descartes has made a distinction between how objects appear to us and how objects really are. He is claiming that there is a gap between appearance and reality. He also claims that we can reach the reality behind appearances by using our rational powers. Is this so? If we are to have knowledge of the world, must we not rely ultimately upon our sense perceptions? Or does reason provide us with a more reliable source of truth that circumvents the errors involved with sense perception? As has been noted, the world described by science can be totally at odds with the everyday world of experience. Does this show that the source of our scientific ideas must be different from the source of our everyday ideas – reason as opposed to sense perception? Or is it simply a matter of having abstracted from the particular ideas we get from the senses? Descartes and his successors can be divided into two camps – rationalists and empiricists – according to how they stand on this issue. In the next chapter we will be examining the empiricist account of knowledge.

The self

A thinking thing

The first thing of which Descartes is certain is his own existence. But what exactly is he? Since the proof of his own existence is grounded on the fact that he is thinking (and thinking includes believing, doubting, perceiving, etc.), then what he must be is a thing that thinks. 'I am thinking therefore I am', if it establishes anything, establishes the existence of a thinking thing. This result, that he is essentially a thinking thing, is counter-intuitive. Most of us consider ourselves most certain of the existence of our own body. However, if the possibility of the evil demon means that Descartes cannot know that material objects exist, then he cannot know that his own body exists. He has already admitted that he sometimes dreams he is sitting by the fire when in fact he is lying in bed. His beliefs about his body are no more immune from the doubts raised by the supposition of an evil demon than those about other material objects.

Descartes is thus certain that he exists and yet is not certain that his body exists. He concludes from this that his self and his body must be distinct things. This means that, despite being intimately joined to his body, he could exist apart from his body.

Substances

Now a thinking thing (a mind) and a body (a material object) are two very different sorts of things; according to Descartes, they are different sorts of substances. For Descartes, and others of his time, the word 'substance' meant something different from what it now means. We think of a substance as being a kind of matter, matter of a particular composition. We will say: 'What sort of substance is this?' meaning, what is its chemical composition? However, for Descartes, a substance was to be understood as something capable of independent existence, in the way that, for example, a colour is not. A colour always has to be a colour *of* something.

What is essential to material things (that is, what persists through all the changes a material object undergoes) is that they are extended (they occupy space). Descartes adds the further claim that what is essential to minds is having thoughts. Minds, Descartes thought, do not occupy space, nor can they even be associated with a position in space, but they do persist through time, since thinking takes time. This has a strange implication for the continuity of Descartes' existence: 'For it could be that were I totally to cease from thinking, I should totally cease to exist' (*Meditations*, 18). Thus if Descartes is unconscious (having no thoughts or experiences) then he, a thinking thing, does not exist.

What then of a person's identity over a period of time? If there are periods when I have no thoughts, these are periods when I do not exist, even though I am aware of no discontinuity, either in my thoughts or in my existence. Should we say that there is a single self, which exists discontinuously, or that there is a succession of different selves? If I am distinct from my body then I cannot use any criteria for bodily continuity to settle the issue. What is the criterion for two thoughts being thoughts of the same mind rather than thoughts of different minds? Many of these questions have not been given a satisfactory answer.

The relationship between mind and body

A further question arises regarding the relationship between Descartes (or, as we would more normally say, Descartes' mind) and his body.

There is a union between mind and body, but how is this union achieved? How does the body affect the mind? For example, how is the body able to bring about certain sensations and feeling? And how does the mind affect the body? For example, how is the mind able to bring about actions by the body? If, as Descartes maintains, mind and body are so different, how are they able to interact? The essence of a material object, such as the body, is extension. The mind, however, has no extension. This seems to mean that there can be no contact between mind and body and no way for the mind to affect the body or for the body to affect the mind.

Free will

Faculties of the mind

There is one further thing to consider in connection with what Descartes says about the self, and that is free will, or freedom of choice. The various faculties of the mind include imagination, memory, understanding and the will. Descartes, perhaps strangely, considers that the will is not limited in the way that the other faculties are. In the case of these other faculties, it is possible to think of them as being more extensive and more perfect than they actually are. In the case of the faculty of will, however, Descartes confesses: 'I cannot complain that the will or freedom of choice . . . is not sufficiently extensive or perfect, since I know by experience that it is not restricted in any way' (*Meditations*, 40). Most of us would protest that our freedom of choice is restricted in all sorts of ways because we cannot do what we want to do. Before concluding that Descartes has made a gross error, we should consider whether he means the same by 'free will' as we do. He goes on to say, 'This is because the will simply consists in our ability to do or not do something (that is, to affirm or deny, to pursue or avoid); or rather, it consists simply in the fact that when the intellect puts something forward for affirmation or denial or for pursuit or avoidance, our inclinations are such that we do not feel we are determined by any external force' (*Meditations*, 40).

Thus what Descartes is discussing is our ability to affirm or deny those propositions presented to it by the intellect. He is not interested in whether we have freedom to bring about the state of affairs we desire. Being able to bring about what we desire is not a measure of the *freedom* of the will but of its power or effectiveness. When Descartes compares his will with God's will he notes that 'God's will is incomparably greater than mine, both in virtue of the knowledge and power that accompany it and make it more firm and efficacious' (*Meditations*, 40). But when considered in itself, God's will is not greater than Descartes' will.

What is willing?

The distinction between the freedom of the will and the power or effectiveness of the will might be made clearer with some examples. A pencil is resting on the desk in front of me. Can I will it to rise a few centimetres into the air? The answer most of us would give is: of course not. Descartes' answer might be that yes, we can *will* it to rise up, since this involves no more than affirming rather than denying the statement 'This pencil will rise into the air'. Whether or not the pencil will *actually* rise is, however, another matter; this depends on the power of the will, on whether, for example, there are the appropriate connections with the object. If it is God who is doing the willing, then the pencil will rise; if it is I who am doing the willing then it will not rise. This contrasts with the case where it is my arm lying on the table in front of me, for when I will my arm to rise up it (generally) does.

My will has power over my arm because it is connected to my arm via the nerves that lead from my arm to my brain. Descartes identified the pineal gland, a small protrusion in the centre of the brain, as the location where mind and body interact. Stimulation of the pineal gland by the 'animal spirits' that flow along the nerves results in the experience of certain sensations; conversely, willing by the mind or soul will cause the pineal gland to stir up the animal spirits and thus cause movements in the body. The (mental) act of willing and the (physical) effects of willing are separated by the same fault line as separates mind and body. The reasoning in the two cases is similar: if two things, which in this case are the act of willing and the effect of that willing, can be conceived as separate then they must be distinct.

Descartes' God

Attributes of God

The conception of God with which Descartes presents us in the *Meditations* may seem unfamiliar and impersonal: 'By the word God, I understand a substance that is infinite [eternal, immutable], independent, supremely intelligent, supremely powerful, and which created both myself and everything else (if anything else there be) that exists' (*Meditations*, 31). There is nothing here about the God of love or the God of goodness. In establishing the existence of God, Descartes is not concerned with religious experience or with revelation; he appeals neither to any religious texts nor to the testimonies of others. Instead, he considers those qualities listed above and tries to establish, through reason, that a being with those qualities must exist. The *Meditations* contain two such proofs, the first in meditation III, and the second in meditation V. This second proof is, in essence, a version of the so-called ontological argument, first put forward by St Anselm (1033–1109). The first is a form of the so-called cosmological proof, although one where the starting point is an idea that Descartes has, rather than the material universe or some features within it. (See chapter 7 for further details.)

The first proof

The first argument is simply stated. Descartes has an idea of God. The nature of this idea is such that, Descartes concludes, God must have caused it. Hence God exists. What is it about his idea of God that leads Descartes to conclude that it was caused by God? Descartes' own self is the cause of his idea of a substance. His idea of God, however, is of an infinite substance and his self is only a finite substance. Since the idea of an infinite substance could not come from that of a finite substance, the cause of his idea of an infinite substance could only be from a substance that was itself infinite.

As suggested above, Descartes' argument is unconvincing, especially when we remember that Descartes has resolved not to entertain beliefs that are open to the possibility of error. The argument does, however, illustrate his rationalist approach: he thinks that we could not have obtained the idea of an infinite perfect being from our senses, since these provide us with ideas of things which are finite and imperfect. The idea of God, claims Descartes, must have been innate in us, since there is nothing in our experiences that could have given rise to our idea of God. In contrast, the empiricists will claim that we arrive at the idea of God by a process of abstraction from the ideas we get from the senses.

The second proof

The second proof, found in meditation V, has a better claim to being founded on clear and distinct perceptions. The perception in question is that existence belongs to the nature of God in just the way that properties belong to mathematical shapes. Existence is as much a part of the essence of God as 'the fact that its three angles equal two right angles' is part of the essence of a triangle. This, Descartes admits, has the 'appearance of being a sophism' (*Meditations*, 46), since in all other things it is possible to distinguish between essence and existence. In the case of God, however, we are not able to separate these two notions of existence and essence. If existence is inseparable from God then God really exists. 'It is not that my thought makes it so, or imposes any necessity on any thing; on the contrary, it is the necessity of the thing itself, namely the existence of God, which determines my thinking in this respect. For I am not free to think of God without existence (that is, a supremely perfect being without a supreme perfection) as I am free to imagine a horse with or without wings.'

Kant (1724–1802) put forward the classic objection to this sort of argument, that it treats existence as a property that things can have or fail to have. We can say of a man that he is tall, well built, blond, easy-going and generous, but his existence is not a further property. The puzzle of treating existence as a property is that if the man in question does not exist, then what is it that lacks this property of existence while possessing all the other properties? Treating existence as a property threatens a population explosion of possible things, some of which exist and some of which do not. Arguably, Descartes' version of the ontological proof avoids this objection by saying not that existence is some further property that God possesses but that it follows from those properties which constitute the essence of God. However, even if Descartes manages to avoid Kant's criticism, he has not shown that God exists. If Descartes has shown anything by this proof, it is the truth of the conditional statement that, if God exists, his existence is necessary. The ontological proof, and objections to it, will receive further attention in chapter 7.

Before leaving the subject of God's existence, the general point should be made that showing a proof of God's existence is flawed does not show that God does not exist. There may be other proofs of God's existence. Whether it is possible for God simply to exist, without there being a proof of his existence, is not clear, although this is certainly possible for things other than God. Whether it is possible to prove God's non-existence is something we shall consider later.

Descartes' legacy

Descartes, as we have seen, initially adopts a sceptical position regarding the reliability of the senses. By the end of the *Meditations* a measure of trust in the senses has been restored: they provide us with knowledge as to the existence of external objects but not a knowledge of their true nature. This is provided by the intellect or reason. Locke (1632–1704), however, and others who followed Locke in the empiricist tradition, gave the senses a central role in the acquisition of knowledge.

Two very different examples of knowledge, one mathematical (say, that 2 plus 2 equals 4) and one scientific (say, that heating a fixed volume of gas increases the pressure), both illustrate that acquiring knowledge depends upon having first grasped the ideas or concepts involved. In the first case it is the concepts of two, four, plus and equals, in the second the concepts of heat, gas, volume and pressure and change. The debate between empiricists and rationalists is about the source of these ideas or concepts. For Descartes, scientific knowledge is essentially mathematical, and the abstract ideas involved cannot come from the senses but must be innate. However, it is a basic tenet of the empiricist tradition that all ideas come from the senses – there are no innate ideas. Ideas, whether particular or abstract, form the building blocks of knowledge and have their origin in perception. Without perception there can be no ideas and hence no knowledge.

Various contemporary discussions can be seen as developments of the empiricist–rationalist debate. Two are of particular interest. The first is to do with how we acquire language. The nub of the problem is that we are able to understand and produce an infinite number of sentences, yet this is based on experience of only a small, finite number of cases. Innate abilities seem to be involved, but are these abilities the sort of thing that Descartes had in mind when he spoke of innate ideas? Or can the empiricist hold that innate abilities are not inconsistent with the claim that all ideas come from experience? The issue becomes less clear-cut if concept-acquisition is seen as the acquisition of a certain sort of ability, namely the ability to discriminate between instances and non-instances of the concept.

The second is to do with the fundamental nature of the universe and its intelligibility. If the universe is essentially mathematical, and so can be understood only in terms of the concepts of mathematics, then this would seem to make the investigation of the fundamental nature of the universe a mathematical, and hence rational, investigation rather than an empirical investigation. There is a long history in philosophy of treating mathematical concepts as innate concepts rather than concepts abstracted from experience. In this case, perhaps Descartes was right and we can understand the universe only through *a priori* concepts.

What should gradually become clearer, as the discussions unfold in subsequent chapters, is the way in which Descartes provided the framework. His influence and importance go far beyond the positive results he achieved. Despite the criticisms that Descartes' work has received, both in his lifetime and ever since, philosophers still think that it is worth returning to. Its ideas are unsettling and provoking.

Summary

- Descartes' aim is a body of knowledge, that is, a set of beliefs about which he can be absolutely certain. He tries to achieve this by setting aside his beliefs and subjecting each to the method of doubt. A proposition will be accepted as true only if doubt is not possible. To assist in this process of radical doubt, he introduces the device of the malicious demon.
- The foundation on which Descartes tries to build knowledge is the *cogito*. Any attempt by the demon to make Descartes doubt his existence is bound to fail, since, in order to entertain such doubt, Descartes must be aware that he exists.
- Descartes thinks that the *cogito* provides him not only with a belief of which he is certain but also with a criterion for knowledge. If he can perceive something clearly and distinctly, in the way that he perceives the *cogito*, then it must be true.

- Descartes thinks that the *cogito* also provides him with knowledge of his true nature or essence, that of a thinking thing. But if Descartes is to have knowledge of the world, he needs to break out of this first-person perspective. This he attempts to do by first proving the existence of God. Knowledge of God's existence would provide Descartes with the bridge from his inner world to an outer world.
- Descartes believes that we can rely on the senses to inform us of the existence of material things, but it is through reason that we arrive at true knowledge of the world.
- Descartes distinguishes two sorts of substances, mind and matter. The essence of matter is extension, the essence of mind is thought. The problem with this dualism is to provide an account as to how it is possible for these two substances to interact.

Questions raised

- In the evil demon, Descartes seems to have provided the sceptic with a powerful weapon. Does Descartes' failure to give a satisfactory answer to the sceptic show that Descartes was setting the standards for knowledge impossibly high? Or must we conclude that the sceptic cannot be answered?
- Can the starting point for knowledge be the first-person perspective adopted by Descartes? Is a project such as his bound to fail? Does knowledge need a foundation in this way?
- Is it the case that I am distinct from my body? Could I exist even if my body were not to exist? Or am I essentially embodied? If minds are distinct from bodies, can there be a criterion for two thoughts being thoughts of the same mind rather than of different minds?
- What is the nature of God and can we prove that he exists? Alternatively, can we prove that he does not exist?

3 Perception and Reality

Introduction

One aspect of the nature of philosophical problems can be drawn out by contrasting the concerns of the philosopher with those of the scientist in giving an account of perception. For the philosopher, the subjective nature of sense perception is important, as is the problem of bridging the gap between subjective experience and knowledge of objective reality. The central question here is: how can the senses provide us with knowledge of physical objects? Descartes, as we have seen, held that it was through the intellect that we arrived at a knowledge of objects, or at least a knowledge of the essential nature of objects. Here different versions of the alternative empiricist approach, that knowledge comes via the senses, are considered. These include representational realism, idealism and phenomenalism.

Philosophical and scientific issues

The subjective nature of sense perception

What is involved in perception? Science has provided us with an increasingly more detailed account of what goes on in the body. The account starts with what happens in the sense organs, for example, the focusing of light by the lens in the eye and the effect this has on the nerve cells in the retina; or the vibrations of bones in the ear and the transmissions of these vibrations through the fluids trapped in the canals in the ear, etc. It continues with a description of how signals are transmitted to the brain along neurones, of how a neurone 'fires' and a spike of electrical activity passes along its axon until it reaches a synapse with the next neurone in the chain, where it opens a molecular gate and allows particles to flow between the neurones. Science is also able to give a picture of what happens in the brain when the signals arrive there, for example, what happens in the visual cortex, and so on.

However, the account given by biologists, biochemists, neurophysiologists, etc. is not the whole story of what goes on in perception. Psychologists tell us that perception is not simply a matter of passively receiving signals from the outside world via the senses. Psychological experiments have demonstrated that what is perceived is dependent on context and expectation. In one experiment, a subject is presented, one at a time but for a brief interval only, with a sequence of characters interspersed with meaningless squiggles. It is found that the same squiggle will be perceived either as a letter or as a number, depending on whether it comes within a sequence of letters or a sequence of numbers.

Given the resources available to science and the astonishing pace of scientific advance, what can we expect philosophy to tell us about perception that the biological and behavioural sciences cannot? What are the philosophical problems of perception?

One thing to notice is that something crucial is left out of the scientific explanations of perception, and that is the *experience* of perceiving. Despite the difference in complexity, there is an essential similarity between our scientific understanding of how the eye works and how a camera works. Both accounts restrict themselves to physical events – there is nothing that allows for the fact that in the case of the eye there is, in addition to all these physical events, also the experience of seeing objects. This experience is subjective, and the physical sciences do not investigate the subjective nature of perception. One might expect this omission to be rectified in psychology, but psychology cannot observe the subject's experiences, only how the subject behaves in the experiments or reports on his or her experiences. Even the reports that a subject gives are examples of the subject's behaviour, that is, physical events. Questions as to the nature of the mental and the relationship between the mental and the physical are questions that will be considered further in a later chapter (see chapter 6).

In the scientific study of perception, it is taken for granted that our senses tell us about the world in which we live and that perception is the means by which we are acquainted with objects in the world. To study perception in biology or psychology is to study the mechanisms by which this acquaintance with the world is achieved. No philosophical study of perception, however, can avoid a critical analysis of this underlying assumption. The scientist assumes that there are objects in the world whose nature is there to be investigated. In philosophy, we consider the evidence provided by perception for the existence of objects and, at least since Descartes, ask the questions: do we perceive objects directly or do we have to *infer* the existence of objects from our experience and, if the latter, is there any justification for such inferences?

Naïve realism

Immediate objects of perception

A naïve realist is someone who claims that we perceive objects directly, that is, someone who claims that the immediate objects of perception are tables, trees, mountains, etc. What is meant by saying that objects are perceived directly or immediately? In everyday usage, the word 'immediately' is taken to mean 'without any time lag'. To bring something about immediately is to bring it about now, this instant. Yet here, it has the sense of 'without mediation' or 'without an intermediate stage'. To perceive something immediately is to perceive it directly rather than indirectly. If, however, one's perception relies on something else that intervenes, or is an intermediary, between the perceiver and the perceived, then the perception is indirect. A mundane illustration of indirect perception is that of seeing an object in a mirror rather than seeing it when it is directly in front of you. The mirror, or rather the reflection produced in the mirror, mediates between you and the object. The suggestion is that, in the case where you see the object indirectly, what you actually perceive, that is, what you perceive *immediately*, is something other than the object, such as a reflection or image of the object.

Clearly the naïve realist is a realist: for the naïve realist, there is no question as to whether or not objects really exist since they are the immediate objects of perception. The qualification 'naïve' is added because such a position seems to show no awareness of a distinction between appearances and reality or of the problems posed by this distinction. If what I perceive directly is the object itself, why do my perceptions differ when the object is perceived under different conditions, such as in different lights, from different angles, when I am wearing tinted glasses, etc.? For example, if I perceive two boats on the river, one close and the other further away, then the appearance of these boats will be different. The nearer one will appear larger, its colours will appear brighter, the sounds it makes will seem louder, and so on, even though the boats themselves are identical. A different example: the appearance of stars in the night sky is clearly nothing like the stars themselves – the discovery that stars were distant suns was just that, a discovery, and not something obvious from the appearance presented to us. If I look at a piece of material under artificial light, it seems to be one colour, and yet this is not the true colour.

If the objects of perception are different, this, on the naïve realist account, should mean that the objects perceived are different objects. The obvious response to this sort of difficulty is to say that, when I move around the object and view it from different angles, the appearance changes but the object itself does not change. However, to say that our senses present us with the appearance of an object from one particular viewpoint seems to be claiming that the immediate object of perception is an appearance, and hence that the object itself is perceived indirectly. If so, this is no longer the position of a naïve realist.

The reality behind appearances

None the less, although it may be granted that the appearances presented by our senses are not an exact match of the world as it really is, one may still want to hold that there is a large measure of agreement between the two – in particular, that the real world is a world of sounds, shapes and colours, tastes, smells and textures. Thus, although our senses may get some of the detail wrong, the differences between the world of appearances and the real world are not differences in kind. These sorts of claims are challenged by modern science. Science presents us with the idea of everyday objects being made up of countless numbers of minute particles, held together by electrostatic forces and in a state of constant motion. At a microscopic level, our own bodies are battlefields, constantly being invaded by bacteria and viruses triggering defensive action from our immune systems. The theories of relativity and quantum mechanics are so bizarre that their descriptions of the world are contrary to the most fundamental assumptions made on the basis of our everyday perceptions. If these scientific accounts are correct (or something like correct), then the way the world appears to us is completely different from the underlying reality. In the face of the scientific view, we must conclude that the world is not remotely like the appearances presented by our senses.

Representational realism

Representational realism is a theory of perception that assumes that the objects we perceive really exist but that what we directly perceive are representations of the objects rather than the objects themselves. John Locke is generally credited with putting forward a representational theory of perception (although it is a matter of debate among philosophers as to whether the theory with which he is generally credited is the theory that he actually proposed – a debate which we will not be entering).

Ideas and qualities

Locke's account of perception is to be found in his *An Essay Concerning Human Understanding*. In the essay Locke relies heavily on an all-pervasive notion of an 'idea'. For Locke, if one is conscious then what one is conscious of is ideas. In perception, the mind is presented with a succession of ideas: ideas of colours, such as whiteness and redness; of shapes, such as stripes and circles; of sounds, smells, tastes and 'feels'. These ideas that come from the senses are, Locke suggests, simple ideas, although the mind puts these simple ideas together to form complex ideas, such as the idea of a boat or a person or a palace. If I am engaged in thinking or reasoning, then again I will be conscious of ideas. This time these ideas may be abstract ones – say, duty or happiness or courage – or less abstract ones – say, my idea of London or of a car or of the sun. Typically, although not necessarily, these ideas will be complex, that is, they will consist of simple ideas associated together.

When I perceive a boat on the river, Locke thought, the boat somehow affects my senses by means of insensible particles (that is, particles that are not themselves perceived by the senses) that travel from the object to my senses. Locke drew a clear distinction (even if he did not always stick to it) between the *idea* in the mind and the *quality* in the object, which is the power to produce the idea. For all ideas in the mind that come from the senses, there are corresponding qualities or powers in objects. Although his account is crude by today's standards, it takes very much the same form as contemporary accounts of perception.

Primary and secondary qualities

Sometimes, says Locke, an idea resembles the quality in the object that was the original cause of the idea. Such qualities Locke termed *primary qualities*. In other cases, there is nothing in the object that an idea resembles, although the object clearly has the power to produce the idea, and such powers are called *secondary qualities*. Locke is not altogether consistent when listing the primary qualities, but a typical list would be: solidity, shape, texture, motion or rest, and number. The list of secondary qualities (or, more accurately, of ideas produced by secondary qualities) is much more extensive: colours, sounds, tastes, odours and so on – anything, in fact, which is not (an idea produced by) a primary quality.

Locke also claimed that the secondary qualities of an object are dependent upon the object's primary qualities. The fact that an object is able to produce the idea of redness in me is the result of some quality in the object, but it is not because the object is red that it appears red. Rather it is, according to Locke, because of the particular arrangement of the minute parts that constitute the object. That is, it is the shape, solidity, motion and number of these minute (and, according to Locke, insensible) parts that give the object its power to produce the idea of red in me. If we were able to observe these minute, insensible parts of the object, thought Locke, we would be able to understand why it is that an object of a particular type appears to us in the way that it does. This, he thought, was impossible, and it would therefore always remain a matter of speculation on our part as to why, for example, certain qualities are to be found together in an object.

Primary qualities as objectively present

Locke was not, in fact, the first person to put forward this distinction between primary and secondary qualities. The distinction is also to be found in the scientific works of Boyle (1627–1691) and Newton (1642–1727). The approach, to which scientific explanation owes its success, is essentially reductionist. A rich and varied range of phenomena is explained in terms of a small number of properties – in this case, the primary qualities of objects. In retrospect it would seem that science has succeeded beyond Locke's wildest hopes in discovering the 'minute particles of bodies and the real constitution on which their sensible qualities depend' (*An Essay Concerning Human Understanding*, 2.23.11). It can explain not only why gold has a certain weight (or density) but also its malleability and colour in terms of other, more basic qualities.

The physicist's list of properties that are fundamental, in the sense that they play an important role in explaining a wide range of phenomena, would be very different from Locke's list of primary qualities. It might, for example, include quantum mechanical properties of spin, strangeness or charm. Further, the properties on this list would not count as a list of primary qualities, as Locke understood the term, since these qualities do not produce ideas in us that resemble them. However, the physicist would agree with Locke with regard to the following claims. First, that a property such as the colour of a chemical substance can be explained in terms of a more fundamental property of the minute parts (perhaps atoms and molecules, perhaps subatomic particles) that constitute a lump of the substance. Second, that the minute parts are not themselves coloured. The typical colour of gold arises not from the atom itself being gold in colour but from some totally different property, such as the energy levels of the outermost electrons in an atom of gold.

The colour that an object appears to have is the end product of a chain of events. Light of a certain wavelength is selectively reflected from the object and absorbed by the rods and cones in the retina of my eye; somehow, after various other electrochemical processes, this results in my having an experience. Just as, in one sense, colours do not really exist, so sounds, as such, do not exist, only the vibrations of molecules of matter. Prior to the arrival of sentient beings, there existed electromagnetic radiation and compression waves, which pass through air and other media, but there did not exist colours and sounds. These did not come into existence until sentient beings, capable of experiencing sounds and colours, arrived on the surface of the earth.

A serious problem for a theory that makes the above distinction between primary and secondary qualities lies in the claim that certain of our ideas *resemble*, while others do not resemble, qualities to be found in objects. According to the representational theory of perception we can compare one idea with another, since we can hold both in the mind, but there is no way that we can make the comparison between an idea and the quality that produced the idea. The quality is not an idea and the mind is acquainted only with ideas. To be able to compare an idea with its associated quality would require that we perceive bodies directly (rather than indirectly through ideas), but this is just what our theory does not allow us to do. Saying that certain ideas, for example, those of colour, are secondary is unproblematic if what is meant is that these ideas can be explained in terms of certain other ideas (be these the 'bulk, texture and figure' of the supposed minute parts or the energy levels of electron orbitals). What we cannot say is what objects are *really* like.

Primary qualities as essential properties

There is another way of distinguishing between primary and secondary qualities, and that is to treat primary qualities as those qualities that are essential to objects. Locke himself seems to suggest such a way of making the distinction when he says 'take a grain of wheat, divide it into two parts, each part has still solidity, extension, figure and mobility; divide it again, and it retains still the same qualities; and so divide it on, till the parts become insensible: they must retain still each of them all those qualities. For division . . . can never take away either solidity, extension, figure, or mobility from any body . . .' (*An Essay Concerning Human Understanding*, 2.8.9). Here, Locke seems to be implying that we can conceive of objects without a particular colour or without being hot or cold, and so on through all the secondary qualities, but we cannot conceive of an object which is not extended in space or which does not have a shape or solidity or motion. This does not allow us to say what objects are really like, but it does suggest the concepts that are appropriate to a description of the reality underlying appearances.

Berkeley's criticisms
Berkeley (1685–1753) takes issue with the suggestion that we can make this sort of distinction between primary and secondary qualities. He argues that being able to see the shape of an object, which is a primary quality, depends on our being able to distinguish the object from its background and hence on seeing the object as being of a different colour from its background. Colour, however, is a secondary quality. This criticism may exploit a difference between Locke and Berkeley over what is meant by 'idea'. Locke uses 'idea' to mean whatever is present to the mind. Thus ideas include both images (not necessarily visual images) and concepts. Now I cannot form a visual image of an object having shape but no colour, just as I cannot form a visual image of an object having colour but no shape, since the boundary of the one is the boundary of the other. None the less, I can *conceive* of an object having shape but not colour – I can, for example, conceive of a hydrogen atom in which the size and the shape of the atom are incorporated but in which colour plays no part.

The role of primary qualities in causal explanations

If we reject Berkeley's criticism, we still have to say how we pick out those qualities that are primary. How do we justify treating shape or texture as a primary quality but not colour? Locke points out that if we pound an almond, its colour will be altered. Now since the immediate effect of pounding will be to alter texture (perhaps by altering the size and shape of the insensible particles that make up the almond), this suggests that the colour depends on the texture. From this it is inferred that texture is the primary quality and colour a secondary quality. Thus Locke's distinction can be seen as a hypothesis as to which qualities will play a fundamental role in causal explanations. If we want to explain the behaviour of a ball rolling down a slope, then its shape, the texture of its surface and its bulk are going to be significant; its colour is not.

Berkeley's idealism

The one-world view

Locke's theory of perception can be said to have inherited Descartes' two-world theory – the physical world of material objects and the mental world of ideas. The fundamental question posed by any two-world theory is: how are the two worlds connected? In the context of a theory of perception, the question is: how can we have knowledge (mental world) of objects (physical world)? The representative theory of perception answers this by saying that objects (physical world) are *represented* by ideas (mental world), but this answer is problematic since we are never in a position to see whether the representation is accurate or even whether there is anything to be represented.

As far as Berkeley was concerned, Locke's theory gave far too much to the sceptic. By allowing that there are two worlds, we give the sceptic a gap through which to drive the wedge that threatens to split the world off from our understanding of it. Berkeley's answer, often given the name 'idealism', is to adopt a one-world view: there is only the mental world, the world of ideas, and there is no separate, independent material world. (In fact, 'Idea-ism' might be a more informative, if clumsier, name for Berkeley's philosophy, since it is based on '*ideas*' and not on '*ideals*' – it is not, for example, about being idealistic!) If this solution works, it immediately removes the problem of understanding the connection between two worlds.

Berkeley points out that his senses provide him with many different ideas but goes on to suggest that the collections of ideas that he experiences do not *represent* objects; rather, they *constitute* them. A stone, a tree, a book and the like are no more than collections of ideas and, as such, cannot have an existence independent of being perceived. Berkeley claims that 'all the choir of heaven and furniture of the earth, in a word all those bodies which compose the mighty frame of the world, have not any subsistence without a mind, that their being is to be perceived or known' (*A Treatise Concerning the Principles of Human Knowledge*, 1,6). The account of matter, which Locke gives, is that of an unthinking substance in which primary qualities exist. 'But it is evident from what we have already shewn, that extension, figure and motion are only ideas existing in the mind, and that an idea can be like nothing but another idea, and that consequently neither they nor their archetypes can exist in an unperceiving substance. Hence it is plain, that the very notion of what is called *matter* or *corporeal substance*, involves a contradiction in it' (*A Treatise Concerning the Principles of Human Knowledge*, 1,9).

Misconceptions of Berkeley's position

It is not as easy as it might seem to mount an effective attack on Berkeley's idealism, and certainly not as easy as Samuel Johnson thought. When told of the theory that material objects were simply ideas, Johnson kicked a stone and said, 'I refute it thus.' There are several reasons why Johnson had not refuted idealism. In the first place, Berkeley did not say that stones (and other objects) do not exist, nor did he say that stones, etc. are figments of our imagination. Berkeley's test for whether there is a stone in front of him will be exactly the same as Johnson's, and that is to see whether he can perceive it, that is, see, touch or kick it. Berkeley agreed with Locke, that the way we know of the existence of a stone is by perceiving it. What Berkeley went on to say was that the thing we know is not something separate from the perception, and certainly not something represented by the perception. It is the perception itself – the stone is, among other experiences, the experience of kicking it. Perception gives us knowledge of objects precisely because objects are perceptions. In other words, using the language of Locke, objects are ideas. Kicking a stone gives us knowledge of the stone's existence because it is a way of perceiving the stone. Berkeley's point is that *any* test for the existence of an object will involve perception of the object. Why then not identify the object with the set of perceptions?

When Berkeley says that there are only ideas (that is, in addition to minds which perceive ideas) and that material objects do not have an existence independently of being perceived, we need to distinguish this carefully from what he might be but actually is not saying here. He is not saying that stones, tables, clouds, mountains, stars, etc. do not really exist. Berkeley would agree with the rest of us that they do exist and that we know they really exist because we perceive them. What do not exist are entities separate from perception. Berkeley's question to Locke and Descartes is: why invent further entities which, in some respects at least, are supposedly like our ideas but which we can never perceive directly? A representational theory of perception might appear to be an extension of a common-sense view of our relationship with the world. Berkeley claims, however, that the stipulation of the existence of objects which we cannot directly perceive is a philosophical hypothesis that runs directly counter to what people understand when they say that objects really exist. When people describe an object that they say exists, they describe their ideas.

'An idea can be like nothing but another idea'

Locke claimed that there was a distinction to be drawn between primary qualities, which resembled the ideas they produced, and secondary qualities, which did not. We saw that there were problems with this claim. What Berkeley says is that nothing can be like an idea except another idea. He meant something like this. Our perception of an object is a mental experience. The physical world that is claimed by the representational realist to exist is something totally different from the mental world. Indeed, it is so different that it does not make sense to talk of a similarity between the mental thing (the idea or perception) and the material thing. Modern-day physicists make a similar claim. For example, some will claim that it is no use trying to picture what an atom is like since ultimate reality does not conform to our every-day conceptions. We may picture a miniature solar system or some sort of fuzzy blob surrounded by circular standing waves, but, whatever the picture, it is not what the atom is really like. The atom can be truly understood not through pictures but only by means of complex mathematics, from which all sensory content has been abstracted.

The real existence of objects

If objects are ideas and if ideas can exist only in the mind, does this not mean that objects can exist only in the mind? And, if so, how can objects be anything other than figments of my imagination? How can the same object be perceived by different people? How can they have an existence that is independent of me? Let us consider how Berkeley's answers compare with Locke's answers to these questions. First, how can the same object be perceived by different people? Locke's answer will be that the same object is perceived by different people when representations of the object, that is, ideas, are produced in each person's mind by the object. Two people know that each has perceived the same object when they are able to describe it to each other. Now Berkeley can give exactly the same account of the experiences of the two people concerned, even though he gives a different account of the source of the ideas.

As for the question: how do we know that an object is not a figment of the imagination?, Berkeley's answer is the same as Locke's. We distinguish between a figment of the imagination and a real object by the perceptions we have. A real object we can touch as well as see; we also have the assurances of other people that they can see it, and so on. Even on a representational account, we do not have direct access to the object, to assure ourselves that it is really there. Berkeley's insistence that there is nothing other than perceptions does not put him at a disadvantage. Indeed, he can be much more certain than Locke in saying that we know that there really is an object, since, he can claim, he merely has to contrast ideas of sense perception with ideas of the imagination.

This still leaves us with some questions to ask of idealism. The first set of questions concerns the source of our ideas. If our ideas, when we perceive objects, are not caused by the objects, what does cause them? The second set of questions concerns the continuity of objects. If objects exist only when perceived, what happens to them in the intervals when they are not being perceived? Do objects pass in and out of existence? If so, does this mean that bits of the world are brought into existence by being perceived, and then pass out of existence when no longer perceived? Did the universe not exist before there were sentient beings to perceive it?

The role of God in Berkeley's philosophy

Berkeley's answer to these questions brings in God: it is God who produces ideas in us and God who enables things to exist when humans, or other sentient beings, are not perceiving them. Calling on God to play such a role would not have been thought unusual by philosophers of the eighteenth century. Descartes relied upon God to underwrite knowledge of material objects, and both Locke and Descartes sub- scribed to the belief that material objects were created by God. The role that Berkeley sees God as playing is similar, at least with regard to its effect, although he is spared some of the effort required of him by, say, Descartes. For Berkeley, God has to do no more than create the appearance of material objects by creating the perceptions in the minds of his creatures, whereas for Descartes God has to create the material objects themselves. Berkeley's system is what we might be left with if we were to apply Ockham's razor (that is, the requirement not to multiply entities unnecessarily) to Locke's representational realism. Berkeley's idealism cuts out the (supposed) unnecessary entities, material objects, while leaving the world, as experienced by us, the same.

One of the ways in which sense perception differs from imagination is that we have no power over what ideas we have or when we have them; they are not subject to our will. Descartes recognized that in imagination we produce the ideas, whereas in sense perception the ideas are produced, or at least appear to be produced, by something else. According to Berkeley, only minds, or spirits, are capable of producing ideas, just as only minds or spirits are capable of perceiving ideas. So if we do not produce the ideas of sense perception, they must be produced in us by some other spirit – in fact, by God. Berkeley attributes the reason our perceptions form recognizable patterns and are not random, the reason they are coherent rather than disjointed (as they are in dreams), to God's goodness. It is, for example, because God is good that my perceptions and your perceptions tie in with each other. It is also because God is eternal, omnipresent and omniscient that the universe existed before mankind arrived on the earth and continues to exist even when not perceived by human beings or other sentient beings.

Objections to idealism

Scepticism about other minds
Let us now turn to objections to Berkeley's idealism. With his idealism Berkeley claimed to have solved the problem of scepticism. If what I perceive is the representation of an object and never the object itself, then I cannot know that the object itself exists. Whereas if, by perceiving the idea (or set of ideas), I thereby perceive the object (since the object is the idea), I *can* know that the object exists. Knowing that an idea exists is something that the sceptic cannot call into question; on this, Descartes, Locke and Berkeley were in agreement. None the less, for Berkeley the object I perceive is something that is independent of me; it is not, for example, a product of my imagination. The idea has been produced in me by something other than myself. The sceptic's question now is to ask how he can be sure of this. My will cannot control whether or not I perceive an object, but this, in itself, shows neither that the idea is independent of me nor that it is produced by something else other than me. After all, I might, as Descartes conceded, have some other faculty that is producing these ideas.

Berkeley is right to point out that, when we distinguish between objects that are real and objects that are imagined or illusory or hallucinatory, we do so on the basis of further perceptions and not by seeing beyond the veil of perception to the 'real' world of objects. But he makes the further claim that these objects really exist because they are independent of us, having been put into our minds by God. How can we know about God? Berkeley cannot say, as Descartes did, that we can have an *idea* of God, since he holds that an idea can only be like an idea; it cannot be like anything else, such as a mind or spirit.

According to Berkeley, we can have neither an idea of God nor ideas of other minds. Berkeley does talk about having 'notions' of other minds, based on an analogy with our own mind, but it is not clear what notions are or how they fit in with his account of knowledge. This means that, even if Berkeley has provided a satisfactory answer to the sceptic regarding the existence of physical objects, he is still left with other sceptical problems. For example, how do we know that there are other minds? We arrive at our knowledge of other people through perception, but if other people are simply ideas then they cannot have minds and perceptions of their own.

The continued existence of things
We might wonder, in any case, whether Berkeley really has solved the sceptical problem about the existence of physical objects. Assuming that I can be certain that a table exists when I perceive it, what about when I look in another direction or go out of the room? I no longer perceive it, so how do I answer the question as to whether or not it still exists? The answer that I know it exists because God is still perceiving it is wrong, because I do not know that God is perceiving it. The most I can say is that *if* it still exists, it is because God, or some other mind, is perceiving it. So sceptical doubt remains concerning the existence of objects that I am not perceiving. In Berkeley's defence it should be pointed out that his position is no worse than that of a representative realist, but nor is it any better.

Scientific enquiry

Before leaving Berkeley's idealism, there are some questions that can be raised concerning both scientific enquiry in general and scientific theories of perception in particular.

If Berkeley maintains that there are no independently existing material objects, then what does he think scientists are doing? What about discoveries made, since Berkeley's time, of another planet in the solar system or of electrons or quarks? There need be no inconsistency between the claims scientists make and the claims made by Berkeley's idealism. Take, as an example, the discovery of the planet Pluto. The presence of this planet was predicted on the basis of observation (that is, on the basis of having certain ideas or perceptions) and the prediction was verified by certain other perceptions – such as a patch of colour at a certain position in the night sky.

In the case of unobservable entities, postulated by science to account for what we do observe, such as subatomic particles, Berkeley's idealism is, if anything, more plausible rather than less plausible than representational realism. No one claims to have perceived subatomic particles directly. Instead their presence is inferred, from a line of water droplets in a cloud chamber or readings on various meters. From Berkeley's position, such particles do not have an independent existence; they are no more than a convenient fiction to make sense of our various perceptions. These fictions are useful in so far as they help us to see patterns in our perceptions. There are philosophers of science who have taken a very similar position to this one.

A related but different question is to ask whether there is any purpose served in trying to give a scientific account of sense perception if one starts from the position of idealism. If God produces the ideas in us, any account involving organs of sense seems redundant. Further, since the sense organs themselves, eyes, ears, etc., are objects, that is ideas, they cannot play a causal role in producing ideas. There is a straightforward response that Berkeley can give. First, he has no problem regarding whether or not sense organs exist. They exist by being perceived. As to the supposed causal role, for example, that eyes enable us to see, this is based on observations such as that, when I put my hands over my eyes, I can no longer see. This discovery is simply the discovery of a certain sequence of ideas or perceptions. The attempt to give a scientific account of perception is the attempt to identify more complex and less obvious sequences of perception. It is interesting to note that, in *A New Theory of Vision*, Berkeley made a significant contribution to the scientific study of sight.

Berkeley's account of causation
The external objects that, in Locke's account of perception, affect our organs of sense to produce ideas in us are, in Berkeley's account,

themselves ideas. In explaining how ideas, such as the ideas of white-ness, hardness, sweetness, etc., appear in the mind, Berkeley cannot (and does not) appeal to a causal relationship between external objects and sense organs or between sense organs and minds. He cannot do this because he maintains that there can be no causal relationships between ideas; ideas are passive. Yet this is not inconsistent with saying, for example, that if we close our eyes we cease having the idea of whiteness or if we cover our ears we cease having the perceptions of sounds.

What Locke sees as an example of a causal relationship, that is, a power in one object to produce a change in another, Berkeley sees as no more than a pattern among our perceptions. To account for the supposed causal powers, Locke appeals to the internal constitu-tion of objects; Berkeley accounts for the regularities that arise in our perceptions by appeal to God, who produces these perceptions in us. This might suggest a considerable difference between Locke and Berkeley on the question as to whether we can give scientific explanations of the world around us. The difference is not as great as it seems. Locke's explanations also make an appeal to God: objects owe their internal constitution to God. The real difference between Locke and Berkeley, at least according to Berkeley, is that Locke interposes an unnecessary level between God and ourselves. God has no need to create objects having various powers, including powers to produce ideas in us, since he can produce those ideas directly. The essential feature of a scientific account is to identify the regularities. Observing that visual sensations cease when we close our eyes is an example of such a regularity.

Hume's scepticism

Ideas and impressions

Hume (1711–1776) argued that there is no satisfactory answer to scepticism. To examine these arguments, we need first to look at how Hume developed Locke's 'way of ideas'. Hume uses the general term 'a perception' to refer to whatever is immediately present to the mind, that is, a mental state of any kind. He divides perceptions into just two types, distinguished by their qualities *as* perceptions, that is, their strength, vividness, liveliness or vivacity. Perceptions that are lively and vivacious – for example, those we get from the senses – are termed 'impressions'. Fainter, weaker perceptions Hume calls ideas. Thus when I am looking at a group of youths kicking a ball, my perceptions are vivid and so are classed as impressions. When I close my eyes and try to re-create the scene in my mind then, although the perceptions I have may be very similar to the previous ones, they will differ in being fainter and less vivid; these copies of the original impressions are ideas. Impressions lead to ideas but ideas do not lead to impressions. An idea cannot appear in the mind without having been preceded by an impression that it resembles.

Relations of ideas and matters of fact

According to Hume, there are two kinds of reasoning, the first involving simply a relation of ideas, the second involving a matter of fact. Propositions whose truth can be decided simply by comparing ideas 'are discoverable by the mere operation of thought, without dependence on what is anywhere existent in the universe' (*Enquiries Concerning Human Understanding*, IV.I.20). Included in relations of ideas are the truths of mathematics as well as those of logic. Matters of fact, however, cannot be discovered in this way. The contrary of a true statement involving a relation of ideas must be false, whereas the contrary of a true statement involving a matter of fact is always possible. For example, the contrary of 'Cats eat meat', although false, is none the less possible, but it is not possible that the sum of 3 and 2 is anything other than 5.

The term 'matter of fact' may be a little misleading, since it might seem to imply that what comes under the term denotes a fact rather than a falsity and hence is a true statement. What Hume means is that the truth of such statements is determined by facts in the world and not solely by relationships between the ideas involved. The truth of a statement such as 'Christopher is tired' cannot be determined by considering the idea of Christopher and the idea of (being) tired. It is determined by Christopher's state at the time. Both the statement 'Christopher is tired' and its contrary 'It is not the case that Christopher is tired' concern matters of fact; both are possible even though (at any one time) only one is true.

This appears to leave Hume with a problem: how can we ever know that a statement concerning a matter of fact is true? The reason this is a problem is that all that is present to the mind are our perceptions, that is, our ideas and the impressions from which they derive. If we cannot determine the truth of matters of fact by comparing ideas, how do we determine it? The answer Hume gives is that all such reasoning relating to matters of fact is founded on the relation of cause and effect.

Cause and effect

For Hume, the paradigm example of cause and effect is provided by one billiard ball hitting a second and transferring its motion to it. On what basis do we make the claim that one event (the motion of the first billiard ball) is a cause and the other event (the motion of the second billiard ball) is an effect, and what exactly do we mean by such a claim? If we consider just our perceptions, we have the impression (that is, a vivid perception) of the first ball moving, followed by the impression of the two balls in contact, followed by the impression of the second ball moving. What we do not have is any additional impression of a connection between these events. Yet, without such an impression, we cannot have an idea. If, none the less, we do have an idea of such a connection, the idea of cause and effect, where does it come from? In other words, what produces the belief that the motion of the first ball causes the motion of the second? We might say that we do not usually identify causes on the basis of a single observation, but nothing important is added to our perceptions by observing a number of such collisions. No new type of impression is introduced. In each case a similar sequence of events is observed, with an event of one type, the cause, always preceding an event of another type, the effect. We do not, for example, perceive any necessary connection between cause and effect or any power in the cause to bring about the effect.

There is a difference from our expectation the first time when we observe for the eleventh time one ball heading towards another, but what are the grounds for this difference? If we try to *deduce* that a certain effect will follow, we must make a further assumption, namely that the eleventh occasion will be like the ten previous occasions. In other words, we must assume that in this respect the future will resemble the past, but this produces a deeper problem. What are the grounds for supposing that there is such uniformity in nature? We may note that, in the past, nature has been uniform, but from this we can infer that the future will continue to be uniform only by assuming the very proposition we are trying to establish – that what has happened in the past is a guide to the future! Thus, claims Hume, although this relationship of cause and effect is central to much of our thinking, there are no grounds for inferring from the occurrence of one event to the occurrence of another event. In other words, we have no rational basis for making predictions about the future. Thus Hume introduces the problem of induction, which we will explore further in the next chapter.

Even though we have no rational basis, we do make predictions about the future, we do expect the occurrence of a second event from the occurrence of the first, we do claim that one event has a power over the other. If these claims are not founded on reason, on what are they based? Hume's suggestion is that they are based on custom or habit. The mind is constructed in such a way that, when it has seen a number of instances of an event of one type being followed by an event of another type, on perceiving the first type of event, it will come to expect the second. The two sets of ideas become associated with each other, and it is this association that leads to the impression (again, remember, a lively perception) of a necessary connection. The impression, however, is not of something in the events themselves; rather, it is an inner perception.

What Hume is saying is that all our knowledge of matters of fact, and this constitutes the bulk of our knowledge, since it includes all but the truths of logic and mathematics, is founded on the tendency of the mind to associate ideas. We are able to 'learn from experience' only because of the habit of mind which makes us expect in the future similar patterns of events to those which have occurred in the past. It is custom 'alone which renders our experience useful to us' (*Enquiries Concerning Human Understanding*, V.I.36). But notice, although this might explain why we come to expect an effect when we perceive the cause, it does not justify the expectation.

Belief in the existence of bodies

Statements that objects exist express matters of fact, not relations of ideas. This means that the existence or non-existence of something cannot be determined by reason. Yet we *believe* in the existence of bodies. What leads to this belief? Hume suggests that there are two different questions here. The first is why do we believe that objects have a continuous existence even though our perceptions of them are discontinuous? The second is why do we believe that objects exist independently of their being perceived? These two beliefs, of continuity and independence, are connected. If I claim that, contrary to what I perceive, objects have a continuous existence, then I must suppose that they exist when I do not perceive them. Hence I must also suppose that they exist independently of my perceiving them.

Hume argued that it is the *constancy* of our perceptions and their *coherence* that give rise to our belief in the existence of bodies. Although our perception of familiar objects may be discontinuous, none the less these objects present the same appearance each time. This constancy of appearance can be accounted for by assuming that the objects continued to exist while they were not being perceived. Often, of course, objects do not present a constant appearance – plants will grow, fruit will ripen and rot, a fire will die down and go out, people will change their hair style or put on make-up or simply adopt a different posture or expression. None the less, throughout all these changes there is coherence in the appearances. We can reconcile the changes we observe in our perceptions and attribute them to changes in objects if we assume that objects exist when we do not observe them.

Scepticism with regard to the existence of bodies

One of the problems posed by Descartes was this: how do we know that the objects we perceive with the senses are really there whereas the objects we dream about are not? What, in other words, are the differences between our waking experiences and our experiences when we are dreaming that give us grounds for claiming the existence of objects in the one case but not in the other? Hume argues to the conclusion that neither set of experiences provides grounds for claiming the existence of objects but goes on to give an explanation (although not a justification) for why our waking experiences lead us to believe in the existence of objects.

A possible explanation for the coherence and constancy of our waking experiences is that our waking experiences are experiences of objects, that is, objects which have an independent existence and which are governed, in their interactions with other objects, by causal laws. But the coherence and constancy do not *show* that our experiences are experiences of objects. They do not show this because dream experiences could be coherent in a way that they often are not and yet, no matter how coherent dreams became, they would not be perceptions of real objects.

Phenomenalism

Hume's arguments appear to demonstrate that there is nothing in our experiences that can prove the existence of external objects, although we can identify the features that lead us to the (unfounded) belief in the existence of objects. Thus Hume leaves us in a position of scepticism with regard to the existence of material objects, since there is no logical inference from sense perceptions to material objects. Phenomenalism tries to supply such an inference by, in effect, offering an alternative account of what is meant by the term 'material object'.

For Locke, ideas represented objects; for Berkeley, ideas constituted objects. For the phenomenalist, what we perceive directly are the data from which objects are constructed. Russell (1872–1970), in *The Problems of Philosophy*, gave the name 'sense-data' to 'the things that are immediately known in sensation: such things as colours, sounds, smells, hardnesses, roughnesses, and so on' (p. 4) (although he later abandoned this terminology). When referring to, say, a particular patch of colour as a sense datum, he is not referring to the stains in the wood which make the table brown or the light waves of a certain wavelength that strike my eye. He is referring to the colour that is directly perceived. Similarly with sounds, the sense data are not the vibrations in the object or in the air but my auditory experiences.

If perception involves inferences, then sense data are the hard facts on which the inferences are based. I may not be certain whether what is in front of me is a sheep or a goat but I can be certain about the sense data I have: the shapes, colours, textures, sounds, smells. I may be mistaken about the dagger I see before me or about the oasis I see shimmering on the horizon but I can be certain about what I perceive directly. If I am mistaken, my mistake lies in the inferences I draw from the sense data, not in the nature of the sense data themselves.

Objects are logical constructions out of sense data

Phenomenalism claims physical objects are logical constructions from sense data. Sense data are what is given, and anything we say about physical objects is reducible to statements referring only to sense data. Notice this is not saying that physical objects *are* sense data (which is, in effect, Berkeley's claim). Sense data and physical objects differ in important ways: the claims we make about each are significantly different. For example, sense data are transient and no two people perceive the same sense data. Sense data do not exist when they are not perceived. Physical objects, on the other hand, are (relatively) permanent; they do exist when they are not perceived and the same physical object can be perceived by different people. You cannot perceive my sense data, although you can perceive similar sense data and, by that means, perceive (indirectly) the same object that I am (indirectly) perceiving.

Berkeley achieved a permanence and an independence (of sorts) for collections of ideas (that is, objects) by placing them in the mind of God, since God perceives them even when they are perceived by no one else. The phenomenalist achieves the same end by supplementing the transience of actual sense data with the permanent possibility of their being perceived. When I close the door of my study I no longer perceive what is on the other side of the door, but, according to the pheno-menalist, what I mean by saying that my desk exists is that there is the possibility of perceiving it. A suitably equipped observer in the right position on the other side of the door *would* perceive it. The claim that the desk no longer exists cannot be based on the lack of anyone perceiving it but on the impossibility of anyone perceiving it.

Another way of saying that physical objects are logical constructions out of sense data is to say that any statement that mentions physical objects can be replaced by a statement that mentions instead the sense data that would be had by a suitably sensitive perceiver in a specified situation. The aim of replacing one statement with its equivalence would be to arrive at one that, because it was couched in terms of sense data, was testable.

The problems begin for phenomenalism when we enquire about the details of these translations. Consider the statement (which we may take to be true) 'my desk existed at 3 o'clock this morning', and further suppose that the desk was not perceived by anyone at this time. According to phenomenalism, this statement is correctly translated by a statement of the following form. 'If <description of a suitable observer placed in a favourable condition *vis-à-vis* making observations of my desk> then the following sense data would have been perceived <description of the sort of sense data that would occur>.' It is not a straightforward matter to fill in these descriptions

Look at an object now and see if you can specify *all* the conditions that enable you to perceive it. Obviously there are certain positive conditions to be fulfilled. You must be conscious, looking in the right direction and properly attending to your perceptions, there must be an appropriate level of illumination, and so on. There are also negative conditions that must be fulfilled. You are not under the influence of certain drugs and not being distracted by other thoughts, there is no other object blocking your view, and so on. This list can surely be continued indefinitely. Moreover, we have cheated in producing them since we have referred to physical objects, and these references must themselves be capable of being translated into hypothetical statements about sense data, thus extending the list still further. Also, we must ensure that the observer is there at the right time. Since time is not an immediate object of perception (not a sense datum), statements about time have to be translated into statements containing reference only to sense data.

In short, phenomenalism does not actually do away with the doubts it is supposed to deal with. According to Ayer (1910–1989), 'The phenomenalists are right in the sense that the information which we convey by speaking about the physical objects we perceive is information about how the world would seem, but they are wrong in supposing that it is possible to say of the description of any particular set of appearances that this and only this is what some statement about a physical object comes to' (*The Problem of Knowledge*, 131–2).

Summary

- Perception involves having experiences, and experiences are subjective in nature. Philosophical problems in perception are concerned with the step from these subjective experiences to claims about the nature of the world. Unless the position of the naïve realist is adopted, whereby it is the objects themselves that are perceived, the existence and nature of objects seems to be a matter of inference from the evidence provided by the senses.
- None of the accounts of perception that has been considered – representational realism, idealism, phenomenalism – seems to provide a satisfactory answer to the question: what do our subjective experiences (or perhaps, more properly, what *can* our subjective experiences) tell us about the objective world?
- Representational realism, whereby ideas in the mind are the representatives of objects in the world, leaves the way open for the sceptic to challenge any claim to a knowledge of the world, even the minimal claim that there are objects at all.

■ Idealism replaces the two-world view of representational realism with a one-world view. The material world, which ideas are supposed to represent, is now redundant. However, although this might solve some sceptical problems, other problems, such as those regarding the existence of objects when we are not perceiving them and the existence of other minds, remain.

■ For Hume, what is given are our perceptions, that is, according to him, ideas and impressions. The differences that exist between imagining an object, perceiving it with the senses, thinking of an object, believing that it exists, he reduces to differences in the strength or vividness of the perceptions. Thus, Hume thinks, our belief that objects exist can be accounted for by showing how it is that the ideas (which make up the content of the belief) have the appropriate level of vividness. What we cannot do, however, is justify these beliefs. For any claim made which goes beyond simply describing our perceptions, we can have no justification.

■ According to phenomenalism, objects are logical constructions out of sense data. This removes some problems, but providing the details of these logical constructions is, to say the least, problematic.

Questions raised

■ How is knowledge possible if we cannot give a satisfactory account of the relation between sense experience and the world? Can we bridge the gap between appearance and reality? Or explain it away? Or arrive at knowledge by some other route? Or must we concede that what we have falls short of knowledge?

■ Hume suggests that all knowledge, whether based on the senses or on reasoning, reduces to probability. Is such a sceptical position really tenable? If not, how do we counter Hume's arguments?

■ Are scientific claims as to the nature of reality justified? Can they be verified? Indeed, is reality intelligible to us at all?

■ Some of the accounts of perception have involved physical processes producing mental experiences. Is this dualist view, which derives from Descartes, a tenable one? If not, what should be put in its place? Should the physical be subsumed in the mental or should the mental be subsumed in the physical?

4 Knowledge, Belief and Logic

Introduction

In this chapter we continue our examination of epistemological issues and introduce topics from other areas of philosophy, including logic, philosophical logic and the philosophy of science.

We begin by exploring the idea that knowledge is justified true belief. From here we move on to consider Kant's distinction between *a priori* knowledge and empirical knowledge and his distinction between analytic propositions and synthetic propositions. This leads on to the idea of a logical truth. Knowledge is extended by using arguments. Logic tells us when we are justified. A valid deductive argument is truth-preserving. An inductive argument provides support for the conclusion but, since the conclusion goes beyond the premises, cannot guarantee it.

Science appears to provide us with extensive and profound knowledge of the universe in which we live. However, its general and far-reaching claims – far-reaching in the sense that they refer to events that are distant in space and in time – are based on local observations. What scientists observe is the behaviour over a narrow time-scale of near, medium-sized objects. What scientific theories encompass ranges from the events inside atoms, lasting for unimaginably short periods of time, to the events in distant galaxies, lasting for unimaginably long periods of time. Can this induction be justified, and can we say what generalizations are possible?

Hempel's paradox of confirmation and Goodman's new riddle of induction both throw doubt on what inductive reasoning can achieve. The claim that science is a body of knowledge is under threat because of criticisms levelled at inductive reasoning. However, according to Popper, induction is not central to science. Popper suggests that the route by which we arrive at scientific laws is less important than the process of testing to which these laws are subsequently subjected. The view that what is distinctive about science is the attempt to falsify would-be laws is questioned by Kuhn, at least with regard to periods of what he would call 'normal science'. Falsification, he suggests, does not play the role attributed to it by Popper.

Propositional knowledge

Knowing how and knowing that

Knowing may involve knowing how to do something or knowing that something is the case. I know that the way to ride a bicycle is continually to make steering adjustments so that I move along a series of circular arcs. I also know how to ride a bicycle. However, these two instances of knowledge are not only quite different but also independent of each other. It is possible to have either without having the other. Further, the way I demonstrate that I know is different for the two sorts of knowing. I show that I know how to ride a bike simply by riding it. Showing that I know that, as opposed to know how, is not always so easy.

The sort of knowledge I have when I know that is also called propositional knowledge, since what I know is that a proposition is true. Belief is also, in this sense, propositional. Although a contrast is generally made between knowing and believing, propositional knowledge is more like a special sort of belief. If I know, say, that grass is green, I also have a belief; I believe that grass is green. If I know that Paris is the capital city of France I also believe this to be the case. On the other hand, I may believe things without it being the case that I know them. I may believe, but not know, that Glasgow and Moscow are on the same line of latitude, that being a vegetarian is healthier than being a meat-eater, that the lottery sequence 1, 2, 3, 4, 5, 6 will not come up, that there is no God, that machines do not think, and so on.

The form that statements of belief take is:

He believes that X.

For example:

He believes that philosophy is a rational activity.

The letter 'X' has been replaced by 'philosophy is a rational activity'. Since we are concerned with the nature of belief rather than with particular beliefs, it is useful to work with the general form – we do the same thing in algebra where we are interested in numbers but not in particular numbers. (Many people find this use of letters to stand for names or numbers or propositions confusing, but it is a powerful technique and worth persevering with.) We need to be clear, however, exactly what sort of thing X is standing for.

Sentences and propositions

In the above example, 'X' was replaced by the sentence 'philosophy is a rational activity'. However, it is not a sentence that is the object of belief but the proposition expressed by a sentence. Why should we bother to make this distinction between a sentence and the proposition expressed by the sentence? One reason is that the same proposition can be expressed by different sentences. For example, the proposition expressed by 'Philosophy is a rational activity' can also be expressed by 'Philosophy is an activity that is rational' or 'The following activity is a rational one: philosophy'. It can be expressed by a sentence in a different language, for example, 'Filosofia es una actividad racional'. To replace 'X', in 'He believes that X', by any one of a number of sentences would be to attribute the same belief. It is also the case that different propositions can be expressed by the same sentence. For example, 'This is fine flour' may mean that it is splendid flour or that it is flour that has been finely milled so that each particle is very small.

Before continuing, let us clarify how we are going to talk about sentences and propositions. Reference to a sentence is made by enclosing it in single quotation marks. Thus one may talk about the sentence 'Violets are blue', for example, by saying that it is a sentence containing three words. On the other hand, reference to a proposition is made by *using* a sentence. Thus, when I *use* the sentence 'Violets are blue', I am passing on information about the colour of a certain type of flower: the sentence 'Violets are blue' is used to express the proposition that violets are blue. In general, the sentence 'p' expresses the proposition that p.

Not all sentences express propositions. Here are some examples of sentences that do not express propositions: 'What is the time?', 'Stand easy!', 'Take the second exit', 'I promise to pay back everything I owe', 'I name this ship *Arkwright*'. These sentences pose a question, issue an order, give a direction, make a promise, name a ship, respectively. None expresses something that can be believed or known. Only sentences used to assert can express a proposition. A crude test for sentences that express propositions is to ask of them 'Can they be true or false?' (This is a crude test because the same set of words can, by employing a different tone of voice, be used to make an assertion or ask a question.) Propositions can be described as being true or false. This is often expressed by saying that propositions have a truth-value – the two possible truth-values being true and false.

Is belief a mental state?

I can ascribe belief in a certain proposition by the sentence

He believes that p.

To believe that p is to stand in a certain relationship to the proposition p; other relationships are possible. Thus: he hopes that p, he fears that p, he thinks that p, he wishes it were the case that p, and so on. Hoping, fearing, thinking, wishing are different mental states that are, as it were, directed at the proposition. 'He knows that p' seems to be part of the same set, suggesting that knowing is also a mental state. However, when he knows that p it must be true that p, unlike when he believes that p or thinks that p or hopes that p. This makes it seem as if knowing is a mental state that somehow guarantees or confers truth. Clearly this is not so. From my own point of view I cannot distinguish instances in which I know that p from instances in which I only think I know that p: the mental states involved in knowing that p and thinking one knows that p are the same. Hence there must be more to knowing that p than being in a certain mental state.

At this point we might want to examine more critically, if only in passing, the suggestion that belief is a mental state. According to Descartes, the mental is what we are aware of. When we hope for something or fear something, these are mental states because there is an awareness of that which we hope for or fear. It is not clear that this is so in the case of belief. I have all sorts of beliefs about myself, about other people and about the world in general without being aware of these beliefs. For example, I believe that I am not capable of running a mile in four minutes, still less in three minutes, but I may never have been conscious of this belief before now. However, in order to have the hope of being able to run a mile in four minutes or in three minutes, I would have to be aware of my hopes.

Knowing involves believing

Knowing that p does seem to be more like believing that p than, say, hoping that p or fearing that p. But is it true to say that knowing is a special sort of belief? Might it not be possible to know that p without believing that p? Surely someone could say: 'I know that everything is made up of minute atoms but I can't believe it'. Or we might say of someone: 'He knows he has won the lottery but he still can't believe it'. Yet it would be misleading to describe these as cases of knowing without believing. The sort of idea being expressed by 'but I can't believe it' or 'but he can't believe it' is that it (i.e., everything being made of atoms or winning the lottery) is difficult to believe or difficult to reconcile with other beliefs. On the other hand, it is sometimes the case that, although the person appears to be claiming that he or she knows, what is actually being claimed is something different, such as, for example: 'It is accepted scientific knowledge that everything is made of atoms.'

One can know only what is true

Let us accept that knowing involves believing (even if we are not sure whether believing is a mental state). Does it involve anything else? As mentioned already, in order to know that p, 'p' must be true. Before Copernicus, many people claimed to know that the earth was the centre of the universe and the sun and other heavenly bodies revolved around the earth. Given that, as we now believe, the sun and stars do not revolve around the earth, did those people really know what they claimed to know? We have to say that they did not really know. At best they only thought they knew. Likewise, if the things *we* claim to know turn out to be false, then we are mistaken in saying that we know them.

We must be careful not to misunderstand the relationship between knowing that p and it being true that p. When Carl Jung claimed that he did not merely believe there was a God, he *knew* there was a God, he seemed to think he was offering some guarantee of God's existence. Believing there is a God is consistent with there being no God, knowing there is a God is not. Claiming to know that God exists does not make him exist since another alternative is possible: God does not exist and I only think I know that he does. Choosing between these two alternatives, of knowing and thinking mistakenly that one knows, can be done only by determining whether or not God really does exist. To state the obvious: one cannot make things true by knowing them.

From the third-person perspective it is possible to separate questions about what a person believes from questions about the truth of these beliefs. Further, one may have evidence relating to the truth of a belief that is not, or was not, available to the person holding the belief. Thus Ptolemy may have believed that the earth was the centre of the universe, whereas we know that it is not. Hence Ptolemy cannot have known that the earth is the centre of the universe. However, from the first-person perspective, what is believed and whether it is true are not independent, since the things we believe are precisely those things we take to be true. From the first-person perspective, it is not possible to distinguish, by means of some sort of direct access to the truth of those propositions for which knowledge is claimed, between what one knows and what one thinks one knows but actually only believes.

Grounds for belief

From the first-person perspective, the evidence for the truth of what is believed is exactly the same as the grounds for the belief. This may not be the case when talking about someone else's belief, since our evidence for the truth of the belief may be different from his or her grounds for believing. Thus it is possible to make two sorts of challenges to someone else's claim to know something. The first is to deny the truth of what is believed. The second is to accept the truth of what is believed but deny that the evidence on which the belief is based is sufficient for knowledge.

Consider Ptolemy's (supposed) claim to know that the earth was the centre of the universe. We have evidence that it is not the centre of the universe and hence that Ptolemy could not know what he thought he knew. On the other hand, someone living at the time of Ptolemy might have had the correct belief that the earth is not the centre of the universe but have based this belief on, say, a personal dislike of Ptolemy. Such a person may have believed but did not know that the earth was not the centre of the universe. In the first case one is looking at the sum total of evidence and concluding that what is believed is false (and so could not be known). In the second case, the sum total of evidence may point to the truth of what is believed but the evidence on which an individual's belief is actually grounded falls short of this.

A priori knowledge

Kant opens his *Critique of Pure Reason* with the admission that all knowledge begins with experience but goes on to argue we also possess knowledge that is entirely independent of experience. Such knowledge he terms *a priori* and contrasts with empirical or *a posteriori* knowledge. These terms should not be seen as implying any temporal order in the acquisition of knowledge. *A priori* knowledge is not knowledge that we acquire prior to or before we have any experiences, it is knowledge that is based on something other than the evidence provided by experience. If *a priori* knowledge is possible, we may be sceptical regarding the senses, yet still be justified in claiming knowledge of those truths that are independent of experience.

Kant thought that one mark of *a priori* knowledge was necessity. Experience can tell us how things are but it cannot tell us whether they must be like that. Compare the two propositions 'Grass is green' and 'Two plus two is four'. Both are true but the second is *necessarily* true. Grass could be some other colour but two plus two could not result in anything other than four. Thus, according to Kant, since 'two plus two is four' is a necessary truth, it must be one that cannot be arrived at through experience. Hence it must be an *a priori* truth, a truth that is independent of experience.

Analytic propositions

Kant also made a distinction between two sorts of propositions: those that he calls analytic and those that he calls synthetic. In his account of this distinction, Kant makes the assumption that propositions always take a particular form, namely that of subject-predicate. A proposition having subject-predicate form divides into two parts: the subject is what the proposition is about and the predicate is the rest of the proposition that says something about the subject. Thus the proposition 'Grass is green' is about grass and the predicate says that it is green. Kant's contention is that, with regard to propositions, there are two possibilities: either the predicate is already present in the concept of the subject or it is not. If the former is the case then the proposition is analytic. An example of an analytic proposition is the proposition that a bachelor is an unmarried man. Here, the predicate 'is an unmarried man' is contained in the concept of a bachelor. Such propositions are termed 'analytic' because they do not say anything new about the subject; they simply provide an analysis of the subject. The knowledge constituted by an understanding of analytic propositions is *a priori*; since it can be obtained by analysing the concept of the subject, it is independent of experience. Propositions that do say something new about the subject, and so add to the concept of the subject something that was not previously there, are synthetic propositions.

Another example to illustrate the difference between analytic and synthetic propositions is the one Kant gives. For Kant, the proposition 'All bodies are extended' is analytic, whereas the proposition 'All bodies are heavy' is synthetic. This may not appear immediately obvious to us. Kant's reason is this: following Descartes, to be extended is part of the concept of body, since extension is the essence of body. On the other hand, being heavy is not part of the concept of body. Hence, to add the predicate 'are heavy' is to add something new to our knowledge of bodies. We are 'synthesizing' a new piece of knowledge and the source of this knowledge is experience. It is our experience of bodies that tells us they are heavy; this is not something we discover from analysing the concept of body.

It is possible to extend this notion of analyticity to other propositional forms, while retaining the spirit of Kant's distinction, by defining an analytic proposition as one that is true by virtue of the meaning of the terms used. To see how, we must first introduce the idea of a logical truth.

Logical truths

Using Kant's notion of an analytic proposition, the clearest examples are logical truths. Consider the following: 'black is black', 'a pink elephant is a pink elephant', 'a deal is a deal'. The truth of such propositions depends on the structure of the sentences that express the propositions. Any sentence of the form 'a is a' is analytic (provided, of course, 'a' is replaced in the same way on each occurrence). We can think of other analytic propositions, having different forms, that are also true simply because of their form. Some simple examples of such forms are: 'p or not p', 'if p then p'. Any proposition that has one of these forms is an example of a logical truth. Logical truths, then, are propositions that are true because of their form. The form or logical structure of a proposition can be revealed by replacing words and expressions by letters. Propositions that are *logically* true are ones whose truth is determined purely by their form and not by the meaning of the (non-logical) terms in the proposition. Quine (1908–2000) expresses this by saying that 'a logical truth is a statement which is true and remains true under all reinterpretations of its components other than the logical particles' (*From a Logical Point of View*, 22–3). (In practice, revealing the logical structure of a proposition is not usually so simple as might be thought from the above account, but it suffices to convey the notion of a logical truth.)

It might seem that a logical truth is not very exciting or interesting; a proposition whose form ensures it is true no matter what it is about must, surely, be trivial. If I wished to be told something significant about quarks, I would feel cheated by being told that a quark is a quark or that either something is a quark or it is not. Of course, even propositions that are, in the above sense, trivial may have a use that is not trivial. For example, one might say to someone that a deal is a deal to remind them that they have entered into a contract. One might say, when looking for a lost item, 'either it is here or it is not here' to encourage a stoical attitude should one fail to find it. A second point to make is that not all logical truths are as transparently true as the ones we have considered.

Having arrived at some idea of what constitutes a logical truth, we can now extend Kant's account of analyticity by suggesting a procedure that will convert any analytic proposition into a logical truth. The procedure will involve replacing one or more terms of the proposition by a synonym (or synonyms), that is, by a term having the same meaning. Consider the proposition: 'No bachelor is married'. When 'bachelor' is replaced by its synonym 'unmarried man', the proposition becomes 'No unmarried man is married'. Treating both 'no' and 'un-' as equivalent to the logical term (or particle) 'not', this is now a logical truth, having the form 'not-not a is a'. Since the logical truth was derived from the original proposition by the substitution of a synonym, the original proposition must have been analytic. We can suggest, as a more general notion of analyticity, the following: an analytic proposition is either itself a logical truth or it can be changed into a logical truth by replacing words and expressions in the proposition with their synonyms. Since terms that are synonymous are terms with the same meaning, a less precise way of describing an analytic proposition is to say that it is a proposition that is true by virtue of its meaning. This reformulation, which owes much to Quine, appears to provide us with a more useful notion of analyticity. However, Quine argues that the distinction between analytic and synthetic is a misleading one and that we are led into deep waters when we try to explain what 'meaning' and, in particular, what sameness of meaning is. Quine's contention is that we are forced to use analyticity to explain what it is for terms to be synonymous rather than the other way round. However, rather than follow Quine into these depths, we shall remain in the relative shallows and see where he resurfaces.

Deductive arguments

Once we have acquired some knowledge, we want to be able to use it to obtain further knowledge. This we do by means of an argument. The term 'argument' may suggest disagreements or quarrels. In philosophy, however, an argument is simply a piece of reasoning. More specifically, it is a set of propositions, called the premises, together with another proposition, the conclusion, which supposedly follows from these premises. Arguments are valid or invalid according to whether or not the conclusion really does follow from the premises. Validity is a property of arguments, whereas truth is a property of propositions. A valid argument is truth-preserving. This means that if true premises are used in a valid argument then the conclusion is also true. Hence, if I know that the premises are true, a valid argument provides me with the knowledge of the conclusion. Before giving a more precise definition of validity, let us illustrate the concept with some examples.

My daughter, Clare, goes into a building to get her exam results. She comes out smiling. From this I deduce that she has got the grades she wanted. Although I may not consciously have thought this through, my argument is this:

Premise 1   If Clare is smiling then Clare has the grades she wants.
Premise 2   Clare is smiling.
Conclusion   Clare has the grades she wants.

This is a valid argument. However, having a valid argument does not guarantee that the conclusion is true; for this, the premises have to be true as well. In the above argument, either premise could have been false. The facts that determine whether the second premise is true or false are straightforward. We know what it means to say someone is smiling and what it means to say that they are not. The facts that determine whether the first premise is true are much less straightforward. The first premise neither states that Clare is smiling nor that she has the grades she wants. What it states is a connection between these two propositions. It would be false if something other than getting the grades she wants would have made Clare smile, for example, being told that her lottery syndicate had just won the jackpot.

Conditionals

The first premise is an example of a conditional proposition. A conditional is a compound proposition made up of two parts, called the antecedent and the consequent. Both antecedent and consequent are themselves propositions and as such they can be either true or false. However, the truth of the conditional as a whole is not dependent on these two propositions being true but on there being the right sort of relationship between them. We can express this relationship in different ways, such as: whenever it is the case that Clare is smiling it is also the case that Clare has the grades that she wants. Alternatively: it is only having the grades she wants that causes Clare to smile; there are no other circumstances that would make her smile in this situation. (It is worth pointing out, although without further comment, that a conditional can be treated as what is termed a material implication, where the truth-value of the proposition as a whole is determined by the truth-values of the constituent parts.)

It is important that the nature of the connection between the two constituent propositions that is asserted by the conditional is fully understood. In particular, it is important to appreciate the difference between the above conditional and the following conditional, which, although formed from the same two simple propositions, has ante-cedent and consequent reversed:

If Clare has the grades she wants then she is smiling.

What this second conditional asserts is that getting the grades will be sufficient to make Clare smile. There may be other reasons for her smiling but, if the conditional is true and she has the grades she wants, it cannot be the case that anything will prevent her smiling.

Validity

Although we need to know something about Clare to determine the truth of the premises, we do not have to know anything about her to determine whether or not the argument is valid. For a deductive argument, validity is a logical or formal property in the same way that being logically true is a formal property of a proposition. Indeed, as we shall see later, although truth and validity are quite separate ideas, validity can be linked to the idea of a logical truth. The form of the argument can be revealed, as we have seen before, by using letters to stand for propositions. If we replace the proposition 'Clare is smiling' by 'p' and 'Clare has got the grades she needs' by 'q', the conditional becomes 'If p then q' and the argument itself becomes:

Premise 1   If p then q.
Premise 2   p.
Conclusion   q.

This is a valid form because, no matter what substitutions we make for p and q, we cannot obtain the result that the two premises are true but the conclusion is false.

By way of contrast, note that the following argument form is invalid:

Premise 1   If p then q.
Premise 2   q.
Conclusion   p.

This is the fallacy known as affirming the consequent. An example of this fallacy is the following:

Premise 1   If it is raining then the sky is overcast.
Premise 2   The sky is overcast.
Conclusion   It is raining.

The argument is invalid because of its form, and this would be unaltered even if both the premises and the conclusion were true. The conclusion, that it is raining, does not follow from the premises since it is *possible* for the premises to be true and yet the conclusion false. In the case of a valid argument this would not be possible. Valid arguments are truth-preserving; they transfer the truth of the premises to the conclusion.

Inductive arguments

In a valid deductive argument, as we have seen, the truth of the premises guarantees the truth of the conclusion. There is another type of argument where the premises provide grounds for the conclusion without guaranteeing it. Such an argument is called an inductive argument. An example of an inductive argument is one in which a general conclusion, such as that all swans are white, is inferred from particular cases, such as that all swans so far observed are white. In a deductive argument, the conclusion is contained in the premises and so the truth of the premises guarantees the truth of the conclusion. On the other hand, in an inductive argument, the conclusion goes beyond the premises and so the premises cannot guarantee the truth of the conclusion. Knowing the truth of the premises of an inductive argument may give grounds for believing the conclusion but not for claiming to know the conclusion. If we allow ourselves the assumption that the future will resemble the past we can exchange an inductive argument for a deductive one. For example, instead of the following inductive argument:

Premise 1   In the past, all As have been Bs.
Conclusion   In the future, all As will be Bs.

we have the deductive argument

Premise 1   In the past, all As have been Bs.
Premise 2   The future resembles the past.
Conclusion   In the future, all As will be Bs.

However, this has not provided better grounds for the conclusion, merely shifted the problem to that of showing that the second premise is true; we still have to show that the future will resemble the past. The only basis for claims about the future is our past experience, but this relies on an inductive argument, whereas the whole point of the premise was to eliminate a reliance on inductive arguments!

Deductive arguments are 'all or nothing' arguments; either the conclusion follows or it does not. Inductive arguments, on the other hand, do seem to offer varying degrees of support for a conclusion. Judged by the standard of deductive arguments, this is not good enough: if they do not offer 100 per cent support, they do not offer any support at all. Given the truth of the premises, it is the form of a valid deductive argument that guarantees the conclusion. The form of an inductive argument can offer no such guarantee. Therefore, any support that the premises of an inductive argument give to the conclusion must depend on the content or meaning of the premises and conclusion. Given our reliance on induction, we certainly need a way of deciding between different particular inductive arguments. The so-called problem of induction is the problem of deciding which inductive arguments give reliable conclusions and which do not. The following two paradoxes show that this is not a straightforward matter.

Paradoxes of induction

Hempel's paradox
In order to be able to use inductive arguments, we need to know what evidence supports the conclusion, that is, what counts as a confirming

instance. The paradox of confirmation, proposed by Hempel (1905–1997) and also known as Hempel's paradox, throws doubt on our ability to identify confirming instances and on the idea that, the greater the number of confirming instances observed, the more confidence we can have in the conclusion. To see why, consider first the proposition 'All ravens are black'. On what grounds could we accept such a proposition as true? Evidence that supports the proposition is the sighting of a raven that is black. On the other hand, the sighting of a raven that was not black would provide a counter-example, showing the proposition to be false. Thus, we can suggest, to see whether the proposition 'All ravens are black' is true we need to observe ravens; the sighting of a black raven is a confirming instance whereas the sighting of a raven that is not black would be a counter-example. The more black ravens we see and the longer we go without sighting a raven that is not black, the more confidence we are likely to have that the proposition is true.

Now consider this proposition: 'Everything that is not black is not a raven'. We can express the same proposition like this: 'All non-black things are non-ravens'. What do we need to observe to establish whether this proposition is true? Since the proposition seems to be about non-black things, it is non-black things that we should observe. A non-black thing that is not a raven (i.e., is a not-raven) is a confirming instance, whereas a non-black thing that is a raven (i.e., is not a not-raven) is a counter-example. As with the previous case, the more non-black non-ravens we see and the longer we go without seeing a non-black thing that is a raven, the more confidence we are likely to have that the proposition is true.

The problem, and what gives rise to Hempel's paradox, is that the two propositions 'All ravens are black' and 'All non-black things are non-ravens' are identical. They divide the world up in exactly the same way. This means that an observation that confirms one also confirms the other, and an observation that is a counter-example to one is a counter-example to the other. A black raven is one sort of confirming instance, but a non-black non-raven is a different sort of confirming instance – though (from the logical viewpoint) one that is equally good. Thus we have the apparent absurdity that observing a pink flamingo, a blue mountain or a white Christmas counts as a confirming instance for the proposition 'All ravens are black'. At the very least, the sudden appearance of all this new evidence challenges our beliefs that we can assess the strength of evidence in favour of a proposition, and that the more confirming instances, the greater should be our confidence.

We can offer some sort of answer to this paradox but not, I suspect, one that would satisfy the logician. For example, we can say that although, logically, the two propositions are equivalent, they are not 'about' the same thing. 'All ravens are black' is about ravens, and so confirming instances and counter examples are to do with ravens. On the other hand, 'All non-black things are not ravens' is about non-black things, and so confirming instances and counter examples are to do with non-black things. We might add that the number of things that are non-black is vastly larger than the number of things that are black and the number of things that are non-ravens is vastly larger than the number of things that are ravens. Even if no raven was black, the majority of non-black things we would see would not be ravens. Irrespective of the actual colour of ravens, it is too easy to find non-black things that are not ravens; the currency is of very little value. What this seems to be pointing towards is the idea that what counts as a confirming instance, and so increases confidence in a proposition, is not purely a matter of logic. It is to do with what the proposition is about, that is, its subject, and what else we know about the subject.

Goodman's riddle

Goodman (1906–1998) claims to present us with a 'new riddle of induction'. The problem of induction has become: when is a general hypothesis confirmed by a particular instance? The general hypothesis that copper conducts electricity is confirmed by a particular piece of copper being found to conduct electricity, whereas the general hypothesis that all men in the room are third sons (Goodman was giving a lecture when he produced this example) is not confirmed by finding a particular man in the room who is a third son. The difference between the two is that the first is a *lawlike* generalization whereas the second is not. Goodman then proceeds to give the following example to show that unforeseen problems arise with trying to distinguish lawlike statements from those that are not.

He asks us to suppose that, up to a certain time t, all emeralds observed have been green. These individual observations therefore support, that is, provide confirming evidence for, the generalization 'all emeralds are green'. Goodman continues: 'let me introduce another predicate less familiar than "green". It is the predicate "grue" and it applies to all things examined before t just in case they are green but to other things just in case they are blue' (*Fact, Fiction and Forecast*, 74). Thus all the particular observations made before time t that were confirming instances for the statement 'all emeralds are green' will also be confirming instances for the statement 'all emeralds are grue'. Thus we have similar evidence for the prediction that emeralds observed after time t will be green and that they will be grue. However, if an emerald examined after t is grue then it will be blue and hence not green. The problem is not that we do not know which of the predictions, concerning emeralds observed after time t, is confirmed by the observation of emeralds made before time t, the problem is to provide a criterion for determining when a generalization is lawlike.

A tempting response to Goodman's riddle is to say that adjectives such as 'grue' are artificial. They can be defined only by using the familiar adjectives 'green' and 'blue' and, moreover, make reference to some particular time t. This means that what seems like a general statement, all emeralds are grue, is a disguised particular statement. Goodman's response is to introduce the predicate 'bleen' that applies to all things examined before time t just in case they are blue and to things examined after time t just in case they are green. He agrees that the predicates 'green' and 'blue' are well-behaved and are admissible in lawlike generalizations, whereas 'grue' and 'bleen' are not, but we cannot base this difference on an implicit reference to a particular time. Rather than starting with 'green' and 'blue' and defining 'grue' and 'bleen' in terms of them, we could start with 'grue' and 'bleen' and define 'green' as applying to all things examined before time t just in case they are grue and to things examined after time t just in case they are bleen. Thus, whether an adjective makes a reference to a particular time is a relative matter.

Scientific knowledge

Falsification of theories

Popper (1902–1994) has suggested that the problem of induction does not undermine the claims of science, since science does not rely on inductive reasoning. Science does not even set about trying to find confirming instances for its proposed laws. What science does, or, more accurately, what scientists do, is to try to disprove or falsify a generalization. Thus, to take the generalization considered above, namely 'All ravens are black', a scientist would not look for black ravens (or, for that matter, non-black non-ravens) but for non-black ravens. The observation of a non-black raven would, as already mentioned, falsify the generalization. A generalization is retained by science only for as long as it is not falsified.

If Popper is correct, then he has provided an answer to Hempel's paradox. The mistake there lay not in thinking that an observation of a black raven was relevant in the way that an observation of a white swan was not. What Popper is in effect saying is that, from the point of view of science, neither is relevant. The only relevant observation is the observation of a raven that is not black (or a non-black thing that is a raven). Any observation that disproves the statement about ravens also disproves the logically equivalent statement about non-black things and vice versa. More importantly, a disproof of either is equally relevant and equally recognizable as a disproof of the other.

Popper's aim was not to seek an answer to the problem of induction but to provide a criterion to distinguish science from pseudo-science. According to Popper, what sets science apart from non-scientific investigations is not the process by which a generalization is obtained from a set of observations. The true mark of science is that it sets out to *disprove* a generalization by producing testable hypotheses. In practice, induction may supply the generalizations to be tested, but the confidence we place in science does not rest on a belief that the induction has been performed well. It rests on the fact that the generalizations have survived rigorous attempts to disprove them. There is nothing wrong if the process of producing new generalizations or new theories is an irrational one provided, once we have a generalization, we can frame and carry out tests by which we might show it to be false.

If knowledge is taken to be a set of true statements then, on Popper's view, science cannot, and should not, claim to be a body of knowledge. At best, its claim is to be a set of statements that have not been shown to be false. As new theories are proposed, tested and rejected, they are replaced by theories which, although they may also be false, are better than the theories that preceded them. Popper holds that, in this way, there can be progress in science even though there is no final, attainable end point.

Kuhnian paradigms

Even this view of progress is rejected by Kuhn (1922–1996), as is the role of falsification expounded by Popper. In order to understand Kuhn's view of science it is necessary to understand a central concept he employs: that of the paradigm. A paradigm is a model or pattern that serves as an example or sets a standard. As Kuhn uses the term, though, it acquires a far richer meaning. Instances that function as paradigms in science are universally recognized scientific achievements. Such achievements not only solve particular scientific problems but also provide the focus for a community of specialists and help determine values and perceptions. Kuhn provides various examples of these paradigms, both major and minor. They include Aristotle's analysis of motion, Ptolemy's computation of planetary position and the Copernican system which replaced it, Newtonian mechanics, Einstein's relativity and so on.

When one of these paradigmatic achievements becomes accepted, it rarely, if ever, provides solutions to all the perceived problems. However, the numerous difficulties or anomalies that come to light are not treated as falsifying the theory, that is, they are not treated as counter-examples, nor do they provide reasons for rejecting the theory. Instead they are dismissed, put aside to be considered at a later date or, in most cases, provide the stimuli for further development of the theory. This activity of dealing with anomalies Kuhn calls 'normal science'. It is what most scientists do most of the time.

It is here that we see some of the ideas of Quine reappearing. Quine's development of Kant's distinction between analytic and synthetic propositions suggests that there is a linguistic and a factual component to what determines the truth of a proposition. Popper's theory of falsification presupposes that individual statements can be tested against reality. Quine rejects this idea and, in its place, offers the picture of the sum total of our beliefs, which includes scientific theories, as forming a web or grid. Evidence that goes against a particular belief will affect the web as a whole. The result may be that it is pulled this way or that. It need not be the case that an individual belief will be dropped. Thus it is the whole web of beliefs that is tested against reality, and it is at this level, and not at the level of individual propositions, that there is a role for both meanings and facts.

Quine's rejection of the sharp distinction between analytic and synthetic propositions is part and parcel of this holistic view. What we take to be an analytic proposition is simply one that we are determined to hold true whatever the disconfirming evidence. This is not, Quine suggests, because there is something special about the proposition. We are liable to refuse to accept a counter-example for any proposition, if accepting it would force us to make much more drastic revisions to our web of beliefs than rejecting it.

In this vein, Kuhn sees the central propositions of a paradigm as buried deep within the web of associated beliefs and so resistant to falsifying evidence. For those committed to Newtonian mechanics, Kuhn notes, the second law of motion behaves 'very much like a purely logical statement that no amount of observation could disprove' (*The Structure of Scientific Revolutions*, 78). None the less, paradigms do get overthrown; normal science is punctuated by periods of 'revolutionary activity'. Yet, when this occurs, it is not simply because the theory has been falsified in Popperian fashion. Even though a significant body of counter-examples has built up, Kuhn suggests, a paradigmatic theory will not be rejected unless there is an alternative. It does not matter if, in the initial stages, the alternative does not appear to offer much of an improvement.

There is certainly no reason to suppose, claims Kuhn, that, as one paradigm is overthrown and a new one adopted, science progresses closer and closer to truth. Once the new paradigm has taken over, the change might be presented, retrospectively, as if it were a logical development, but in fact it imports a whole new set of beliefs about the world. Even though many of the terms used in the earlier theory also appear in the later theory, the meanings of these terms will have changed, making comparisons between the two difficult. Thus Einstein's general relativity, which supplanted Newton's theory of gravitation, cannot be seen merely as a development or extension of the earlier theory that brings us closer to a true account.

While Popper concedes that science may never reach the goal of providing an objective, true account of nature, he does see science as approaching ever closer to it; Kuhn, on the other hand, denies that there is any reason to suppose that there is such a goal. Progress is, as it were, a local phenomenon, not a large-scale movement towards some end. It is in this different view of science that Kuhn sees a way of solving the problem of induction, although the solution itself is not spelt out.

We might express a similar point by saying that some of the truths of science are conventional truths, that is, they are true because of a convention as to the meaning of the terms which express the truth. The implications of such a suggestion are that first, if a different convention had been adopted, then we would have a different theory to explain the same facts, and second, that a scientific theory is under-determined by these facts. Can we have two different scientific theories which both give an equally good account of the known facts? If we answer 'yes', then we seem to be saying that scientific theories do not straightforwardly represent the world, for surely both accounts cannot be true.

Summary

- Propositional knowledge is a special sort of belief. A claim to knowledge must be rejected if the belief is false. It must also be rejected if the grounds for the belief are inadequate.

- Kant argued that there are some propositions whose truth can be known independently of experience, that is, that *a priori* knowledge is possible. Extending Kant's definition, an analytic proposition is one whose truth is determined by the meanings of the terms used in the proposition. Quine, however, argues that the distinction between analytic and synthetic is fatally flawed.

- Valid deductive arguments are truth-preserving: if the premises are true then the conclusion will also be true. Inductive arguments are not valid. In an inductive argument, there is always a gap between premises and conclusion. The existence of this gap poses a threat to claims to knowledge based on induction.

- Hume's problem of induction is that there is no inconsistency in a general statement being confirmed in all cases up to a certain time and yet being falsified subsequently. To deduce the conclusion of an inductive argument requires the additional premise that nature is uniform, that the future resembles the past. Yet any justification for this premise would have to appeal to inductive reasoning. Hempel's paradox and Goodman's new riddle of induction add further problems.

- Popper tries to avoid the problems of induction by suggesting that scientific theories are never confirmed, they can only be falsified. For Popper, we can never reach the point where we can claim that a law of science is true, no matter how many confirming instances there have been. The best we can achieve is a statement that has been tested but not yet disproved.

- Kuhn argues that we are not entitled even to this degree of confidence. For any theory that is accepted by scientists as correct, there will be a number of known counter-examples. These counter-examples will lead to the rejection of a successful theory only if there is an alternative theory to go in its place. Thus, the laws of science cannot be seen as true statements – or, at least, not as statements which we know to be true.

Questions raised

- According to Quine, one of the unfounded dogmas of empiricism is that there is a cleavage between the analytic and the synthetic. He sees this as connected to the claim that individual statements can be tested against experience. Quine's position is that it is the complete set of beliefs that is held up against reality. Does it make sense to suggest that logic and mathematics, not to mention the way that we describe the world, could have been completely different?
- When we use words to describe how things are now, there is an implicit assumption as to how things will be in the future. Does this mean that we are not justified in describing things in the way we do?
- How do we reconcile the extraordinary success of science as a whole with what appears to be very shaky epistemological under-pinnings? Should we place less confidence in science? Should we accept that science provides genuine knowledge but alter our conception of knowledge to accommodate this? How is this answer affected by the suggestion that in a hundred years many of the scientific theories we now accept as true will have been shown to be false?

5 Space, Time, Causality and Substance

Introduction

In the previous two chapters we have concentrated on epistemological issues, whereas in this chapter we begin to shift the focus onto metaphysics. Although metaphysics deals with very abstract questions (such as 'what exists?'), it cannot remain unaffected by advances in mathematics and science. The topics treated here, although traditionally coming within metaphysics, are just as likely to arise within the philosophy of science.

The four terms that appear in the title of this chapter are four concepts that Kant claims will provide ordering principles for any possible experience of an external world. For him, they are *a priori*, since experience is impossible without them. While their importance remains, the content of these concepts has changed considerably from the time when Kant was writing. For example, the two major advances in physics that occurred in the twentieth century, relativity and quantum mechanics, have completely altered our notions of space, time and causality. The philosophical implications of these two theories are still being assimilated. We no longer use the term 'substance' in the way that Kant and his contemporaries would have used it, yet, although the Kantian concept of substance might seem to be a technical concept within philosophy, it is a concept that is deeply embedded in the way we think of the world.

An examination of some aspects of space and time entailed by the scientific theories of relativity and quantum mechanics reveals a world far removed not only from the mechanics of Newton but also from our everyday conceptions. The differences are great enough to call into question the claim that we can have objective knowledge of space and time simply through a consideration of the form that our experience takes. The discussion is introduced through Zeno's paradoxes of motion, which, although nearly two and a half thousand years old, are still the subject of competing explanations. In them is raised the question as to whether space and time are continuous.

The success of Newtonian physics encouraged the view of the universe as one vast mechanism in which all future events are predetermined. We consider the degree to which this picture, with the connection it implies between predictability and determinism, is affected by twentieth-century scientific developments in quantum mechanics, where it is claimed that underlying subatomic events are random. This is followed by a discussion of free will, which considers the threats posed by both determinism and quantum randomness.

The discussion of substances looks at the substance–attribute distinction. Although the terminology is unfamiliar, this is a distinction that is central to many metaphysical questions, as well as being embedded in our conception of the world. The discussion introduces concepts that will be useful in later discussions, for example, those dealing with persons and God. There is also a connection to the discussion on free will and determinism.

The aims and limits of metaphysics

Historically, mathematical knowledge, and in particular the geometry of Euclid, has been the supreme example of a system of knowledge. Descartes, as we have seen, tried to construct certain knowledge on the pattern of Euclidean geometry by first establishing a foundation of indubitable propositions. Such propositions were to be established not by observation and induction but through reasoning. Descartes acknowledged that observation and experiment had roles in the pursuit of knowledge but thought that only reason could show us the essential properties of objects. The world as perceived through the senses was constantly changing and, in any case, the senses could not be relied upon.

What we have here are the germs of two different ideas regarding the role philosophy can play in relation to knowledge. One idea is that philosophy, in the form of epistemology, underpins (or undermines) the claims made by science (or would-be, pseudo-science). Descartes' work certainly gave an emphasis to epistemological considerations. A second idea, however, is that philosophical study is the means of acquiring knowledge, at least of a certain type. This idea goes back at least as far as Plato, for whom the senses acquainted us only with the world of shadows and not directly with the reality that lies behind the shadows.

Some philosophers have attempted to construct elaborate metaphysical structures based not on scientific observation, but on reason and speculation. Such metaphysical speculation was criticized by Kant for overstepping the limits of reason. Hume was even more opposed to metaphysical speculation, claiming that abstract reasoning should be restricted to 'quantity and number'. Regarding any book that contains neither abstract reasoning concerning quantity or number nor experimental reasoning concerning matter of fact and existence, Hume's suggestion was: 'Commit it then to the flames: for it can contain nothing but sophistry and illusion' (*Enquiries Concerning Human Understanding*, 12.3.132).

If we turn to contemporary views on the source of knowledge then, notwithstanding the problem of induction discussed in the previous chapter, it is generally considered that knowledge is scientific knowledge and that scientific knowledge is based on observation and experiment. None the less, it is also recognized that mathematics is the language of physics and that mathematical knowledge is based not on observation but on abstract reasoning. Since reasoning in philosophy is akin to mathematical reasoning in the degree to which it is abstract, perhaps philosophy can also provide knowledge of the world, albeit abstract knowledge.

It is also worth making the point that the branches of science have arisen out of philosophy and that philosophical reasoning has often provided the stimulus for the development of new scientific theories. Not that the traffic has been all in one direction: scientific studies have exerted both direct and indirect influences on philosophy. Indeed the interaction between science and philosophy has been both rich and complex.

A priori concepts

For Locke, as might be expected, our ideas of space and time come from the senses: 'we get the *idea* of space, both by our sight and touch' (*An Essay Concerning Human Understanding*, 2.13.2), and 'we have the notion of *succession* and *duration* . . . from reflection on the train of *ideas* which we find to appear one after another in our own minds' (2.13.4). The ideas of space and time are examples of what Locke calls simple modes, meaning that each particular idea of space or time is a variation on the same simple idea, which comes from things themselves. What ideas we have of space and time will depend on what space and time are like and how they affect us.

On the empiricist view, philosophy has little that is original to say about the nature of space and time as opposed to how we get our ideas of space and time. Kant adopts a very different position. For him, space and time are not ideas derived from experience but are *a priori* 'forms of intuition' which make our perceptions possible: 'Space is not an empirical concept which has been derived from outer experiences. For in order that certain sensations be referred to something outside me . . . the representation of space must be presupposed. The representation of space cannot, therefore, be empirically obtained from the relations of outer appearance. On the contrary, this outer experience is itself possible at all only through that representation' (*Critique of Pure Reason*, 68). Similarly, only 'on the presupposition of time can we represent to ourselves a number of things as existing at one and the same time (simultaneously) or at different times (successively)' (*Critique of Pure Reason*, 74).

In order to understand what Kant is claiming, we need to appreciate that he is using certain words in a technical sense. When I have knowledge of something, that something must be represented to my mind. An 'intuition' is Kant's term for that direct apprehension the mind has of whatever is present to it. However, in order for the mind to apprehend anything, it must provide it with a form. Space and time are the forms that are given to our perceptions. All our perceptions must be temporally ordered, that is, they must bear a temporal relationship to other perceptions, and any perception that presents itself as of 'something outside me', and hence as part of a world that is independent of me, must be spatially ordered, that is, it must bear a spatial relationship to other perceptions of things outside me.

Although Kant's use of the word 'intuition', to mean a mind's direct apprehension, seems strange to us now, it would have been readily accepted at the time. It is worth pointing out here that modern philosophers use 'intuition' with a different but again somewhat technical sense compared with its everyday meaning. For contemporary philosophers, intuitions are not inexplicable insights based on the most cursory evidence but, roughly, the unconsidered thoughts we might have on a subject. Thus, we shall refer later to our intuitions about space and time, meaning simply what someone who is not philosophically sophisticated, and who does not have scientific expertise, thinks about space and time. We shall also talk about our intuitions of right and wrong, which are the thoughts we have about what is right and wrong, without recourse to any moral theory.

To return to Kant, he thought that even when we have perceptions with a spatio-temporal form, we still have to understand what it is we are perceiving. We achieve this understanding by categorizing our perceptions. Kant argued that we are able to have coherent experiences only through the use of *a priori* categories or concepts. These concepts are not derived from the particular experiences we have, as the empiricists would argue, but structure our perceptions to produce our experiences. Thus it can be said that our experiences conform to these concepts rather than the other way around. For reasons we shall not examine here, Kant identified twelve such fundamental concepts, but it is the concepts of substance and cause that we shall consider. Thus, for example, we cannot understand the concept of a book or a man or a cow without having the *a priori* concept of a substance, a 'thing' that has properties. Nor can we understand the concept of a particular thing without realizing that it must have been produced by something – for which we need the *a priori* concept of causality. According to Kant, we arrive at these concepts through reasoning about what must be the nature of any experience.

The ideas of space and time are not listed among Kant's twelve categories since, although they have a similar function and they are even more fundamental, our grasp of them is immediate rather than mediated by reasoning. The nature of space and time is readily accessible to us through seeing the forms that our perceptions take.

The twelve categories and our forms of intuitions, space and time, are not only the means by which our subjective experiences are ordered. They are objective in that the nature of objective reality conforms to them. This claim to being objectively valid needs closer examination. First, however, we must appreciate that, when Kant talks of an objective reality, he is referring to a reality that is knowable by us or, as he calls it, the world of appearances and not the world as it is in itself. Any knowledge must be from a certain perspective, and we can know the world as it appears to us and not as it is in itself. This does not, however, mean that our knowledge is subjective since, or so Kant believed, he has given the forms and categories that any understanding of reality must have.

Kant believed that Newtonian mechanics correctly described reality and so his account of space and time is based on the account given by Newton. Yet scientific theories developed in the twentieth century did not merely replace the theories of Newton, they showed many of our fundamental beliefs about space and time that were incorporated in the theories – beliefs that seemed obvious beyond doubt – to be false. Although this does not show that Kant was wrong, it does illustrate the dangers of trying to give an *a priori* grounding to scientific theories.

Space and time

We begin our examination of the nature of space and time, however, not by looking at the science of the twentieth century but by looking at Zeno's paradoxes of motion, which date back about two and a half thousand years.

Zeno's paradoxes of motion

Zeno lived in the Greek city of Elea in Lower Italy around 470 BC. His famous paradoxes of motion purport to show that, whether we assume, on the one hand, that space and time are infinitely divisible or, on the other hand, that space and time are not infinitely divisible, motion is impossible. There must be something wrong with this claim since, of course, motion is possible, and yet his two alternative assumptions, from which the impossibility of motion appears to follow, are not only mutually exclusive, they also exhaust all the possibilities. The problem is that of finding what is wrong with his arguments. While many philosophers claim that these paradoxes have now been resolved, others claim that the proposed explanations miss the point and problems still remain.

The dichotomy

Zeno produced four paradoxes of motion, recorded by Aristotle. In the first two, a paradox arises from the assumption that space and time are infinitely divisible. Since these first two paradoxes raise similar problems, only the first will be discussed. This, often referred to as the *dichotomy*, is about a runner who has to run a given length. Suppose, for the sake of argument, this length is 64 m (a convenient power of 2). Then in order to cover the whole distance, the runner has first to cover half the distance, i.e., 32 m. Once he has covered half the distance, he then has to cover half the distance remaining, that is 16 m – then 8 m, then 4 m, then 2 m, then 1 m, and so on. We can continue halving the distance to be covered indefinitely, since the process of division is unending, and so the runner has to cover an infinite number of distances in succession in order to complete the race. Doing an infinite number of things in succession seems, on the face of it, impossible. The runner, in other words, will never reach the end of his run; he will never cover the 64 m.

Infinite series

It was to be more than two thousand years before mathematics was able to come up with satisfactory treatments of the infinitesimally small and the infinitely large, but the mathematics of infinite series certainly resolves some of the problems raised by Zeno in the first two paradoxes. In the first paradox, the set of distances the runner has to cover is $(32 + 16 + 8 + 4 + 2 + 1 + 0.5 + 0.25 + \ldots)$ m, where the ellipses indicate an infinite number of terms, each half the size of the previous one. Moreover, if our runner manages a constant speed of 8 m per second, he will take 4 seconds to reach the halfway mark, 2 seconds to reach the three-quarter mark and so on. This series $(4 + 2 + 1 + 0.5 + \ldots)$ seconds can be treated in the same way.

Both the above series are examples of geometric series. Some geometric series, such as the above, are said to be convergent and will have a finite sum even though there are an infinite number of terms, 32 m for the distance, 8 s for the time. The mathematics of infinite geometric series, and in particular the condition for convergence, is now fully understood (it appears in A-level mathematics specifications) and would seem to dispose of Zeno's first two paradoxes. This, however, is not the case, for while we might have a clear understanding of infinite series of numbers, we do not necessarily have a clear understanding of the physical concepts of space and time or of what it means to say that space and time are infinitely divisible.

The infinite divisibility of space and time

If space is infinitely divisible, this means that, between any two points, there is an infinite number of other points. (Actually, we can make what appears to be a much more modest claim: between any two points, there is always a third. This amounts to the same thing, since this process of finding another point can be repeated indefinitely.) We can now ask whether each point, in this infinite set of points, is extended. Does each have a size, even though infinitesimally small, or do they have no size at all? Either answer seems to raise a problem. If they have no size at all, then how can any number of them have size, that is, how can space be extended? If, on the other hand, they do have a finite length, no matter how small, then an infinite number of them will result in an infinite length. So the problem raised by Zeno's first two paradoxes can be redefined in this way: if space is infinitely divisible, that is, if you can go on dividing up distance indefinitely, then the end product of such a process is an infinite set of points. Either each point has no length at all (in which case even an infinite number of them will not stretch anywhere) or each point has a very small length (in which case an infinite number of them will stretch infinitely far). It was for this reason that Hume concluded that 'no finite extension is infinitely divisible' (*A Treatise of Human Nature*, 75).

Quantized space and time

Quantum theory provides independent grounds for questioning the continuity of space and time. The starting point for quantum theory was the realization that the energy radiating from a hot body had to be in discrete chunks or 'quanta'. The size of these quanta is dependent on the frequency of the radiated energy, the constant of proportionality being called Planck's constant (after Max Planck, one of the pioneers of quantum theory). Planck's constant is a very, very small number. One of the results that comes out of quantum theory is that the smallest time that has any physical meaning is 10^{-43} seconds – the Planck time – and the smallest distance to have any significance is the distance travelled by light in the Planck time, that is 10^{-35} metre. Now the Planck distance and time are incredibly small: if we were to write out the number 10^{43} in full it would consist of 1 followed by 43 noughts.

A time of 10^{-43} seconds is what we get if we divide a second up into 10^{43} parts! None the less, despite the incredibly small size of these 'bits' of space and time, they are finite.

The arrow
The idea that space and time might be 'chunky', and are not thereby infinitely divisible, removes the problems posed in Zeno's first two paradoxes; we cannot divide space and time indefinitely and so we do not end up with an infinite number of distances or times. However, the third and fourth paradoxes are intended to show that the assumption that space is not infinitely divisible also results in paradox. In the third of his paradoxes of motion, the *arrow*, Zeno asks of an arrow in flight whether, at each instant of its flight, it is moving or at rest. His answer is that it must be at rest, since the arrow cannot move in an instant of time. Thus the supposed motion of the arrow must consist of a succession of instants for each of which the arrow is at rest, that is, there are no instants when it is moving. From this, Zeno again concludes that motion is impossible.

If the consequence of the quantum view of reality is that space and time are 'chunky', does it have an answer to Zeno's third paradox? Zeno's paradoxes appear to present two alternatives, both of which are equally untenable; does modern physics claim that there is a third possibility, which escapes the problems faced by the first two? The answer would appear to be 'no'. Instead of providing a third way, the physicist has, in effect, assumed that there is nothing untoward about one of these alternatives. Zeno's third paradox is not solved by quantum mechanics but simply treated as not being paradoxical after all. Scientists and philosophers have accepted the bizarre nature of quantum reality in deference to the success of quantum theory in producing explanations and testable predictions with regard to macro-objects. The 'leaps' made by Zeno's arrow, which changes its position every instant without being in any of the intervening positions, are made at the subatomic level by particles, whose energy changes from one value to another in an 'instant' without taking any intervening values. Thus, if our view of motion is of *continuous* movement, then at the quantum level there is no such thing.

The stade
The fourth paradox, the *stade*, is more difficult to explain and to interpret, but one interpretation is that it shows there could not be a minimum length or time interval. If this demonstration succeeds, it

turns the screw still tighter. The earlier paradoxes have supported the conclusion that space and time cannot be infinitely divisible, whereas showing that there is no such thing as a minimum interval (for space or time) shows that space and time must be infinitely divisible.

The argument takes the form of a *reductio ad absurdum*, in which we begin by assuming the contrary of the result we are trying to prove. If the paradox is to prove that there cannot be a minimum time, we shall suppose, contrary to this, that there *is* a minimum time. Before proceeding, we must explain more clearly what is meant by saying that there is a minimum time. The passage of time is marked by events happening. If, in a certain interval of time, two events happen consecutively, the interval cannot be a minimum time interval since the interval between the start of the first event and the start of the second event is a shorter interval. Hence, by a minimum time interval we mean an interval of time within which two (or more) consecutive events cannot occur.

Without going into too many details, we begin by imagining a group of objects moving past another group, for example, a column of soldiers marching down the length of a stationary column of soldiers. It will take a certain time interval for one of the marching soldiers to pass each of the stationary soldiers. The faster the column marches, the smaller this time. It seems intuitively obvious that if we increase the speed of the column, this length of time will become smaller and smaller. Since we have assumed that there is a minimum time interval, the time for one soldier to pass another will eventually be reduced to this minimum time interval.

We now imagine a third column of soldiers, also marching past the stationary soldiers with the same speed but in the opposite direction. Consider an individual soldier in this third column. For every stationary soldier he passes (which he does in the minimum time), he will pass two soldiers marching in the opposite direction. Hence we have our contradiction. For in the minimum time interval (that is the time interval when only one event can occur) we have two events occurring. Since this contradicts the original assumption, there can be no such thing as a minimum time.

Relativistic considerations

The assumption that resulted in the first paradox was that it is impossible to do an infinite number of things in a finite time. The assumptions here are, if anything, more obvious. These are, first, that the passage of time will be the same whether the events are experienced by a soldier in the moving column or a soldier in the stationary column. Second, that lengths will be the same. Third, that if two objects are moving in opposite directions with the same speed (relative to a stationary object) then the speed of a moving object relative to the other will be twice its speed relative to the stationary object. Each of these assumptions is founded in our everyday experience yet, according to Einstein's theory of relativity, each is false. The reason we are not aware of this is that effects become noticeable only when speeds approach that of light. In the paradox of the *stade*, for the soldiers to pass each other in as small an interval as the Planck time, their speed would be in excess of the speed of light. Thus the assumptions that produce the above paradox are not warranted. The air of paradox may, for some, be transferred to the view of space and time provided by relativity! This will receive further consideration below.

Twentieth-century physics

Let us return to the claim that many of our accepted beliefs about space and time have been shown, by twentieth-century physics, to be wrong. A few of these beliefs can be indicated here. First, it is believed that space and time are quite independent concepts. If one event occurs at a certain place and time and another event occurs at a different place and different time, the spatial separation and the temporal separation are quite distinct, with no trade-off between them. Second, space and time provide the framework within which bodies exist and events occur. While the space between objects and the time between events will vary, it is believed that space and time themselves are not affected by the bodies they house. Generalizing from this, it is believed that the nature of space and time is the same throughout the universe and does not exhibit different properties in different regions. Third, it is believed that now is 'now' throughout the whole universe, by which is meant that everyone will agree as to which events occur at the same time and which events precede other events. Each of these beliefs is, according to relativity, false.

As a way of pursuing this point, let us turn to another belief, not perhaps as fundamental but none the less firmly based on everyday experience. This is the belief, raised in the context of Zeno's fourth paradox, about the way that the speed at which an object appears to me to be moving differs according to the speed at which I am moving. When I am standing at a level crossing, an inter-city train will appear to rush past, whereas if I am in another train going in the same direction, the inter-city train will slowly draw up alongside and only gradually pull ahead. What matters here is my speed *relative* to the speed of the other train. This phenomenon may seem to be perfectly general, and we might expect it to apply not only to other objects but also, for example, to light. If a rocket is fired from an aircraft, the speed of the aircraft is added onto the speed of the rocket. In the same way, we would expect that, if light were emitted in all directions from a fast-moving object, a ray of light travelling in the same direction as the object would have a greater speed than a ray of light travelling in the opposite direction. This, however, is not the case. Measuring the speed of light (in a vacuum) will always produce the same answer no matter what the relative motion of the observer and the source of the light. Einstein (1879–1955) developed his theories of relativity in part to account for this counter-intuitive result.

Defining simultaneity

Einstein questioned the assumption that time was invariant for all observers. Timing events depends on being able to say when two events are simultaneous. Einstein began with an analysis of this notion of simultaneity. When we say that the murderer struck at 9.27 we mean that two events – the murder and the hands of a clock showing 9.27 – were simultaneous. If these two events occur at or near the same location, the notion of simultaneity is unproblematic. Problems arise, however, when two events are spatially separated. We might observe, from earth, that the transmission from a space probe ends at 10.18, when it passes behind Uranus, but these two events – the space probe passing behind Uranus and the hands of a clock on earth showing 10.18, are not simultaneous. The reason for this is, of course, the signal transmitted by the space probe just prior to its moving into the planet's shadow takes time to reach us on earth, whereas light from the clock reaches us, as near as makes no difference, instantaneously. In order to say the time at which the probe moved behind Uranus, we need to know how long the signal took to reach earth and then subtract this from the observed time of 10.18.

Only simultaneous events that occur at an equal distance from an observer will *appear* simultaneous, but, provided the observer knows how far away the events occur, the actual time interval between the events can be determined from the apparent interval. However, although one observer may determine two events to be simultaneous, another observer may not. It is a consequence of Einstein's special theory of relativity that, when the speed of one object relative to another is a significant fraction of the speed of light, observers on the two objects will obtain different measurements for both length and time. To an observer on spaceship A, the lengths of objects on galactic cruiser B will appear shorter than they will to the crew of the galactic cruiser and the onboard clocks will appear to be going more slowly.

The dimensions of space and time

It would seem to follow that if special relativity is true (and there has been a considerable amount of confirming evidence) then we cannot talk about *the* temporal order of two events. Given events that occur far enough apart in space but close enough in time, it is possible for the observers to disagree about the temporal order of events. One might observe event D to precede event E, another that E precedes D and the third that D and E are simultaneous. This undermines the Kantian claim that there is only one time.

The strangeness does not stop there. The special theory of relativity treats time as a fourth spatial dimension. Space and time are not treated as separate but as somehow linked in a four-dimensional spacetime.

The independence of dimensions

Let us first clarify what talking of space as being three-dimensional means. Any point in space can be specified by three numbers, called co-ordinates. These three co-ordinates give the distances, in three directions, of the point from some origin. For example, these three directions could be North–South, East–West and up–down. The reason we need three directions is that these three directions are independent of each other but more than three directions would not be. With respect to some origin, say Big Ben in London, I can move in an East–West direction without affecting my North–South distance or my up–down distance from Big Ben. As well as the three spatial dimensions, time provides a fourth dimension. Thus I can talk about the spatio-temporal displacement from the origin, which might be Big-Ben-at-midnight-on-31-December-1999. In the way that the three spatial dimensions are independent of each other, so time is independent of each of the spatial dimensions.

The four-dimensional Newtonian universe

The Newtonian universe is four-dimensional and in it the spatio-temporal position of any event can be specified by means of three spatial and one temporal co-ordinate. None the less, as we have seen, the temporal dimension is quite different from the spatial dimensions and, in this respect, Newtonian mechanics corresponds to our intuitions as to the distinct nature of space and time (where I am using the term 'intuition' not in the sense that Kant used it but to refer to our unexamined beliefs about space and time). However, on the relativistic account, space and time have become spacetime and the three dimensions plus one dimension have become four dimensions on a par with each other.

Four-dimensional spacetime

One of the features of spacetime is that both spatial and temporal intervals between events can vary for different observers. For example, suppose terrorists set off two bombs, one in London at noon and one in Birmingham at 4 p.m. The spatial interval between these two events is the distance between London and Birmingham, approximately 110 miles, and the temporal interval is four hours. However, these intervals are as measured by an observer on the earth. If these two events are observed from a different frame of reference, say that of an alien space cruiser travelling through the solar system at more than half-light speed, both the observed distance and the observed time between the events will be different. What is the same for both the observer on earth and the alien in the space cruiser is what is known as the spacetime interval between the two events. The spacetime interval inextricably combines space and time. (For those interested, this is calculated by squaring the observed distance, subtracting from this the square of the observed time interval multiplied by the speed of light, and finding the square root of the result.)

So far we have been considering the views of space and time entailed by Einstein's special theory of relativity. His general theory of relativity, which is a theory of gravitation, has still stranger consequences. According to this theory, the effect of a massive body is to distort spacetime, that is, to 'curve it'. We can only begin to get some sort of picture of what this means by an analogy. Suppose, instead of being three-dimensional, space was two-dimensional: everything happened on the surface of a plane. Curved (two-dimensional) space would then be produced if this plane were wrapped around a sphere or onto a shape something like a saddle. The effect of curving space in this way would be that the shortest distance between two points would now be a curve. Euclidean geometry would not apply: for example, the sum of the angles of a triangle would not be 180 degrees.

Further consideration of the nature of space and time lies outside the scope of this book. However, what we have seen should be enough to cast doubt on the idea that we can determine the nature of space and time through the application of reason alone. Kant may be correct in his claim that our perception of an independent world must be spatially and temporally ordered, but the suggestion that we can arrive at an objective account of the nature of space and time simply by attending to the forms of our perceptions looks suspect in the light of developments in physics. Investigation of the nature of space and time would seem to be a scientific one, albeit one that requires philosophical input and leads to philosophically interesting results.

Causality

Types of causes

Aristotle identified four types of causes (a better term might be explanations), of which only two, the final cause and the efficient cause, need concern us here. In the physical sciences, explanations as to why something happened is in terms of an efficient cause, that is, some prior event or set of circumstances that brought about the event in question. In other areas, such as biology and human action, explanations may be couched in terms of a final cause. Such explanations are also termed teleological. Examples are: he put the money in the slot in order to get a drink; birds developed feathers in order to fly better. In these cases, it is the end point or result that explains the preceding action or event.

Nowadays, when we talk about a cause we mean what Aristotle referred to as efficient cause, an event or state of affairs that produces another event or state of affairs. Teleological explanations can be replaced by causal explanations in various ways. The teleological explanation of a man putting money in a slot is to cite the end or purpose, namely that of getting a drink. This is replaced by a causal explanation that attributes to the man a present intention or need or desire to get the drink. The present intention, need or desire, together with certain beliefs, causes the action of putting the money in the slot. In this way, an explanation that seems to rely on the idea of the end point exerting a 'pull' on preceding events is replaced by one where preceding events exert a 'push'. The exact nature of this 'push', and whether it is possible to resist such a 'causal push', remains to be considered.

An interesting example of reversing teleological explanations is provided by evolutionary theory. If one looks at an evolutionary line, one can see various stages in the development of features, such as wings, feathers, webbed feet, eyes and so on. It is tempting to see the changes as being purposeful: each step along the chain was there because of its contribution to the final feature. Darwin, however, proposed a quite different explanation: individuals pass on to their offspring various characteristics. However, although characteristics are inherited, the offspring are not exact copies of their parents. Some of these offspring are better equipped to survive and reproduce than others. Thus characteristics that arise by chance that make an individual more fitted to the environment will be passed on and other characteristics will not. The steps along the evolutionary chain can be explained by saying first, that they arose by chance, second, that they provided an evolutionary advantage to their possessor and third, that the relevant characteristics could be inherited. The subsequent discovery of genes provided the mechanism by which evolutionary change occurred.

Evolutionary psychologists have tried to explain what are seen as deep-seated behavioural and social patterns in human beings and, more contentiously, what are claimed to be significant differences in the behaviour of men and women by reference to evolutionary pressures. One supposed difference is that men are more likely than women to have casual affairs, to philander. A teleological explanation for philandering is in terms of the goal of sexual gratification; a 'psychological' causal account is in terms of desires and beliefs; the account given by evolutionary psychology is along the following lines. The defining difference between male and female is that females have the larger sex cell. Larger sex cells tend to mean fewer sex cells, whereas smaller sex cells tend to mean more of them. The result is that males (and in particular, men) can be more profligate with their sex cells and can engage in sexual activity (that is, activity that, if successful, leads to reproduction) far more often than females (and in particular, women). The argument then runs that men and women devise different strategies for maximizing their chances of passing on their genetic material. Philandering is one of the strategies that, it is claimed, will be adopted by men. Talk of developing strategies begins to sound like a teleological explanation, but it is not; the expression is being used metaphorically. The point is that, if philandering is a successful strategy for men in that it results in greater effectiveness in passing on genetic material, then more males will be born with the philandering characteristic. A man may think that in pursuing a woman he is bringing about the outcome that he desires, but his behaviour is explained in terms of inherited characteristics that, in the past, have proved to be evolutionally successful.

The influence a cause exerts on an effect

Although causal explanations are commonplace, it is not obvious what is meant by saying that A causes B. Does it mean that the occurrence of A is a sufficient condition for the occurrence of B? This would mean that whenever A occurred, B would occur. Does it mean that the occurrence of A is a necessary condition for the occurrence of B? This would mean that whenever B occurred, A must have already occurred. Does it mean that A is both a necessary and a sufficient condition for B? Is it to be analysed in some other way involving necessary and sufficient conditions or in some way that does not involve necessary and sufficient conditions at all?

The account given by John Mackie (1917–1981) is that a cause is part of a complex set of conditions which, together, are sufficient to produce the effect: 'the so-called cause is, and is known to be, an *insufficient* but *necessary* part of a condition which is itself *unnecessary* but *sufficient* for the result' ('Causes and Conditions', 16). This he referred to as an INUS condition. An example he uses to illustrate this is of a fire in a house, the cause of which is an electrical short-circuit. In saying that the short-circuit is the cause of the fire, we are not saying that it was a sufficient condition. The short-circuit alone would not have caused the fire; other conditions had to be right. For example, there had to be combustible material near to the short-circuit, there had to be a supply of oxygen and so on. There also had to be an absence of certain conditions, such as an effective sprinkler system. In saying that the short-circuit was the cause of the fire, we are not saying that it was a necessary condition for the fire. The fire could have been caused by a short-circuit somewhere else or by a candle falling over and so on.

The short-circuit, then, was not a sufficient condition for the fire. However, the set of conditions immediately prior to the fire was sufficient for the fire (otherwise it would not have started). This set of conditions was not necessary for the fire since, as already suggested, it could have been started in some other way. Yet, if we consider this set of sufficient conditions more closely, we can identify some components as unnecessary, that is, without them the fire would still have started.

By claiming that the short-circuit is the cause of the fire, we are claiming that the short-circuit is a necessary component of that set of sufficient conditions. That is, the same set of conditions but without the short-circuit would not have started the fire.

We can consider a further example. Suppose we are investigating the cause of a death. There are a number of conditions that would be sufficient to bring about death, such as decapitation, asphyxiation, electrocution, drowning and so on, and clearly none of these is a necessary condition. For each of these sufficient conditions we can identify a necessary component, which we claim is the cause of the death. Thus, he died (through drowning) because he had a concrete block attached to his legs. He died (through asphyxiation) because some food stuck in his throat, and so on.

This suggestion, that in claiming that A is the cause of B we are claiming that A is an INUS (an insufficient but necessary part of an unnecessary but sufficient) condition for B, is certainly an important one that makes clear some important features of causation. However, before moving on, there are a number of issues to be raised. First, there is the assumption that the cause precedes the effect. Yet, we have already seen that there is no unique temporal ordering of events. Whereas, from some frames of reference, A precedes B, from some other frames, B might precede A. The topic of causality within the context of relativity is a difficult one that we shall not explore here. What we can say is that Mackie is giving an account of what is ordinarily meant by the claim that A caused B, and the assumption, in Mackie's account, that A precedes B is already there in the claim that he is analysing.

The second issue revolves around what is meant by saying that something is a necessary condition. We have said that 'A caused B' does not mean 'A is necessary for B', but Mackie's account does use the idea of A being a necessary part of a sufficient condition for B. We might express this by saying that if A had not occurred, and yet everything else had remained the same, B would not have occurred. This is to express necessity in terms of a *counterfactual*. A counterfactual is a conditional in which the antecedent is false. Thus 'The occurrence of A was necessary for the occurrence of B' can be expressed by the counterfactual 'If A had not occurred then B would not have occurred'. When introducing conditionals in the previous chapter, it was noted that a conditional can be treated as a material implication where the truth-value of the conditional is determined by the truth-values of the antecedent and consequent. Such an approach is not very useful when applied to counterfactuals. One possible treatment, provided by David Lewis (1941–), uses the structure of possible worlds, which are claimed by Lewis to exist.

Finally, let us turn to the issue of a set of conditions being sufficient for a certain event. How wide do we have to cast the net to ensure that we have a set of conditions that is sufficient? There is no general answer to this but, if anything is sufficient, the state of the whole universe at some time prior to the event surely must be. The fact that the majority of events making up the state of the universe at a certain time are *not* necessary components of a sufficient condition for (and so play no part in causing) the particular event is irrelevant. It is a short step from here to the claim that the state of the universe at one time is sufficient for the state of the universe at a subsequent time. This claim amounts to determinism.

Determinism

Determinism is the view that every event is the effect of earlier events, that is, for every event there is an antecedent set of conditions that suffice to bring about the event. The laws of nature are usually invoked to account for why the prior set of conditions is sufficient to bring about the event – if the event were not to occur, given the prior set of conditions, this would be a contravention of a law of nature. If this is true, then future events are fixed by laws of nature and the present state of the universe and so are unalterable.

The success of Newtonian mechanics led Laplace (1749–1827) to suggest that, armed with the laws of physics and a knowledge of the position of every particle in the universe at a particular time, it would be possible for a super-intellect to predict every future event. Einstein makes a more modest claim that restricts itself to a region of the universe: if you knew everything about the contents of a sphere of radius 300,000 km, then, with the laws of physics, you would know what was going to happen at the centre of that sphere in the next second. One second is the time that light would take to travel from the outside of the sphere to the centre and, according to special relativity, nothing can travel faster than light.

The Laplacian claim is an epistemological one; it is a claim about what we can know. This epistemological claim is a claim about predictability. However, it presupposes the truth of a metaphysical claim about the universe. The metaphysical picture or model is of a mechanistic universe that runs like clockwork. In the way that the mechanism of a clock determines the subsequent actions of that clock, and so makes them predictable, so the mechanism of the universe determines the subsequent states of the universe. In the case of the universe, the envisaged mechanism is a vast collection of particles whose interactions are governed by rigid laws. The view that developed in the nineteenth century was that the state of the universe at any particular time was constituted by the position and momentum (i.e., mass times velocity) of each particle at that time. Subsequent states of the universe were determined by laws of physics.

As mentioned, the success of Newtonian mechanics laid the foundations for the Laplacian view. Newton showed how the heavenly bodies were governed by exactly the same laws that governed earthly bodies. Success in predicting certain physical phenomena led to the expectation that, in principle, all future events could be predicted: it was simply a matter of finding out the laws and finding out about the state of the system at a particular time. None the less, there is a difference between such claims as 'the state of the universe at a certain future time will be such and such' and the claim that every state of the universe is determined by the previous state. The first type of claim can, in principle, be verified, the second cannot. Repeated success with regard to more modest versions of the first type of claim may increase confidence in the second claim, but the problems relating to induction that were considered in the previous chapter undermine this. Predictive success may lead us to believe that the universe is determined but is none the less consistent with a universe that is not fully determined.

The view of a mechanistic, and hence determined, universe was undermined in the twentieth century by various developments in physics. Although predictability and determinism have been closely linked, the reason for this is that the proposed laws of physics, which enabled successful predictions to be made, were deterministic laws. In the twentieth century, physicists (and chemists and biologists) examined systems that, although governed by deterministic laws, were not predictable – so-called chaotic systems – and also systems that, although not governed by deterministic laws, were predictable.

The butterfly effect

In order to predict a future state of the universe, it is necessary to have exact knowledge of the present state, likewise when predicting the behaviour of a small region of the universe. However, any knowledge of the state of the universe (or a region of it) is by observation and measurement, and these involve errors. Using a ruler, one cannot measure lengths of around a metre to much better than the nearest millimetre. Apparatus can be designed to improve on this, but a measurement with no margin of error is not possible. In many cases, a small margin of error in the specification of the initial state will result in a small margin of error in the predicted state. I may not know the exact force that the charge exerts on a shell or the exact angle of elevation of the barrel, but I can get pretty close to the target. By making my knowledge of the initial conditions more exact, I can get closer to the target. Some systems, however, are not like this. We assume that whether a coin comes down heads or tails is determined by the distribution of mass in the coin, the initial impulse on the coin, the effects of air resistance, the height at which it is caught and so on. Yet we are not able to predict the outcome. Minute changes in the initial conditions result in a radically different outcome: heads rather than tails. This sensitivity to initial conditions is also known as the 'butterfly effect': the idea being that a small, apparently insignificant event in one place, a butterfly flapping its wings over China, results in a large effect, say a tornado over California.

Statistical laws
Perhaps more important are cases where the laws on which predictions are based are not themselves deterministic. Thermodynamics introduced laws into physics and chemistry that were not deterministic but statistical in nature. The second law of thermodynamics states that any closed system will become more disordered, the degree of disorder being measured by the entropy of the system. The basis of this is that disordered states (states with higher entropy) are more likely than ordered states (states with lower entropy). It is a statistical law not a deterministic law. However, although the second law of thermodynamics is accepted as a law of nature, it need not undermine the claim that physical systems are determined, since it can be seen as summarizing what happens in a system that contains large numbers of particles, each of which behaves deterministically. We are not able to follow the behaviour of each individual particle because of limitations in our measuring instruments and computational power. None the less, using statistical laws we can predict the behaviour of collections of particles, and we can do this precisely because every particle behaves deterministically.

Quantum mechanics poses more profound problems. Atomism, the idea that all of matter is made up of indivisible particles, was put forward in the fifth century BC by Democritus. In the seventeenth and eighteenth centuries, this developed into a more sophisticated atomic theory that everything we see around us is made up of compounds formed from a relatively small number of elements. If we were to take an element and divide it into smaller and smaller parts, we would eventually arrive at an atom, an indivisible particle. All atoms of the same element are alike but different from atoms of any other elements. In the twentieth century it was discovered that, although an atom is the smallest particle of an element, atoms are not indivisible but are made up of still smaller particles. Early models of the atom treated subatomic particles as being like the objects we see around us: electrons were thought to circle a nucleus of protons and neutrons in the way that the planets circle the sun. However, this view led to impossible results. Electrons do not behave like planets or billiard balls. Under some conditions, electrons behave as if they are not particles at all but waves. They 'interfere' with each other in the way that waves do (reinforcing or cancelling each other out at different positions in space) and, when fired at slits in a target, produce the sort of interference pattern one gets from light. Indeed, light also exhibits this dual wave/particle nature, depending on the nature of the experiment and the instruments used to detect it.

Uncertainty

Laplace required that the positions and momenta of each particle be known, but Heisenberg's uncertainty principle states that the more precisely one knows the position, the less precisely one can know the momentum of the particle. Unlike in the earlier discussion of chaotic systems, this is not a matter of there being an error associated with any measurement. The uncertainty principle is somehow about the nature of ultimate reality itself and not about our errors of measurement. Further, whereas the statistical nature of the second law of thermodynamics could be seen as summarizing the collective behaviour of individual particles that behaved deterministically, it is difficult to see quantum mechanics in this way. It is true that some physicists, most notably Einstein, never accepted this and continued to believe that there is an underlying, if unobservable, determinism, but this is very much a minority view. To take just one example, if we have a certain mass of radioactive material, we know that after a certain time, known as the half-life for that particular element, half of the atoms will have undergone radioactive decay. Yet which atoms decay and which do not seems to be totally random.

Of course, science may discover some underlying deterministic process that accounts for the apparent random quantum events, but as things stand at present, the most fundamental processes studied by physicists are random, as well as being, in many other respects, bizarre. Since the ultimate constituents of the objects in the world we see around us are these strange subatomic particles that are governed by non-deterministic quantum mechanical processes, the claim that the universe is determined has a less obvious appeal than it did towards the end of the nineteenth century. None the less, random processes at the quantum level result in law-like processes at a macro-level. The half-lives of radioactive elements have precise values even though it is impossible to predict which atoms will decay. Thus, although without the picture of a mechanical universe we are less likely to be seduced by the idea of determinism, macro-determinism is not incompatible with quantum randomness.

Free will

A deterministic universe seemed to pose a threat to free will; an essentially random universe also poses a threat to free will, despite the fact that, initially, quantum mechanics might be seen as rescuing free will from determinism. In order to see whether either poses a genuine threat, we need to examine more closely what is meant by the claim that we have free will. We can begin by saying that to have free will is to have the ability to make a choice between alternatives. This requires, first, that, prior to the choice being made, there are two distinct sets of possible future events and, second, that the choice made will be the factor that determines which of these two possible sets of events actually occurs. In those cases where I act freely, my choice is the necessary part of a set of conditions sufficient to bring about that which I have chosen. I will not be able to exercise free choice in all circumstances. In some cases where I choose to do something, the resulting set of circumstances will not be sufficient to bring about the fulfilment of my choice. However, having free will does not depend upon every action being free, only that I can sometimes act freely.

We can now see the nature of the threats to free will posed by determinism and by the random events at the quantum level. Determinism threatens the first condition: if the future is decided, then my choice can have no effect. Quantum randomness threatens the second condition: no matter what I choose, what actually happens is random. It is possible to counter both threats. To say that the future is determined is to say that the state of the universe at one time is a sufficient set of conditions for an event to occur at a later time. However, if my choice is a necessary part of this sufficient condition, then there is a sense in which there are two possible futures: the future that occurs when I choose one way and the future that occurs when I choose the other way. The threat of quantum randomness can be countered by pointing out that the randomness does not extend upwards; at a macro-level there are causal laws, and so it is possible for my choice to produce a particular effect.

Even if free will is possible, there are numerous cases where we do not act freely. Freedom requires the power to control events, and this power can be limited by the impersonal forces of nature or by the power exercised by other people. These are cases where I am aware that I am not free. There are also cases where I seem to be able to exercise choice effectively but where this is an illusion. There are cases where I get the outcome I have chosen but where this would have been the outcome no matter what I had chosen. My choice, in other words, was not a necessary part of the sufficient set of conditions that brought about what I had chosen. In one sense I am lucky, in that I chose what was going to happen anyway, but my sense of having free will is illusory, just as flotsam carried here and there by the storm may have the illusion of freedom if each change of course is preceded by the intention to change course in just that way!

Free will is also illusory if I could not have chosen other than I did. We can think of different sorts of cases where this would be so: the addict who thinks he has made the free choice to have another 'hit' or another drink; the philanderer who thinks he has chosen to seduce someone but whose behaviour has been determined genetically; the paranoid schizophrenic who thinks he has chosen the appropriate response to a chance remark. In each of these cases there are particular features we can point to that show there was no freedom of choice. The pseudo-choice made may have been effective in bringing about the outcome chosen; if the addict, philanderer or paranoid had chosen differently, some other outcome would have been produced. None the less, it was a pseudo-choice and not a genuine choice simply because the individual could not have chosen otherwise. I am assuming that in each of the above examples there are *plausible* grounds for saying that the individual could not have chosen otherwise. However, a more important concern can be raised here: if determinism is true, then every choice we make is a pseudo-choice. If whatever happens is the inevitable outcome of the set of preceding events, then the real threat posed by determinism is not that actions have been determined but that choices that determine the actions have themselves been determined. The fact that actions have been determined is not a problem for free will providing that, in some cases, a necessary part of the set of determining events has been the choice made by the person performing the action. However, if the choice to act in one way rather than another has been determined, then how can this be seen as a free choice? This might be expressed by saying that we are free in one sense, in that we often do what we choose to do. But we lack ultimate freedom or true freedom since our choices themselves are determined. Determinism means that we cannot be free to choose otherwise than the way we do choose.

What is meant by 'could have chosen otherwise'?
We can illustrate the various distinctions made so far with a set of examples all based on the following circumstances. A political detainee, call him Malcolm, has been held under house arrest for a period of time when one of his guards informs him that he can, over the next twenty-four hours, go wherever he wants. Consider now the various ways Malcolm might respond and how differences in actual or possible circumstances and outcomes show whether or not he makes a free choice.

Example 1   Malcolm says that he will go to the nearby house of his friend and fellow political detainee. Reluctantly his guard concedes to his request – he had been hoping Malcolm would opt to visit his wife instead. Malcolm could have chosen whatever he wanted. Whatever he had chosen to do, in so far as it was within the power of the political authorities to grant, he would have done. Here we say that Malcolm acted freely.

Example 2   Malcolm says that he will go to the nearby house of his friend and fellow political detainee. However, unlike in the previous case, his guard then informs him that his friend's house is out of bounds. Malcolm has clearly made a choice, and we have no particular reason for saying that the choice was not made freely, but it turned out that he was not free after all. Choosing to go to his friend's house did not result in his going there.

Example 3   Malcolm says that he will spend the time with his wife, who is detained in another part of the country. He is escorted there and later escorted back. He has made a choice and what he has chosen has happened. However, suppose his guard had been under instructions to find an excuse to move Malcolm out of the capital for the duration of the state visit of the president of a country sympathetic to Malcolm's political demands. Although Malcolm had been asked what he wanted, he was going to be taken to see his wife anyway. This means that his freedom was illusory. He chose freely and did what he had chosen to do, but this was not the outcome of his choice since it was going to happen anyway.

Example 4   The question as to how he would like to spend his twenty-four hours of freedom is put to Malcolm in an interview on state television. Opposite him, but out of view of the cameras, is his wife. She is gagged and held by two members of the security police. One of them holds a hypodermic needle to her arm in which is contained a lethal dose of poison. Sweat breaks out on Malcolm's forehead and his fists clench. These signs of tension are picked up by the television cameras. Malcolm says that he has not been detained at all and that he will happily spend the next twenty-four hours in the same way that he has spent the last few years, that he has no wish to go anywhere. The interview ends. The needle is taken away from his wife's arm. Here Malcolm is not free and does not make a free choice. This could be disputed since it could be argued that he does make a choice, although the options are not what they appear to be to those watching on television. In saying what he does, Malcolm is choosing to save his wife's life rather than make a political protest against his decision. Circumstances have forced him into the position where his choice is limited but his choice within these limits is free. After all, he could have chosen to ignore his wife's plight and to speak out against the regime holding him under house arrest.

Example 5   As before, the question is put to Malcolm in front of the television cameras. He gives a similar response, but this time he answers in a relaxed way and with no appearance of being compelled. However, what neither he nor the viewers are aware of is that he had previously been hypnotized while under the influence of drugs, and his response was the result of this.

It is this final example that we must focus on. Given the effectiveness of the drugs-plus-hypnosis programme, Malcolm could not have chosen otherwise. It is irrelevant whether, in practice, any such techniques exist that are 100 per cent effective. What matters is that we have described a case where the reason a person is not free is because he could not have chosen otherwise. What appeared to be a choice was a pseudo-choice since it was determined by past events. Yet, if determinism is true, then each of the choices in the other examples is also determined by past events; each of Malcolm's choices is a pseudo-choice, whether it is the choice to visit his political ally, the choice to visit his wife or the choice to stay where he is. Assuming the truth of determinism, each choice is the inevitable outcome of the way that Malcolm is and the circumstances in which he has to choose. Determinism seems to entail that in no case could Malcolm have acted otherwise.

If the condition for Malcolm to have made a free choice is that Malcolm could have chosen otherwise, is there an alternative account of this? In other words, is there a meaning of 'could have chosen otherwise' that is not precluded by determinism? Is there a meaning of 'could have chosen otherwise' that is consistent with saying that Malcolm could not have chosen otherwise in example 5 but that he could have chosen otherwise in the other cases? We begin to see possibilities when we note that some person other than Malcolm might have acted differently if he or she had been in Malcolm's situation in any of the examples except the last. The point of claiming that the hypnotic technique is 100 per cent successful is that it produces the same result no matter on whom it is tried. On the other hand, not everyone would choose to save the life of their wife (or husband) rather than speak out to further their political cause, even if most would.

To say that Malcolm could have chosen otherwise is to say that some other people put into Malcolm's position would choose otherwise. Of course, if determinism is true, it is not possible to place someone other than Malcolm in the same position that Malcolm is in; exchanging Mary for Malcolm would require the whole of history to have been different. Further, if Malcolm were replaced by someone exactly like Malcolm, the replacement would make the same choice as Malcolm.

This interpretation of the meaning of 'he could have chosen otherwise' will not satisfy some. They will want to answer that in order for *Malcolm* to be free it must be the case that *Malcolm* could have chosen otherwise. We do not show that *Malcolm* is free by claiming that *someone else* would have chosen differently. For them, Malcolm is trapped in the rigid grip of prior circumstances, both internal and external. For them, freedom can come only with the loosening of the bonds that would occur if the universe were not determined. However, it is not clear what circumstances they would accept as enabling free choice.

There is a further point that can be made before leaving this issue. So far, the importance of human freedom has been taken for granted, and we have not enquired as to why free will is important. One of the reasons for its importance is its link with responsibility. Malcolm would not be considered responsible for appearing, in the last example, to support the political regime that he has spent his life opposing, since he was not free. Likewise in example 4, Malcolm's responsibility for not speaking out against the regime is limited by the extent to which Malcolm is considered not to have been free to make a choice. If it is thought that Malcolm was free – the freedom in question being to save his wife's life or speak out against the regime – then he was responsible and some would judge he had done the right thing, others that he had done the wrong thing.

More generally, we can say that the choices we make when we are choosing freely reveal our character and show what kind of person we are. Malcolm's 'choice' in example 5 tells us nothing about Malcolm, whereas his choice in example 4 (limited though it was) does. Example 5 tells us nothing about Malcolm because anyone in the same position would have done the same; example 4 does tell us about Malcolm because some people in that position would have made the same choice whereas others would have made a different choice. This, indeed, is the reason why the interpretation of 'could have chosen otherwise' as 'there are others who would have chosen otherwise' is important. If others would have chosen otherwise, this means that there is a difference in the character of those who would have chosen differently. Although, or perhaps because, Malcolm's choice and Mary's choice are equally determined by the combination of external circumstances and internal character, the difference in determination gives one aspect of the way in which Malcolm and Mary are different.

Substance

The substance–attribute distinction

When considering Kant's notion of an analytic proposition, we introduced the idea of the subject-predicate form of a proposition. In the proposition 'Socrates is sitting', the subject is 'Socrates' and the predicate is 'is sitting'. It has been claimed that there are two ways of being, corresponding to this grammatical distinction between the two parts of the proposition. In other words, that it is possible to exist as a substance or as an attribute. The subject of the proposition refers to a substance, in this case Socrates, whereas the predicate refers to an attribute, that of sitting. This distinction between substance and attribute can be found in the works of many philosophers from Plato onwards. Kant considered that the concept of 'substance', like that of 'causality', was one of the categories that made perception of the world possible. Like other important concepts in philosophy, it is not without its problems.

The substance–attribute distinction cannot be defined simply in terms of the grammatical distinction. The traditional explanation distinguishes between those things that can exist independently, that is substances, and those things that cannot, that is attributes. Attributes, it is suggested, can exist only in a substance. This way of making the distinction is at least plausible. We do not encounter independent instances of laughing, only instances of someone who is laughing. Likewise, colours are to be found on the surfaces of things or in transparent or translucent things. Smiles are to be found on faces, scratches and bruises are to be found on bodies, thoughts (as we saw when considering Descartes' *cogito*) are to be found in minds, heaviness is to be found in objects, and so on. All of these: sitting, smiles, scratches and bruises, thoughts, heaviness, are attributes and, as such, are attributes *of* something else. They cannot exist alone and, as it were, unsupported.

The independence of substance

However, while attributes cannot exist independently of a substance, it seems equally true that substances cannot exist independently of attributes. Socrates can exist without the attribute of sitting but only by having another attribute in its place, such as standing or walking or crouching, etc. What is impossible is Socrates with *no* attributes. Socrates does not need the particular attribute 'sitting', but equally, sitting does not need the particular substance Socrates. There are a number of different ways we can go from here.

Substance as a substrate

One move involves backtracking on the claim that Socrates was a substance after all. When we refer to Socrates, we are referring to something with all sorts of attributes: male, lived between 470 and 399 BC in Athens, teacher of Plato, died by drinking hemlock, and so on. However, we have agreed that attributes cannot have independent existence, hence there must be (or so the argument goes) something, some substrate, in which all these attributes adhere. This substrate is the true substance. The conclusion of this line of reasoning is that there are at most two types of substance: matter and mind (and many philosophers would claim there is only one). Material attributes inhere in matter, mental attributes inhere in mind. Such a position is known as 'substance dualism' (see chapter 6).

This view presents us with problems. What we think of as matter does seem to have at least one attribute, that of being extended. Hence either we have to say that matter is not substance, the true attributeless substrate, or we are back to the idea that substance cannot exist independently of attributes. Locke ridicules the claim that we understand the notion of substance if all we know is that it is something in which attributes inhere (Locke uses the term *accidents* rather than attributes, but this also, like the term substance, now has a rather different meaning): 'Had the poor *Indian* philosopher (who imagined that the earth also wanted something to bear it up) but thought of this word *substance*, he needed not to have been at the trouble to find an elephant to support it, and a tortoise to support his elephant: the word *substance* would have done it effectually' (*An Essay Concerning Human Understanding*, 2.13.19). Locke sees the attempt to understand this notion of a substance as one of the dead-ends of scholasticism. His concern is with ideas of particular substances and with why it is that certain sets of ideas are bundled together.

An alternative to trying to find an attributeless substrate is to take another tack and see whether there is anything else that could be truly independent. In an age when it was believed that God created everything, it was natural to think that the only independent being was God himself – nothing else could be independent since everything relied on God for its continued existence. God, on the other hand, was thought to be 'self-caused' and hence independent. Thus, for many past philosophers, God is the only true substance. (The nature of God, as construed by philosophers, will be examined in chapter 7.) It is interesting to note that Descartes is inconsistent in what he takes to be examples of substances, sometimes allowing that things like horses and stones are substances, sometimes maintaining that only mind and matter are substances, and sometimes that God is the only true substance.

The persistence of substance

Another approach to trying to pin down this notion of a substance focuses not on being able to exist independently but on persistence through change. Suppose we have Socrates sitting followed by Socrates standing. Then we have a change – of attributes – yet through this change we have something enduring, namely Socrates. A substance, then, is something that endures through change. By way of contrast, if we have Socrates sitting (and Plato not sitting) followed by Plato sitting (and Socrates not sitting), what we have is *not* one instance of sitting which endures through a change of substance (Socrates to Plato) but two different instances of sitting. If I take pleasure in your sudden discomfort, the smile that is wiped off your face is not wiped onto mine – my smile is a different one! If a cat produces a scratch on my arm, identical to the one that has just healed, it is none the less a new scratch and not a return of the old one.

This approach may seem more promising than the previous one, but it is not without its problems. We are used to the idea that everything is transient and nothing endures. Plato thought that the world of experience contained only change and that the unchanging, the pure forms, existed on some other plane. The same pressure that drove philosophers to seek an attributeless substrate also drives them to seek something permanent and unchanging as an example of a substance.

The essence of a substance
Socrates may endure through some changes, from sitting to standing, from having a head of hair to becoming bald and so on, but he will not endure through all change. Drinking hemlock results in a change through which Socrates does not endure. Yet something does endure, namely the body of Socrates, which changes from being alive to being dead. Some of Socrates' attributes can change, and Socrates endures through such changes, but other attributes are such that, if they are lost, Socrates ceases to be. In other words, some attributes are essential to Socrates in that they define that particular substance, whereas others are not. Another way of saying this is to say that some attributes constitute the *essence* of Socrates.

This idea of essences or essential properties can lead to all sorts of difficulties. While Socrates is alive, 'Socrates' and 'the body of Socrates' pick out the same object in the world (assuming that 'Socrates' is not the name of a mind). Yet being alive is an essential property of Socrates, whereas it is not an essential property of the body of Socrates. Consider another example: suppose I am holding a knife in my hands. It is an essential property of this knife that it has a blade, but having a blade is not an essential property of the lump of metal from which the knife has been made. On the other hand, it is not an essential property of this knife that it has a certain weight but it is an essential property of the lump of metal that it has a certain weight. Remove some of the metal and, providing I do this judiciously, I have the same knife although a different lump of metal. Thus, what counts as an essential property of a substance seems to depend on how we pick the substance out.

The notion of a substance enduring through change is not something that is essential to scientific theories. Causality is seen in terms of events or states of a system. What seems to endure through change at the everyday level disappears entirely at the atomic and subatomic level. True, there are fundamental particles, but these are defined purely in terms of their attributes; in any case, their status as substances is undermined by the uncertainty principle and the wave/particle duality that 'smears' their individual existence. The search for the aether was a search for a substance to support wave properties, but this search was abandoned by science long ago.

None the less, our perception of the world is that it is filled with persisting, independent objects having certain qualities or properties that alter through time. The terminology of substance and attribute does not appear in our everyday discourse, but important aspects of the ontological commitment implied by the terminology remain. The concepts of substance and attribute, if not the terms themselves, underpin our everyday understanding of the world and our ability to act within it. They also underpin the conception we have of ourselves as individuals. Descartes' proof of his own existence relied upon an intuitive grasp of the distinction. The reason he can take 'I am thinking' as his starting point rather than 'there is some thinking going on' is because thinking, being an attribute, cannot exist by itself, and so if there is an attribute then there must be a substance. All that is needed is to identify the substance. Descartes' approach reflects a deep-seated belief about ourselves: we are not simply thoughts or 'awarenesses' but are things that think and are aware. Individuals are not simply collections of attributes.

Summary

■ Paradoxes, as we have seen in the previous chapter, challenge our assumptions as to how things are. Zeno's paradoxes are no exception to this. By appearing to demonstrate that motion is impossible they challenge assumptions as to the nature of space and time. The most obvious challenge is to the notion of continuity, but, as we have seen, the fourth paradox indirectly questions some of the assumptions that were rejected by the theories of relativity.

■ While our subjective experiences may conform to the assumptions about space and time that embedded in Newtonian mechanics, the reality, as found in relativity and quantum theory, is very different.

■ An important analysis of what we mean when we say that an event is a cause is that it is an insufficient but necessary part of an unnecessary but sufficient set of conditions for bringing about the effect.

■ The nineteenth-century deterministic view of the universe is called into question by statistical laws of thermodynamics and quantum uncertainty. While many of the events we observe are caused, it cannot be be proved that every event has a cause.

■ The ability to exercise free will depends on a relationship of cause and effect. My choice must be part of the cause of the event chosen.

■ Generally when a person does X because he or she chose to do X, then they could have acted otherwise. However, free will is illusory unless he or she could have chosen otherwise.

■ What may be meant by saying that a person could have chosen otherwise is that another person in the same situation would have chosen otherwise. This analysis makes the links between free will and character and between free will and responsibility.

■ While the grammatical distinction between subject and predicate seems to provide the basis for a metaphysical distinction between substance and attribute, it is not so easy to fill in the details. It would appear that substances need attributes as much as attributes need substances. None the less, the idea of a substance does seem to capture an important aspect of the world and of us as agents within it.

Questions raised

- Is Kant's claim that our *a priori* forms of intuition of space and time not only order our subjective experiences, but also have an objective validity, simply wrong, or did he make a mistake as to the nature of these intuitions?
- If the state of the universe at one time completely determines its state at a later time, does this take away moral responsibility? Can we be responsible for our actions when these are the result of choices that derive from our character, over which we have no control?
- If we consider ourselves as substances that persist through change, do we have an essential property that we retain through all changes? If so, what is it and is it different for each individual?

6 The Mind

- Introduction
- Descartes' real distinction of mind and body
- Distinctive aspects of the mental
- Materialism
- Functionalism
- Summary
- Questions raised

Introduction

In this chapter we begin with a problem raised by Descartes when he claimed that the mind and body are distinct: how do mind and body interact? For Descartes, the distinction between mind and body is the distinction between two different kinds of substances. The metaphysical position of many philosophers writing in this area is that of materialism, which claims that the only type of substance to exist is material or physical. Contemporary investigations into the nature of mental phenomena constitute a distinct branch of philosophy, the philosophy of mind. Within the philosophy of mind, a more specific materialist thesis can be found which, in its simplest form, claims that minds are simply brains. The mind/body problem has thus become largely the problem of explaining, or, as some philosophers would see it, explaining away, the mental in a material world. It should be treated as an open question as to whether there are mental phenomena at all.

Another type of theory that tries to account for mental phenomena is functionalism. Its account of the way that the mental is related to the brain draws on an analogy with the way that the software of a computer is related to its hardware. The analogy suggests that the brain should be seen as an organic computer and mental phenomena as the programs that it runs. While the operation of a computer can be understood in terms of the physics and chemistry of its hardware, it can also be understood in terms of the set of instructions that constitutes the program being run. These two sorts of explanation are largely independent of each other. Indeed the same set of program instructions can be run on very different hardware bases. Functionalist accounts define the mental in terms of the causal role that it plays and, although it is consistent with dualism, most functionalists have assumed that the Cartesian picture of the mind is deeply flawed and that the causal functions will be carried out by physical states.

Descartes' real distinction of mind and body

Our starting point is Descartes' distinction between mind and body: minds and bodies are different types of substances with different essential properties. A mind is something that thinks; a body is something extended, something that occupies space. It does not follow from this that physical objects cannot have thoughts or that minds cannot be extended; yet this is what Descartes believed. According to him, minds do not have spatial properties and bodies do not have mental properties. None the less, as he recognized, mind and body interact with each other. If they are two completely different kinds of substance, what is the nature of this interaction and how can it occur?

The problems faced by substance dualism in trying to give an account of mind/body interactions fall into two classes. In the first are the problems associated with explaining how changes in physical objects can be brought about by mental events. In the second are the problems of explaining how mental changes can be brought about by physical events. Let us concentrate on the first class of problems. Our understanding of the changes that occur in material objects is provided by science. This understanding is extensive and it seems there is no need for a contribution from non-material causes. There appear to be no 'gaps' into which mental causes could fit or mechanisms by which they could operate. A fundamental type of interaction between bodies is collision. A collision requires that bodies have locations in space and obey an exclusion principle that prevents different bodies occupying the same location at the same time. The difficulty with any account of mind/body interaction based on collisions is that it assumes the mind not only has a location but also must be able to exclude a material body from that location. If the mind lacks *all* material properties then clearly it cannot take part in this sort of interaction. Even if we are prepared to allow that mind might have spatial location (for example, in the brain) we cannot allow that the mind has the material property of exclusion and still maintain that it is non-material. Further, if the mind did possess this property of exclusion, then either the mind and the brain would have to have different locations or they would have to be identical.

There is another sort of interaction that does not depend on the notion of one body excluding another, namely the interaction between a body and a field. Examples of such interactions are a particle being deflected by a gravitational field or a charged particle being deflected by a magnetic or electric field. We could hypothesize that the mind is (or exerts) some sort of field and the body is acted on by (and, in turn, acts on) this field. Some believers in psychic phenomena seem to see the mind in this sort of way. It is, however, difficult to sustain such a claim and still maintain that the mind is not physical. After all, although there is a sense in which electric and gravitational fields are 'immaterial', they are none the less physical. Problems with the notion of a 'mind field' become apparent as soon as we start to ask questions such as: What is the extent of this mind field? What sorts of laws does the field obey – is it the same strength throughout or does the strength vary in some law-like way? The understanding of magnetism is not advanced by saying, simply, that a magnetic field is an aura surrounding a (magnetic) body. In the same way, if we are to give an account of how the mind can affect material objects in terms of the interaction between a particle and a field, it is not enough to say that the mind is some sort of aura.

Supposing we were able to devise experiments to answer the sort of questions raised about the 'mind field'. The greater our success in answering these questions, the less plausible is the claim that the mind is a separate non-material substance. In general, the more seriously we treat the possibility of the mind being able to interact with the body, the more difficult it is to treat the mind as non-physical.

A radical claim made by some materialist philosophers is that we should not assume that there are mental phenomena, for which some sort of account has to be given. Rorty (1931–), for example, claims that, outside of philosophy, the concept of the mental performs no useful work. On this sort of view, the language that relates to mental concepts, that is, to beliefs, hopes, desires, etc., could be dispensed with altogether and replaced by more precise concepts grounded in neurophysiology.

None the less, there are philosophers who cannot go along with an out-and-out materialist position, although few, if any, would support a version of dualism based on the idea of two separate substances. Modern-day dualism is based on the distinctness of two different types of phenomena; mental phenomena are not reducible to physical phenomena, and even if we were to explain all the physical interactions in the universe, the explanation would be incomplete. In order to understand the position of the modern dualist, let us look at what it is claimed will be omitted by descriptions that are purely physical.

Distinctive aspects of the mental

Intentionality

Mental states, such as beliefs, desires, hopes, fears, etc., point beyond themselves; they are about something else. Thus, for example, I believe that I am sociable, I desire to remain healthy, I hope to be happy and I fear death. To express this in another way, my belief is about being sociable, my desire is about good health, my hope is about happiness and my fear is about death. The first claim to be considered, then, is that the mental is characterized by this feature of 'aboutness' – a feature to which philosophers refer by the term 'intentionality'. This can be coupled with the claim that a purely physical description cannot provide an account of intentionality.

To avoid the danger of confusing the concept of 'intentionality' with that of being 'intentional', it is worth noting briefly the similarities and differences between the two. Both concepts contain the idea of pointing to, or being directed at, something else. An intentional action is one carried out for a purpose, the intention being what the action is aimed at. To know someone's intentions is to know what they are trying to achieve. However, although our mental states have intentionality, they are not intentional. For example, I believe I am sociable, thus my belief has intentionality, but I do not have this belief intentionally. Our beliefs, hopes, etc. are not intentional, since we cannot acquire them at will, but they do have intentionality, since a belief or a hope is always a belief or hope about something. It may be possible to bring about *some* mental states intentionally – for example, we may watch a horror movie in order to produce a feeling of fear – but such cases are not typical. (To add to the confusion, philosophers also talk of *intension*, with an 's'. The intension of a concept is its meaning, and this is distinguished from its *extension*, which is the set of things to which it is correctly applied. These two terms, intension and extension, will not be used in the present text, but the reader may encounter them elsewhere.)

Is it true that intentionality is a defining characteristic of mental states? It is surely possible to think of cases where I simply feel happy or worried or even afraid, that is, mental states (happiness or anxiety or fear) that are not about something. On the other hand, there are also physical, non-mental things which appear to have intentionality. Words on a page, pigments on a canvas, deposits on a photographic plate, tea leaves in a cup, vibrations in the air, puffs of smoke in the sky, electrical impulses down a wire, flags hoisted on a pole, grooves on a disc, magnetized oxides and so on; all these can be about something else and so, on the above definition, have intentionality.

Intentionality, therefore, cannot be used, in any simple way, to distinguish the mental from the non-mental. If we had to decide whether a phenomenon was mental or non-mental, we could not use intentionality as a test. What, then, of the related claim that a purely physical description cannot include intentionality? The following argument might be advanced.

The wind blowing across sand may produce a pattern that resembles another object, but this sand-pattern is not *about* that object. Erosion may produce rock-patterns that look like the face of Jesus or that of a pop star, but these rock patterns do not depict Jesus or the pop star. It is only through mental states that physical states acquire intentionality. For example, it is only when patterns in the sand or in rocks become objects of awareness that they become representations of other things. The ability of physical things to acquire meaning and become symbols is dependent on the intentionality of mental states.

This argument is not conclusive. It may be true that, in a universe in which there were no human beings, there would be no intentionality. However, this does not mean that minds or (non-physical) mental states are needed for intentionality. It is clearly the case that human beings can use one physical object to represent another, but it begs the question to say that intentionality requires a non-physical human mind. If human beings are purely physical then (non-physical) mental states cannot be needed for intentionality. Yet this question, as to whether human beings are purely physical, is at the heart of the debate between materialists and dualists.

Phenomenological aspect

Another suggestion as to what is missing from a purely physical world, devoid of mental states, is what is called a 'phenomenological aspect'. We can observe the way another person reacts to touching a hot stove; we can see the blisters appearing on the skin; we may even be able to monitor the activities in the nerves and in the brain; but none of this is the same as actually experiencing the pain. Likewise with aches, scratches, tickles, caresses. We may be able to give a physical description of what is happening in the body, but this does not convey the phenomenological quality of the experience: that is, what it feels like to ache, to be scratched, tickled or caressed. Whereas the various electrochemical activities occur in the body – in particular, in the brain – the phenomenological quality is experienced in the mind.

Nagel (1937–), in an article entitled 'What is it Like to be a Bat?', claims that, in order for something to have conscious mental states, there must be something that it is like to be that thing. To say, for example, that bats have conscious mental states is to say that there is something that it is like to be a bat. We can deduce that, since a bat's perceptual apparatus is very different from our own, what it is like to be a bat must be very different from what it is like to be a human being. However, what we cannot do is to deduce, purely from the differences in physical characteristics, exactly what the mental characteristics will be. We cannot, in other words, deduce the phenomenology of a bat's world.

Qualia

The term *qualia* is given to the components of phenomenological content. Thus a particular ache, itch, tickle, pain will be experienced as a particular *quale* (the singular term for *qualia*). Likewise, sounds, colours, textures, smells will be experienced as *qualia*. It seems to follow from this that *qualia* are private to each individual. You and I might perceive the same thing, say some red flowers in a blue vase, and we might describe what we see in the same way, but we experience different *qualia*. These different *qualia* may not even be similar; in other words, the phenomenological aspects that the world presents to each of us may be very different. For example, my *quale* when I perceive something red may be similar to your *quale* when you perceive green. There even appears to be the possibility that my experience of red is like your experience of a tickle or the taste of chocolate!

The infallibility of the first-person viewpoint

The privacy of experience
The suggestion that only I can know what my experiences are, is put forward by both Descartes and Locke. They claim that not only do I, and I alone, have direct access to my experiences but also that, concerning the content of these experiences, I am infallible. Thus, I cannot make a mistake as to the phenomenological content of my experience in the way that I can make a mistake as to the cause of that experience. If I claim to see a cow, I may be mistaken. Perhaps what is in front of me is some other large mammal or a holographic image or a lifelike model. Perhaps there is nothing there and my perception is the result of having taken a drug or of some trick of the light. On the other hand, if I claim simply that I have the visual perception as of a cow then, surely, I cannot be mistaken.

This means that, when we talk about our experiences, we each use a language whose words have meaning only by referring to the private objects of our own minds. If I say that I see a cow, I am referring to a public object and as such I am open to correction by others. If no one else can see the cow that I claim to see (and there are no peculiar circumstances that account for my seeing something that no one else can see) then I have made a mistake. Suppose, instead, I say that I have the visual perception as of a cow. Now, even though no one else has a similar visual perception, I have not made a mistake; I am infallible when it comes to claims about my own experience. Instead of using the word 'cow' to refer to something in the world, I use the expression 'the visual perception as of a cow' to refer to something in my mind, a particular *quale* (or set of *qualia*).

The private language argument
Wittgenstein (1889–1951), in his famous 'private language argument', offered a telling criticism of these sorts of claims. His central point is

that the possibility of making a mistake and of being corrected is essential to language, and, if he is right, then language cannot be private in the way suggested above. Let us see why not. First we note that the expression 'the-visual-perception-as-of-a-cow' uses the word 'cow'. If this serves to make an implicit reference to cows, then 'the-visual-perception-as-of-a-cow' has to bear some sort of resemblance to a cow. In which case, my use of the expression is, after all, open to correction by others. For example, I can be asked to describe my perception, and if what I describe is nothing like a cow, then I am wrong in saying that I have the-visual-perception-as-of-a-cow. This implicit reference to public objects must mean that I am *not* using a private language to describe my experiences after all.

Suppose 'cow' in 'the-visual-perception-as-of-a-cow' does not have this sort of implicit reference – any more than the 'eat' in 'leather'. Then the expression 'the-visual-perception-as-of-a-cow' is simply a name, not a description, and could be replaced by, for example, *quale* X. This name, *quale* X, gets its meaning by referring to the private object of my experience. It is a term that only I can understand. Names, like other words in a language, are not used once and then discarded but are reused. However, the occasions on which they are reused are not arbitrary or random; in order to have a stable meaning, there must be rules governing their use. They do not, for example, acquire a meaning through some act of will on our part somehow forcing a meaning upon them. When we learn the meaning of a word, we do not learn necessary and sufficient conditions for the proper use of a word. Instead we learn a public criterion or a set of public criteria for the correct use of a word.

The problem for a language of private mental events is: what will justify any future use of the name '*quale* X' to refer to the content of my experience? If *quale* X is the name of a private experience, there can be no public criteria. I can say that it seems to me that '*quale* X' is being used correctly to refer to my present experience, but what seems to be right may not be right. Unless there is a way of checking whether the word is being used correctly, there is no criterion for its use and hence no rule. This means that the terms in my private language are meaningless.

The private language argument does not, in itself, show that the mental can be reduced to the physical. What it does show is that, if the mental, characterized by its phenomenology, is distinct from the physical, it cannot be totally divorced from the physical. Phenomenology may introduce something new – how things seem to be in addition to how, in physical terms, they are – but phenomenological aspects are not totally unconnected with the physical. What the private language argument also shows, assuming it to be correct, is that some of the theories of perception discussed earlier can be ruled out. For example, the naïve realist assumes the existence of a private language in order to talk about the immediate objects of perception, these objects being mental. Representational realists also suppose that it is possible to talk about ideas as things in their own right as well as representations of objects in the world.

Conflicting criteria for what counts as mental phenomena

We have considered two ways in which a purely physical description may fall short of being a complete description of the world we actually inhabit. The first is that the mental adds intentionality, the second that it adds phenomenology. We now need to address the following problem. Some of the states that we might want to call mental exhibit intentionality and are phenomenological in nature. However, there are some that, although they have a phenomenology, do not exhibit intentionality and others that exhibit intentionality but which do not have a phenomenology.

Pains and tickles, for example, are not *about* anything. On the other hand, although a strong fear or a strong desire or a strong conviction has a phenomenology, it is not always the case that beliefs, desires or fears have a phenomenology. What, for example, is the phenomenological aspect of my belief that I am less than 6 feet tall? Does it differ from that of my belief that I am over 5 feet tall? I have held both beliefs for all my adult life but there is no particular experience I would associate with either belief, and certainly no experience that I have been having ever since I became an adult. There is a phenomenological difference between desire and fear, but the change that comes about when a person, who previously feared death, now desires it, may not be a phenomenological one at all. Instead, the difference may lie in the causal links with behaviour.

Do intentionality and phenomenology pick out two different aspects of mental things? In which case, why do some mental states exhibit one but not the other? Do they pick out two different sorts of thing altogether, which just happen to have some members in common? If so, which, if either, is 'mental'? Is the mental something that exhibits either intentionality or phenomenology (or both)? If so, why are we generally not aware that it has this disjunctive property? These are questions that the dualist has to answer. However, they do not pose a problem for the theory, or set of theories, to which we now turn, materialism. All that materialism has to do is to account for these two features in physical terms.

Materialism

Materialism, as a general metaphysical position, can be expressed in a number of ways, but, in essence, it is the view that everything can be accounted for in material or physical terms. Materialists claim that a physical description can, at least in theory, give a complete account of all that exists, including the mental. They assume that the mental is related to activities in the brain. The different versions of materialism amount to different ways of identifying mental states, if there are any, with brain states.

Eliminative materialism

The most extreme form that materialism takes is given the name 'eliminative materialism'. Less extreme versions of materialism view the mental, in some way or another, as constituting a set of phenomena for which some sort of account has to be given, even if the account is in physical terms. Eliminative materialism, on the other hand, does not concede even that there has to be an account of the mental. Instead, as its name suggests, it assumes that a successful materialist account eliminates all reference to the mental. It does not treat terms such as 'beliefs', 'desires', etc. as having an accepted reference but as terms that acquire meaning only within a theory; what the terms purport to refer to are theoretical entities and, since the theory is fundamentally wrong, they have no meaning at all.

An analogy may make this point clearer. One of the important discoveries in the emerging science of chemistry was that of the element oxygen and its role in combustion. Before this discovery, there were a number of theories as to what happens when something burns. Initial observations suggested that burning resulted in a loss of matter. One theory was that materials that burnt easily did so because they contained a substance called 'phlogiston'. It was thought that such combustible materials were 'phlogiston-rich' and that burning involved the loss of phlogiston. When more careful measurements were made, these appeared to show that burning resulted in a gain rather than a loss in mass. Retention of the theory thus required the assumption that phlogiston had negative mass! Although not directly relevant here, it is interesting that the phlogiston theory survived for some time despite contrary experimental evidence. (See the section in chapter 4 on Kuhnian paradigms.) The relevant point of the analogy is that, although the term 'phlogiston' was used as if it were the name of some existing substance, it turned out that there was nothing to which it referred. The theory of burning that replaced the phlogiston theory eliminated any need for the term 'phlogiston'. Eliminative materialists say that the same is true of terms such as 'belief' and 'desire'.

Folk psychology

At the root of the eliminative materialist's position lies the claim that we attempt to understand and predict each other's behaviour by appeal to a body of common-sense laws. This body of laws is, in effect, a scientific theory, labelled 'folk psychology' (or FP, for short) by eliminative materialists. These laws employ terms such as 'belief', 'desire' and 'hope', and the concepts designated by them constitute the theoretical framework. These terms do not function like, say, 'dog', 'brick' and 'cloud', whose meaning can be conveyed by pointing at the relevant objects, but are like 'phlogiston', whose meaning was acquired through its role in a theoretical framework. If FP is a true theory, then not only do such theoretical terms have a meaning but there is also something to which they refer. On the other hand, if the theory is false, there is nothing to which these theoretical terms refer. It turned out that 'phlogiston' had no referent; eliminative materialists claim that 'belief', 'hope', etc. also fail to refer. Eliminative materialism claims that, eventually, FP will be replaced by a better theory and our use of these terms will disappear.

What justification can be offered for the claim that 'belief', 'desire' and other terms referring to mental states are theoretical terms and that supposedly commonplace views incorporating these terms constitute a theory? The eliminative materialist will point to the way we use the conceptual framework for mental phenomena to try to explain and predict human behaviour. The theory hypothesizes an 'internal' causal process that mediates between the outside conditions that affect an individual and the behaviour he or she produces. These internal processes involve (1) an awareness of an opportunity for acting in a certain way, (2) a belief that acting in this way will result in a certain outcome and (3) a desire for that outcome. When these constituents are present then, other things being equal, the result will be a particular action. Thus, the way FP functions defines it as a scientific theory.

Suppose we accept that FP is a theory. Does it follow from this that the terms in our common-sense conceptual framework are theoretical terms? If they are, are there also grounds for thinking that FP will be shown to be a radically false theory, which will mean that these theoretical terms will need to be discarded? Even given that FP is not a reliable theory, why should it be assumed that FP needs to be rejected rather than modified? It is possible for many of the theoretical terms to survive a modification of FP.

These are technical questions, and it would not be appropriate to try to answer them fully here. However, two brief points can be made. The first is that terms used in the context of a theory need not all be theoretical terms that derive their meaning solely from that theory. They may be terms which refer to phenomena which the theory has to explain; they may be terms which figure in several theories or which can be carried over, relatively intact, from one theory to its replacement. Propositional attitudes could fit into any one of these categories.

The second point relates to the scope of neuroscience. The assumption being made is that neuroscience will replace FP eventually. It is certainly true that neuroscience is a development of well-established sciences and can draw upon the bodies of knowledge to be found in these. However, whereas oxidation theory and phlogiston theory offered rival accounts of the same set of phenomena, namely burning substances, it is not obvious that this is the case with FP and neuroscience. It is possible to see FP and neuroscience as complementary, rather than rival, theories that operate at different levels and with different sets of theoretical terms.

Identity theories

If materialism cannot eliminate mental phenomena, then its aim must be to give an account of mental phenomena in physical terms. The simplest account that can be given is to say that mental phenomena are identical with physical phenomena. Yet even this simple-sounding claim encompasses different sorts of relationships between the mental and the physical, as will be made clear following an account of the type–token distinction.

The distinction between type and token

To illustrate this distinction, consider the question: How many words are there in the sentence 'Run rabbit, run'? Whether the answer given is two or three will depend on the interpretation of the question. The answer 'two' would be justified by saying that there are two words, 'run' and 'rabbit', the second 'run' being simply a repetition of the first word and not a different word. Here, the assumption is made that the question is asking for the number of different *types*. On the other hand, the answer 'three' would be justified by saying that there are two 'run's and one 'rabbit'; two plus one is three. Here the two occurrences of 'run' count as two different words, that is, they are two different *tokens*, even though they may be tokens of the same type.

With this in mind, consider the question: How many different brain states have I had in the last hour? The answer to this question will differ depending on whether it is the number of different types or of different tokens that is required. Similarly with the question: How many different mental states have I had in the last hour? This answer will also differ depending on whether a count of types or tokens is required. Supposing that, for both questions, I obtain an answer for the number of types and the number of tokens. On the assumption that brain states are identical to mind states, should the number of brain states and mind states be the same if I compare type with type or token with token? No. In fact, it is not possible to say whether they should be the same or different, since the assumption I have been asked to make, that of identity between brain and mind states, has not been specified unambiguously.

What are the possibilities? First that the identity holds at the level of types, in which case there is no requirement that the two token-counts produce the same answer. Second, that the identity holds at the level of tokens, which removes the requirement for the two type-counts to produce the same answer. Third, that there is a more complicated identity relationship, so that neither count need produce the same answer.

Type–type identity

The first possibility to be considered is that a type–type identity holds between mental and physical phenomena. Various theoretical identities in science are type–type identities, and the following example might help explain what is involved. An early puzzle for science was to give an account of heat. There is a phenomenological aspect to heat, namely the sensations of hot and cold that are produced in us. In addition there is also the 'thing' itself, that is, heat. One idea saw heat as a substance (perhaps a gas or a fluid) that can be absorbed by bodies and transferred between them. As it turned out, this idea was wrong. It was discovered that the heat in a body is the amount of kinetic energy possessed by the particles that constitute the body. This theoretical identity is a type–type identity whereby a particular type of phenomenon, heat, is identical to a particular type of physical property, kinetic energy.

One version of materialism claims that the identity of mental phenomena and brain states is a type–type identity. Thus, it is claimed that pain is identical to a set of axons, known as C-fibres, being in an excited state. (In fact, this suggestion seems to be based on flawed neurophysiology, but as an illustration it is apt enough. Reference to an identity between pain and the stimulation of C-fibres is certainly prevalent in the philosophical literature, and flawed neurophysiology need not result in a flawed philosophical account.) As with the identity between heat and molecular motion, the identity is an identity of types, a mental phenomenon, pain, and a physical state of the brain (or part of it).

None the less, the identity of heat and molecular motion is different, in important ways, from the proposed identity of C-fibre excitation and pain. Heat, that is, molecular motion, can exist even if there are no sentient beings around to experience it. Sentient beings are a prerequisite for the *sensation* of heat, since sensations are part of experience. Although the sensation of heat is the means by which we detect heat, the theoretical identity holds not between the sensation of heat and molecular motion but between *heat* and molecular motion. With pain it is different. The sensation of pain is *not* the means by which we detect pain; here we cannot drive a wedge between the sensation and something else of which it is a sensation. If there is an identity between pain and C-fibre stimulation, then there must be an identity between the sensation of pain and C-fibre stimulation. This leads to difficulties.

In the case of heat, we can say that if there is molecular vibration then there is heat, although there may or may not be the sensation of heat. In the case of pain, it seems distinctly odd to say that if there is C-fibre stimulation then there is also pain but there may or may not

be the sensation of pain. Yet this is the position we might be forced
into by claiming an identity between pain and C-fibre stimulation. It
is well known that injuries that would normally cause pain may, in
some circumstances, fail to do so, for example, when the person is
involved in a game or is in a life-and-death situation. Now it may be
that, in such situations, stimulation of C-fibres is suppressed and this
is why there is no pain. But it is also possible that there is no feeling
of pain despite C-fibre stimulation. For the identity to be true requires
that there can be pain but no feeling of pain. Conversely, a patient
may complain to a doctor of a pain yet, if the doctor were unable to
detect any physiological indication (including C-fibre stimulation), there
would be no pain. We would have to say that the sensation of pain
was not always a reliable indication of pain.

A further point is this. In the case of a theoretical identity, such as
the identity of heat and molecular motion, recognizing the truth of
the identity leads to an understanding of the phenomenon. We know
that heat is transferred from one body to another. By realizing that
heat is molecular motion, we understand *how* heat is transferred, what
aids the transfer and what hinders it. That is, we come to understand
something of the nature of heat. With the supposed identity of pain
and C-fibre excitation, it is difficult to see what has been explained.
In what sense do we achieve a greater understanding of the nature
of pain? We certainly do not see why, whenever we have C-fibre
stimulation, we have pain. What the materialist might claim is that we
have a greater understanding of pain through seeing that it is a physical
phenomenon. However, the idea that pain is physical is what drives
the identity claim rather than what follows from it. Studying C-fibre
stimulation, how it arises and how it relates to, say, bodily injury, will
certainly contribute to our understanding of how the body works, but
it is not clear that it leads to a greater understanding of pain. This
point is not affected by identifying pain with some other physical
state, perhaps more complexly specified than saying that C-fibres are
being stimulated.

For the type–type identity thesis to be true it must hold not only
for pains but for all mental phenomena, including intentional states.
Thus each possible belief will be identical to a brain state of a different
type and similarly for other intentional attitudes. An illustration will
show what this commits us to. A belief that snow is white is one type
of belief, and this must be identical to a brain state of a certain type,
say, brain state number 137, in some catalogue of brain states. A
different belief, say, a belief that grass is green, will be identical to

another brain state (say, number 143). A dislike of snow would be identical to yet another brain state (say, number 815).

Now, even if we were to build up a body of empirical evidence relating certain types of beliefs, such as that snow is white, that grass is green, etc., to certain brain states, say numbers 137 and 143, respectively, this would show only contingent connections and not identities. Such connections might be useful; reading a person's brain state may be a way of detecting when a person lied about his or her belief. What we could not do is use the brain state as a criterion for holding a particular belief. Suppose a person is in brain state 137 but claims that he does not believe that snow is white. There remains the logical possibility that he is sincere and that all the other evidence we have, for example, his behaviour and past experiences, is consistent with what he says. It could be decided that all this other evidence counted for nothing, but this would amount to changing the meaning of 'belief'. This would not be a matter of showing that a type–type identity held between beliefs and brain states but of ruling or postulating that it did.

One of the problems with the claim that a type–type identity holds between brain states and mental states is that the division of brain states into types and the division of mental states into types have to mirror each other exactly. On the face of it, there seems no reason why they should. Yet all that materialism need be committed to is this: that a person's mental state is, in some way, strongly connected with the person's brain being in a particular state. This commitment can be met by claiming that mental states are supervenient on brain states.

Supervenience
What it means for mental states to be supervenient on brain states is that the same mental state can arise out of different brain states but different mental states cannot arise out of the same brain state. Changes in brain state may not change the mental state, but changes in mental state can occur only with a change in the brain state. The way in which mental states might be supervenient on brain states can be understood as analogous to the way in which pictorial content is supervenient on the pattern of ink dots on newsprint. A picture of the Eiffel Tower is produced by a particular pattern of ink dots. The same picture can be produced by other patterns of dots, for example, a greater number of smaller dots. Thus we cannot talk about a type–type identity between this type of picture, that of the Eiffel Tower, and this type of pattern of dots. On the other hand, the same pattern of dots cannot produce a different picture. (There are, it is true, certain

patterns of dots that can be seen in different ways, say, as a duck or as a rabbit. However, this is not the case of the same pattern of dots producing two different pictures, that is, with a difference in pictorial content. Rather, the dots produce a single picture that can be seen as one thing or as another. The pictorial content is the duck–rabbit illusion.) Supervenience implies that mental states can be realized by different physical states. These may be different physical states at different times in the same human being, or different physical states in different human beings, or different physical states in humans and non-humans. Aliens from another world may have radically different body chemistry but the same (types of) mental states.

Another analogy, which should appeal to those who have some knowledge of computer programming, and which is germane to a characterization of the mental, is the relationship between a high-level language and a low-level language, or machine code. The same high-level language statement, which might be to test whether a name from one list matches up with a name from another list, can be implemented on different types of computers, even ones that use a different machine code and hence a different machine-architecture and different sets of basic instructions. The high-level instructions are supervenient on the low-level ones and hence, ultimately, on the computer hardware.

Token–token identity

Although the suggestion that there is a type–type identity between brain states and mental states is eliminated by the possibility of realizing the same (type of) mental states by different (types of) brain states, this does not preclude a token–token identity between the two. Thus, it is claimed, each particular mental state (token) is identical to a particular physical state (token). Yet, even though the mental state is a token of a type (of mental state) and the physical state is a token of a type (of physical state), there is no relation between the two types. This, it is suggested, excludes the possibility of there being laws relating physical events and mental events.

Functionalism

Functionalism takes a different approach to the mental from those we have seen so far. Instead of trying to eliminate all reference to the mental or trying to identify mental states with physical states, it tries to incorporate the mental into a physical framework. ('Incorporate' is an appropriate word here, meaning to embody, to combine into one substance.) The mental is to be understood not in terms of what it *is* but in terms of what it *does*. In general, what mental states do is act as intermediaries between inputs (such as those produced by the action of external bodies on the sense organs), outputs (that is, behaviour) and other mental states. Thus, mental states play a causal role, and it is the specific nature of the causal role played which characterizes the mental phenomenon in question. If two mental-state tokens play identical causal roles then they are tokens of the same type, even though different brain states may be involved. There is rarely, if ever, a simple relation between input and output, and so mental states mediate not only between stimulus and response but also between other internal functional, that is mental, states.

The mind as a computer program

Functionalism has been closely associated with the development of artificial intelligence and has, in its turn, been influenced by it. The science of artificial intelligence produces theories of intelligence that are expressed through computer programs. The criterion for the success of these computer programs is a functional one, that is, whether or not they produce the appropriate output from the given input. Since the program (that is, the set of instructions) plays a causal role between input and output, it is, functionally, analogous to the mind (or the mental faculties). Thus artificial intelligence provides us with a model of the relationship between the mind and the body (or, more particularly, the brain). The computer hardware consists of circuit boards, buses, silicon chips, etc., and the state of the components at any particular time – switches being on or off, each node of the circuit having a certain potential, etc. – corresponds to a brain state. This is the physical part of the system. On the other hand, the functional state, that is, the particular instruction being executed, corresponds to a mental state.

There are a number of interesting and suggestive aspects to this analogy. First, the program plays a causal role, and, given the input, the output can be predicted and explained by reference to the set of instructions in the program.

Second, although the program is stored in the hardware (on magnetic disks or tapes or in ROM or RAM), it is something separate from the hardware. This is at least suggestive of a solution to the problem of intentionality, since instructions have intentionality. Perhaps the intentionality of a sequence of magnetized patches derives from its function and, in a similar way, a sequence of sounds or a set of marks on paper has intentionality because of *its* function.

Third, understanding the steps in the program and understanding the changes at the level of the hardware are two different ways of understanding the system. The two accounts can be both independent and complete. If we consider only the machine states, there are no gaps in the causal chains that have to be filled in by unobserved non-physical causes. Equally, we can understand the functional role played by the program in accounting for the output that results from the given input with no reference to what is happening at the level of hardware.

Fourth, although each step in the program has a corresponding machine state, this is not a case of type–type correspondence. Rather, since the same computer program can be run on different hardware systems, it would appear to be supervenient on the hardware. In other words, the functional features of a computer are not tied to any particular hardware configuration. Indeed, functionalism is not committed to hardware (in the sense of some configuration of a material substance) at all and so is consistent with dualism. None the less, functionalism is generally associated with materialism.

These points may lead us to ask whether the brain is or, perhaps, is nothing but, a computer. This is a difficult question to answer, but the greater the number of tasks that computers can be made to perform which were previously considered peculiar to human beings, the more indirect evidence there is for such a claim.

Can machines think?

Is it possible for machines to think? Or, in other words, is it possible for a machine to have mental states? The answer will, of course, depend on how we understand the notion of the mental. If we adopt the position that mental states are identical to brain states, then whether we can make a machine that can think will depend on whether it is possible to produce a machine capable of replicating brain states. Is it possible, for example, to have brain states without having brains? In other words, can we make the notion of a brain state sufficiently abstract to allow such states to be instantiated in things other than brains? In particular, we might ask, is it possible for brain states to be realized in computers? If a brain state is constituted by structural relationships, say between components capable of carrying out simple logical operations (or combinations of such operations), then computers that have such components will be capable of replicating brain states. On the other hand, if a brain state is constituted by the presence of cells of a certain type, interconnected in certain ways, along with particular organic molecules, chemical solutions of a particular strength and acidity, etc., then brain states will not be replicated by computers, at least not by those of the type we now have.

The Turing test

From a functionalist position, we need simply to consider whether machines can be devised that are capable of mediating between input and output in the appropriate way. From this stance, a test for whether a machine could think would be to see whether a computer – or, more accurately, a computer program – could produce output that is indistinguishable from that produced by a human being in the same circumstances. This is the basis for the Turing test, proposed by Alan Turing (1912–1954). A human subject and a computer are placed in separate rooms and an interrogator puts questions to both of them via a terminal. If the interrogator is not able to identify the computer on the basis of answers alone, then the computer is deemed to have passed the test (or perhaps the human has failed it!) and to have same mental attributes as a human.

Would passing the Turing test really be a demonstration of being able to think? What is being claimed by saying that a computer can think? For example, is consciousness being claimed? On a functionalist account of mind, if a computer is able to perform like a human being in every respect, then the computer has a mind that is like a human's in every respect. If consciousness is a mental phenomenon then it must carry out a certain function. It follows that any machine able to perform the same function has the same mental property, that is, it is conscious.

The Chinese room

Searle (1932–) argues that passing the Turing test is not sufficient to show that the computer has conscious thoughts. Searle asks us to imagine a room (the so-called Chinese room) in which there is a book containing a large set of instructions. Through one opening into the room come pieces of paper with marks on them. There is a person in the room whose task is to compare these marks with those in the instruction book and then carry out the instructions indicated. This will involve making marks on other pieces of paper, these pieces of paper then being passed out through a second opening. Now suppose that what is written on the pieces of paper coming into the room are questions in Chinese – perhaps they are questions posed by an interrogator in the Turing test – and what the operator writes on the pieces of paper are the appropriate answers, also in Chinese.

The operator in the Chinese room is doing nothing more than manipulate symbols (it is assumed that he or she does not understand Chinese) and so the Chinese room plus operator can be likened to a computer. We now suppose that the answers produced satisfy the interrogator administering the Turing test. Does this mean that the Chinese room can understand Chinese in the way that a person understands Chinese? We can assume that the operator can think, but the operator does not understand the questions being asked or the answers he or she provides. And if the operator does not understand Chinese, it is difficult to find anything else on which to hang this understanding. In this respect, the Chinese room is not like the native speaker of Chinese who responds in similar fashion to the same set of questions.

Suppose we put the following question to the Chinese room, in Chinese: Do you understand Chinese? The answer it will give, also in Chinese, is 'Yes'. However, if we put the same question to the operator, in the operator's native language, the operator will answer 'no', again in his or her own language. Thus the understanding of Chinese and, with it, the consciousness of the meaning of the symbols, is not something that the operator has. Computers, like the operator in the Chinese room, may be good symbol manipulators (that is, they can manage the syntax of language) but this is not the same as grasping the meanings of the symbols being manipulated. One of the features we associate with understanding the meaning is consciousness. Computers and the Chinese room may perform the appropriate mental functions, but this does not seem to be enough to justify attributing consciousness. Consciousness seems to be something that cannot be captured by any functionalist account.

A defence of functionalism

Dennett (1942–) argues that the implausibility of saying that a computer can be conscious arises from the way that Searle has set up the Chinese room example. One of the problems of trying to devise programs that will enable a computer to pass the Turing test is what is known as the 'frame' problem. Understanding a language does not merely involve manipulating symbols; it also requires a lot of background knowledge. Speakers of a language are able to recognize which items of this background knowledge are relevant to a particular sentence. It has proved to be difficult to program this into a computer. Hence the idea that the Chinese room operator could produce answers to questions simply by looking up appropriate instructions in various manuals is a considerable oversimplification of what would be needed to pass the Turing test. Dennett maintains, in effect, that the more we flesh out our account of what would need to go on inside a computer for it to be capable of passing the Turing test, the more plausible it is that such a computer would think and be self-aware.

Dennett's criticisms of Searle's Chinese room thought experiment are accompanied by other criticisms of arguments that attempt to show the mental is not reducible to the physical. Dennett also tries to make the idea that the mental can be explained in terms of the physical more plausible. Whether he succeeds in this is a question over which philosophers will continue to disagree. The reader must examine the arguments and decide for her or himself which is less implausible.

Summary

- There are different ways of trying to characterize the mental. For example, mental states exhibit intentionality, that is, they are about something, and mental states have a particular phenomenological quality for the person who experiences them. Claims have been made that the first-person perspective provides privileged access to one's mental states and that one cannot make a mistake as to one's experiences. This appears to assume the possibility of a private language, a possibility that is rejected by Wittgenstein.
- The view most commonly, although not universally, accepted by philosophers is that of materialism. Materialism either denies that mental phenomena exist at all or it reduces mental phenomena to physical or material phenomena.
- Eliminative materialism assumes that supposed reference to the mental is by means of terms that have meaning only in the context

of an informal scientific theory. Moreover, it argues that this theory, folk psychology, is a poor theory and will be replaced by a more developed version of neuroscience. When this happens, terms such as 'belief' and 'desire' will disappear, since they lack genuine reference.

- Other types of materialism claim some relationship between brain states and mental states. This relationship may be type–type identity, token–token identity or supervenience. Functionalism, which strictly speaking is not committed to materialism, identifies the mental not, directly, with different states of the brain but with certain functional states that mediate between sensory inputs, behavioural outputs and other functional states.

- The Turing test proposes placing a computer and a human being in separate rooms or cubicles and then interrogating each of them. If the interrogator is unable to distinguish the machine then the machine is deemed to have a mental life similar to that of a human being. Searle has argued that being able to manipulate symbols in this way does not show understanding, whereas Dennett has argued that the sort of operations required are much more complex than the simple manipulation of symbols envisaged by Searle.

Questions raised

- What are the fundamental constituents of the universe? Is a universe in which there are conscious beings one with more than physical elements? Can the mental be reduced, without residue, to the physical?

- Although Cartesian dualism is a view many philosophers argue against, most people who are not philosophers probably hold some version of dualism. Most people also think that there is interaction, in both directions, between mind and body. Is it possible to rescue this dualism by giving some explanation as to how this interaction works?

- According to some accounts the human brain is a Turing machine and the relationship that the mind bears to the brain is similar (or perhaps identical) to the relationship that computer software bears to the hardware. If this is so, then (given the obvious fact that we are conscious) it is possible for a machine to be conscious. This means it is also possible that we shall one day produce machines that are conscious. Is the Turing test a suitable test of whether or not this has occurred? If machines do exhibit consciousness, does this mean that we will have responsibilities towards them that we do not have towards other machines? Would such machines acquire rights?

7 God

Introduction

Any number of claims have been made regarding God. For example, that the existence of God is a more fundamental truth than the existence of the world we see around us. Or, that God exists eternally and necessarily, whereas the existence of everything else is contingent and transitory. Or, that God is the creator of heaven and earth and everything depends on God for its existence. Or, that God is self-caused and is the first cause in the chain of causation linking successive states of the universe. Clearly, God is a good subject for metaphysical enquiry.

Whether it is possible to prove that God exists is a metaphysical and epistemological issue and not a matter of religious faith, belief or revelation. Questions we must consider include: what do we mean by

'God'? Is the notion of God coherent? What is the evidence for God's existence?

One of the claims made about God is that God is a person. Persons are able to enter into a particular sort of relationship with each other and, rather than trying to lay down a criterion for being a person, we shall consider the nature of this relationship more closely. The question then arises: do the qualities of omnipresence, omniscience and omnipotence even allow for such interpersonal relationships, let alone enhance them?

Referring to God

Names

Before considering the evidence to which we might appeal in deciding whether God exists, we need first to deal with another problem. This might be called the problem of reference, and it is as follows: we are trying to find the answer to the question 'Does God exist?'. For this, we must understand the question and, in particular, we must understand what is meant by the word 'God'. 'God' functions as a name, and it is tempting to think that we can really understand a name only by being acquainted with whatever is named. However, this would mean that if we can understand the question then we already have an answer: God must exist in order for us to know what we mean by asking whether God exists. On the other hand, if God does not exist, we can neither understand the question we are asking, nor even what is meant by saying that God does not exist.

Frege's theory of names

Any existential statement, whether a positive one, with the form 'N exists', or a negative one, with the form 'N does not exist', raises the problem of reference. Positive existential statements appear to be saying of something that it exists; negative existential statements appear to be saying of something that it does not exist. Thus the first is superfluous, the second absurd. Frege (1848–1925) offers a way of dealing with this problem. He suggests that, when we talk about the meaning of a name, we are confusing two things that should be kept separate: the sense of the name and its reference, that is, what the name refers to. The two are connected in that the reference of a name is determined by the sense that the name has. The sense of a name is given by a description or set of descriptions.

Consider an existential statement made of a legendary figure, for example, that King Arthur existed. According to Frege's theory of names, the meaning of 'Arthur' is a cluster of descriptions. This cluster might include the following: 'The person who united the British kings to fight the Saxon invaders', 'The person who gathered around him the group of men known as the knights of the Round Table', 'The person who ruled at Camelot' and so on. The claim that King Arthur existed is the claim that the name has a reference, that is, that there is one, and only one, person who fits all (or, perhaps, most) of these descriptions.

The theory that there is a description, or set of descriptions, that constitutes the sense of a name, and that the sense of a name is used to pick out who or what the name refers to, is rejected by Kripke (1940–). To appreciate some of the force of Kripke's objection, it is helpful to introduce the terminology of 'possible worlds'. The basic concept is quite simple. Consider what is actually the case, that is, the facts. Many of what we think of as facts are contingent facts. Britain's present head of state is Queen Elizabeth, but this could have been otherwise since the position could have passed on to some other member of the royal family, or the monarchy could have been abolished altogether. The Berlin Wall has been knocked down but could be still standing; mankind still exists but could have been destroyed by a nuclear holocaust; and so on. Pointing out something else that might have happened can be taken as implicitly referring to a possible world in which it did happen. Many possible worlds are almost identical to our own, for example, the possible world in which I had two slices of toast for breakfast this morning instead of one. Other possible worlds are vastly different, for example, the possible world in which the dinosaurs were not wiped out or in which life did not develop.

Rigid designators
What happens when we take a description, which in the actual world picks out a certain individual, and try to apply it in a possible world? Sometimes the description will pick out exactly the same individual in the possible world. An example would be the description 'the person writing this book' applied to possible worlds that differ from this only in regard to distant events. In the actual world and these possible

worlds, I am picked out by the description. However, it is conceivable that someone else could have written the book you are now reading, and this would be a possible world in which I did not write it. When the above description is applied to this other possible world, someone other than me will be referred to. Kripke expresses this point that descriptions can pick out different individuals in different possible worlds by saying that descriptions are not *rigid designators* over all possible worlds. On the other hand, he claims, names are rigid designators. After all, if they were not, I could not talk about a possible world in which Jon Nuttall did not write the book you are reading. If, to push the point a bit further, the name 'Jon Nuttall' meant 'the person who wrote the book you are reading', there is no possible world in which this book was written by someone other than Jon Nuttall.

Take another example. As it happened, Suker was the top goal scorer in the 1998 World Cup. Thus 'Suker' and 'top goal scorer in the 1998 World Cup' refer to the same person. However it is only a contingent fact about Suker that he was top goal scorer – he might have been off-form during June and July 1998, Croatia might have been eliminated early in the competition, he might not have been selected and so on. In other words, we can imagine possible worlds in which Suker was not the top goal scorer. Yet, to be able to make such a statement, we need to be able to designate Suker in these possible worlds. The name 'Suker' does this for us; it is a rigid designator since it points to the same person in different possible worlds. On the other hand, 'top goal scorer in the 1998 World Cup' will refer to other individuals in other possible worlds. There is a possible world in which David Beckham is not sent off against Argentina, England goes on to win the World Cup and Michael Owen is top goal scorer. In this possible, if somewhat unlikely, world, the description 'top goal scorer in the 1998 World Cup' refers to Michael Owen and not Suker.

If names are rigid designators and descriptions (in general) are not, then we cannot explain how a name acquires a reference by producing a description that is supposed to be the sense of the name. Kripke points out that a name may have a reference even when all the descriptions that we take to be true of the person to whom the name refers turn out to be false. The example he gives is that of the prophet Jonah. The Bible has a lot to say about Jonah, including that he was swallowed by a whale. However, according to Kripke, the 'scholarly consensus regards all details about Jonah in the book as legendary and not even based on a factual substratum, excepting the bare statement that he was a Hebrew prophet' (*Naming and Necessity*, 67). Even the name 'Jonah' is virtually certain not to have been Jonah's name! The question posed is how 'Jonah' can refer to someone. What is it that makes the biblical stories fictional accounts of an actual person rather than fiction pure and simple?

The causal chain theory of reference
The account Kripke gives is known as the 'causal chain' theory of reference. The first link of the chain is formed when a name is given to a person. This may be done in a formal way by means of some ceremony, say a Christening, or some act, such as that of registering a baby's name with the appropriate authority. Alternatively, a person may acquire a name in a less formal way. Those acquainted with the person will use the name to refer to him or her, and so the name acquires a reference. The succeeding links of the chain are forged when other people pick up on the use of the name. It is not necessary that they should be acquainted with the person to whom the name refers provided that they are aware that the person from whom they learn the name is using it referentially and that they themselves use it with the intention of referring to the same person.

In this way it is possible to learn a name through being given false information about someone. Thus, for example, friends of Jonah may have wished to play a trick on him by saying that he was a very miserable person who was swallowed by a giant whale. Such stories may reach people who do not know Jonah or anything about Jonah. On Frege's account one would have to say that, for such people, the sense of 'Jonah' is 'the miserable person who was swallowed by a whale' and there is no reference (unless there did exist, somewhere, a miserable person who was swallowed by a whale, in which case, 'Jonah' would refer to him and not to Jonah!). However, on Kripke's account, provided there is a causal chain (of the appropriate sort) leading back to Jonah, then this is the person to whom the name refers. Moreover, the name succeeds in referring to Jonah even though Jonah was called something other than 'Jonah', was not miserable and was not swallowed by a giant whale.

The concept of God

Consider the question 'Did King Arthur exist?' There are two different types of interest that might prompt this question. One is whether the name 'King Arthur' refers to a historical figure; this is the question that is settled by establishing the existence of a causal chain, of the appropriate type, leading back to a particular person. However, the second interest is whether there was someone who did (most if not all) the things that Arthur is said to have done. In other words, the second concern is with whether there was an individual who satisfied the cluster of descriptions that are commonly attributed to King Arthur. This question can, after all, be asked without subscribing to the theory that such a cluster gives the sense of the name 'King Arthur'.

In order to settle the question 'Does God exist?' it might be that we need to engage in historical research to determine whether there is a causal chain leading from our use of 'God' to, say, Moses' use of 'God'. This, however, need not be our only, or even our primary, concern. For suppose we establish that there is such a causal chain and that God, like Jonah, existed. We still want to know certain things about God. For, just as we have discovered that Jonah did none of the things the Bible said he did, so we might also discover that *God* did none of the things the Bible said he did. Thus we might conclude that God existed but that he did not create heaven and earth or all the flowers of the field, etc. We might conclude that we are wrong to attribute omniscience, omnipotence, omnipresence, perfect benevolence, etc. to God. This still leaves, and perhaps gives added urgency to, the question: does there exist a transcendent being who is omniscient, omnipotent, omnipresent, perfectly benevolent, etc., who created heaven and earth and who would be the proper object of our worship? In other words, we have a *concept* of God, and when we ask whether God exists, what we really want to know is whether that concept is instantiated or not.

There is clearly scope for disagreement as to what exactly is the concept of God. There are, after all, many different religions all claiming knowledge of God, and these religions have different beliefs about God. None the less, the claim is also made that the members of different faiths all believe in the same God, even though they have different beliefs about him. I shall sidestep the question as to whether this suggestion can be defended and take the concept of God to be the following. God is a person, is immaterial (except when incarnated in his son Jesus Christ – a complication we shall ignore here), created everything that exists, is all-powerful (omnipotent), is all-knowing (omniscient), is present everywhere (omnipresent), has perfect free will and is perfectly good. The question to which we want the answer is this: is there a single individual to whom these (or possibly most of these) descriptions apply?

Religious language

First, we need to be sure that we understand expressions such as being omnipotent or being a person. Do words have their ordinary meaning when used of God? When we say of God that he is all-powerful and that he is a person, do we mean 'all-powerful' and 'person' in the usual sense, or are we using these words in some special way to convey different meanings from their ordinary ones? Can the objection that it is incoherent to say of an infinite spirit that it is also a person be countered by saying that 'person' is not to be understood in its usual sense? If it is said that religious words have a special meaning, how are these special meanings determined?

Meanings arise from religious experience

One claim is that religious words acquire a special meaning through religious experiences and that those who do not have such religious experiences are incapable of understanding them. Thus those who claim God has revealed himself to them through a mystical experience describe him as both a person and an all-powerful spirit, but qualify this by saying that he is not a person in the way that you and I are persons. God is a person, but only someone who has had a similar mystical experience can understand what this means.

The effect of this is to turn religious language into a secret language, a language that can be understood only by the initiated. This is not because it is not taught to the uninitiated but because it could not be. It is private, in the way that the 'sensation language' considered in the previous chapter was private, although this time it is supposedly private to a group of people rather than to an individual. None the less, the problems that attended the idea of a private sensation language also attend this notion of a secret language. If those who speak this secret language are to communicate with each other, then there must be public criteria for correct use of the words of the language. Correct use cannot be determined by reference to a private experience. Indeed, without public criteria there could be no guarantee that those in on the 'secret' had shared a similar experience. A blind person may demonstrate a grasp of the concept blue by using the word 'blue' correctly without having had the experience of seeing blue. In the same way, it is not necessary to have certain religious or mystical experiences to be able to grasp religious or mystical concepts.

Meanings arise from a model

Can religious words be given new meanings in the way that science gives new meanings to many everyday words? One way in which science gives words a different meaning is through definition. Examples of this are 'work', 'energy', 'force', etc. The purpose of this is to make the meanings more precise. An alternative would be to coin completely new words, which science also does: 'moment of momentum', 'hysteresis', 'quark', 'photon', etc. Now there are technical words used in religious language, but it is not these that cause a problem. It is not, for example, being suggested that there are new, more precise definitions of words such as 'spirit' and 'person'.

Swinburne (1934–) suggests a different way in which science changes the meanings of words and that is through their use in models. In the kinetic theory of gases, the molecules of the gas are treated as if they were billiard balls. Yet when we treat gas molecules as billiard balls, we are not assuming that they are like billiard balls in every respect. Another example Swinburne gives is the description of light as both a wave and a stream of particles. Here 'wave' and 'particle' cannot have their normal meanings, since when we describe something as a wave we exclude the possibility of its being a stream of particles and when we describe something as a stream of particles we exclude the possibility of its being a wave. Swinburne wants to make the point that, for example, when we say God is a person, we are assuming a model. We are no more saying that God is like other persons in every respect than a physicist is saying that a molecule of gas is like a billiard ball in every respect.

While there is something to be said for this suggestion, there are also significant differences between scientific language and religious language. The status of models in science is somewhat controversial: some commentators argue that they are of no fundamental importance, that what is important is the mathematical formulation of a theory, whether this is quantum theory or the kinetic theory of gases. Others argue that models play a more significant role. None the less, it is clear that the model of an atom as a billiard ball and the models of light as a stream of particles or as a wave form only part of the scientific accounts of these phenomena. Further, we are able to understand the extent to which these unperceivable entities are like 'billiard balls', 'particles' or 'waves' precisely because of the mathematical formulation in which the analogies are spelt out.

It has been suggested that quantum mechanics is the most successful scientific theory ever, but it has achieved this success in spite of the difficulty of conceiving fundamental particles as exhibiting properties of both waves and particles. Quantum mechanics is more than a theory that makes the claims that the world at the subatomic level is one we cannot properly conceive, in which particles behave like waves. By itself, such a claim would give us neither an understanding of the subatomic nor, and this is more important, any reason to believe that there was any such thing as subatomic particles. It is the mathematical formulation of quantum mechanics and the testable predictions that are derived from it which underpin the special use of words such as 'wave' and 'particle'. It has yet to be shown that any special use of religious words has a similar underpinning. Hence, we shall assume that the words used to analyse the concept of God have their normal meaning.

Attempts to prove God's existence

The ontological argument

The ontological argument was first formulated by St Anselm. Its basic idea is that the nature of God is such that he must exist. Sometimes a description picks out something that exists, examples being 'the present queen of England', 'the 1998 winner of the World Cup', 'the capital of Moldova'. Sometimes descriptions fail to pick out anything that exists, examples being 'the present king of France', 'the 1066 winner of the World Cup', 'the capital of Eriador'. In general, a description that has a reference has it contingently: there is a possible world in which there is no queen of England but in which there is a king of France. In the ontological proof it is claimed not only that 'God' does have a reference but also that this is not a contingent matter; the concept of God is such that it must be instantiated.

Anselm claims that our concept of God, as an all-powerful, all-knowing being, is a concept of something such that we could conceive nothing greater. If it seems a contingent matter as to whether or not this description succeeds in referring to anything, suppose that God does not exist. This would mean that God is an all-powerful, all-knowing, etc., *non-existent* being. Can we not conceive of something greater than this? Yes we can, we can conceive of an all-powerful, all-knowing, etc., *existent* being. Something that exists in reality, Anselm argued, must be greater than something that exists just in our imagination. Hence, since God is that than which nothing greater can exist, it must be that God exists.

As we have seen (chapter 2), a slightly different version of the ontological argument is found in Descartes' meditation V. Here the concept of God is expressed in terms of perfection rather than greatness: God is a being which possesses all perfections and so, since existence is a perfection, it must be one that God possesses and so, again, God must exist.

Kant's criticism of the ontological argument

Kant's criticism of the ontological argument applies to either version, since both versions treat existence as a property. In St Anselm's version it is a property, the possession of which makes its possessor greater. In Descartes' version possession of the property makes the possessor more perfect. Kant's point is that existence is not a property at all. If we think of God as an all-powerful being, then all-powerfulness is part of the concept of God. If we also think of God as all-knowing, all-knowingness is a second property to add to all-powerfulness. However, if we further think that God exists, we are not adding a third property, that of existence. What we are doing is saying that there is an instance of the concept; there is someone who is all-powerful and all-knowing. A person who believes in God, that is, believes God exists, does not have one concept of God (that is, one that contains the idea of existence) and the atheist a different concept of God (that is, one that does not contain the idea of existence). The believer and the atheist share the same concept but disagree as to whether the concept is instantiated.

Necessary existence

An objection that can be made against Kant's criticism is that the ontological argument is not attributing existence to God but necessary existence. There are all sorts of things whose existence is, or has been, disputed, such as fairies, the Loch Ness monster, flying saucers, aliens and so on. Whether or not any of these things do exist is a contingent matter. Perhaps aliens from another planet do exist but, if so, they do so only contingently, and we find out whether they do by examining the empirical evidence. What is being claimed in the case of God is not simply existence but necessary existence. God, it is claimed, is a necessary being and God's existence is discovered not empirically but through reason.

What we are being asked to believe is that there are two types of existence. There is contingent existence, which is the sort that people, mountains, clouds, stars and electrons have, and necessary existence, which is the sort that God has. However, some philosophers have argued that it is not legitimate to use the terms 'necessary' and 'contingent' in this way; at best, it leads to confusion. If the terms have a use, it is applied to propositions, where they give the *modality* of the proposition. A proposition, as we know, can be either true or false. The modality of the proposition gives the *way* in which the proposition is true or false. A proposition that is true may be true contingently, such as 'grass is green', or true necessarily, such as 'a bachelor is unmarried'. Some philosophers, such as Quine, object even to this notion of modality. Others accept that it is legitimate to say 'necessarily God exists' or 'God exists' is necessarily true, but it is not legitimate to say that God has necessary existence. There are different ways in which propositions can be true (or false) but not different types of existence to be had.

It is important to note that, by giving the modality of a proposition, we are saying nothing about its truth-value. The modal values, that is, necessary and contingent, are independent of the truth-values, that is, true and false. To say that God exists is a necessary proposition, is to ascribe a modality. Even supposing that this ascribes the correct modality, this still leaves open two possibilities: that the proposition is necessarily false and that the proposition is necessarily true.

Let us consider how a proposition such as 'N exists' can be necessarily true. First, let us remove complications arising from the fact that 'exists' is a present-tense form of the verb 'to exist'. 'Margaret Thatcher exists but Julius Caesar does not exist' is true now, but the converse was true around two thousand years ago. However, I can also use 'exists' in a timeless way to say that Julius Caesar exists but the Greek god Zeus does not. In this atemporal sense of 'exist', what would it mean to claim that 'Julius Caesar exists' is necessarily true?

One way of capturing the idea of necessity is through the device of possible worlds. A proposition that is contingently true is one that is true on this world but not true on some other, possible world. A proposition that is necessarily true is one that is true on all possible worlds. The claim that 'Julius Caesar exists' is necessarily true entails that Julius Caesar exists on all possible worlds. He might do different things on different possible worlds. On some he crosses the Rubicon, on others he does not. On some he is stabbed by Brutus, on others he is not.

We can now see that the proposition 'Julius Caesar exists' cannot be necessarily true. There are possible worlds in which Caesar's parents never meet or meet but do not have children. There are possible worlds where the population of Italy is wiped out in 80 BC by an asteroid or where human beings never evolve or where life never gets started on earth. In all these (and many more) possible worlds, 'Julius Caesar exists' is false.

I have argued that, when we ask whether God exists, we want to know whether our concept of God is instantiated. Is our concept of God such that it will be instantiated in all possible worlds, including, of course, the actual world? Let us begin by assuming that concept of God is simply that which exists. Then 'God exists' means 'that which exists, exists'. This is a necessary truth; it is analytic. What ensures necessity rather than contingency is the form of the proposition. However, although the proposition 'God exists' is necessarily true, this does not mean that the concept of God, i.e., that which exists, is instantiated, since there might be nothing that exists.

If the concept of God is no more than the concept of that which exists, then the concept is instantiated in all possible worlds where something exists. If there is no possible world in which nothing exists (say, because a world in which nothing exists is not a world at all) then this concept is instantiated in all possible worlds. This, however, falls a long way short of saying that our traditional concept of God is instantiated in all possible worlds. We cannot simply invent a concept that includes the stipulation of existence and, in doing so, ensure that the concept is instantiated. Let us see further why not. Suppose I say that 'n-unicorn' (short for 'necessary unicorn') means 'a horse-like animal that has a horn on its head and exists'. Then 'an n-unicorn exists' is necessarily true, since all this means is that the proposition 'a horse-like animal that has a horn on its head and exists, exists'. What it does not mean, however, is that a horse-like animal that has a horn on its head exists! The necessary truth of positive existential propositions about n-unicorns does not prove that unicorns exist, since there may be nothing that instantiates the concept of an n-unicorn.

Even if, by definition, 'God exists' is true in all possible worlds, this does not mean that the concept of God is instantiated, either here or in any other possible world. There is a difference between the proposition 'Julius Caesar exists' and propositions such as 'black is black' or 'the number 17 exists'. Changing what happens in the world changes whether or not it is true that Julius Caesar exists, whereas no changes will make it the case that black is not black or that the number 17 does not exist – even in a world in which there are no more than 16 things and none of them is black, the propositions are still true. Even if we suppose that 'God exists' is true in our world, we can see what changes might be made to produce a possible world in which there is no omnipotent being, no omniscient being and so on. If the concept of God is incoherent and contains a contradiction, then 'God exists' cannot even be true in our world. Indeed, it would be the case that, necessarily, God does not exist. Although an exhaustive consideration of the question as to the coherence of the concept of God will not be attempted here, we will return to the issue when we consider the claim that God is a person.

The cosmological argument

In the cosmological argument, we start not from our concept of God but from the nature of the world around us. Aquinas (1224–1274) suggested several ways in which we could infer the existence of God. The existence of things in the world is contingent, but why should contingent things exist? The existence of contingent things becomes intelligible only if their existence is seen to derive from something that exists necessarily.

God as first cause

The existence of any particular object can be explained by giving the cause of its existence. We can generalize this: the sum total of what exists at a particular time (that is, the state of the universe now) results from the sum total of what existed at an earlier time (that is, the state of the universe previously). Thus there is a temporal series of states of the universe, each (with possibly one exception) preceded by a state, which is its cause. Either this series is infinite or there was a first cause. If, for the moment, we assume that the idea of a series of causes stretching back in time for eternity is incoherent, then there must have been a first cause. According to the cosmological argument, this first cause cannot have a contingent existence but must have a necessary existence. Hence God, the first cause, the creator of heaven and earth, exists.

Is the notion of an infinite set of causes stretching back in time incoherent? At one stage, a strong rival to the big bang theory (which holds that the universe came into being a finite number of years ago) was the so-called steady state theory. This theory claimed that the universe had existed for ever and accounted for the observed expansion of the universe by postulating the continuous creation of matter. The consensus appears to be in favour of the big bang theory, but this is on the basis of experimental evidence, not because of any incoherence in the notion of the universe having existed for ever.

Even if the possibility of a universe without a beginning cannot be eliminated on the grounds that it is an incoherent idea, it does now seem to be eliminated on empirical grounds. Some see the evidence in support of the big bang theory as evidence for God's existence: if there was a big bang in which the universe was created then there must have been a cause of the big bang, that is, God. If God is the first of a temporal succession of causes, then God was not preceded by anything. If we can allow the possibility that God came into existence uncaused, then we can allow the possibility that the universe came into existence uncaused. One answer is to say that God did not come into existence uncaused, since God, uniquely, is the cause of himself. Yet the idea that something can be the cause of itself seems, if anything, less intelligible than there being no cause. The idea that God is his own cause has been put forward to explain how God necessarily exists, but we cannot explain anything by appealing to a concept that is itself inexplicable and, perhaps, incoherent. That something can be the cause of itself goes against our understanding of cause and effect, which is a relationship holding between two different events.

It has been suggested that, when Aquinas talked of a first cause, he was not referring to a temporal succession of causes but to a hierarchy of causes. Consider an explanation for my own existence. There is a chain of events leading back into the past, which would include my parents meeting each other, their parents meeting and so on, each of which was the effect of the previous one. This chain provides one sort of explanation. However, there is also a set of conditions that is in place now: I have food, drinking water, shelter and so on. In other words, there is a complex social structure, the existence of which also provides an explanation for my existence. The existence of the social structure, like my own existence, is a contingent matter. It might be thought that the (contingent) existence of a complex social structure stands as much in need of an explanation as my existence. The existence of the complex social structure can be explained in terms of the existence of the species of human beings within the set of species that makes up life on earth. This in turn can be explained in terms of the existence of the biosphere. The existence of the biosphere can be explained in terms of the existence of the solar system. Thus we get the idea of a set of explanations spreading out from the fact to be explained, the fact of my existence. Each level supports the previous one and is, in turn, dependent on the next one. The existence of each level is, however, a contingent matter.

The point made in the cosmological argument is that, no matter which of these levels of contingent explanations we reach, we have not reached the ultimate explanation. Even when we reach the level of the fundamental laws of physics, which govern the working of the whole universe, we are still dealing only with contingencies. The ultimate end is God, who exists not contingently but necessarily.

The key assumption of both the above versions of the cosmological argument is that there must be an explanation for the existence of things. They assume, in other words, that the universe is intelligible. Further, it is assumed that explaining one contingent thing in terms of another contingent thing falls short of an adequate explanation: only God can provide an adequate explanation. However, in order to go from the premise 'If there is an adequate explanation it is provided by God' to the conclusion 'There is a God', a further premise is needed, namely 'There is an adequate explanation'. What the cosmological argument fails to do is to give any justification for this additional premise. The existence of anything may simply be a brute fact; the existence of one thing rather than another thing may also, in the end, be a brute fact for which there is no further explanation.

The teleological argument

The final argument for God's existence to be considered is the teleological argument, often called the argument from design. Historically, the teleological argument has arisen out of a sense of awe and wonder at the natural world, perhaps because of some feature of it that exhibits complexity or adaptation to circumstances or that carries out a certain function (preferably one we consider to be important). Whatever induces this sense of wonder seems to present itself as something that could not have been brought into existence by the impersonal forces of nature. In other words, it is something for which there appears to be no plausible explanation other than that it has been designed, for the function it serves, by some intelligent being.

There are several versions of this argument; one of the more famous is that given by William Paley in 1802. He supposes that, when walking across a heath, he stumbles on a stone. The presence of the stone calls for no special explanation, yet the same would not be true if he had come across a watch. The nature of a watch, Paley argues, is such that it must have had a maker, 'an artificer or artificers, who formed it for the purpose which we find it actually to answer, who comprehended its construction, and designed its use' (quoted in Dawkins, *The Blind Watchmaker*, 4). In the same way, Paley continues, living organisms and parts of living organisms have both a complexity of construction and a purpose, leading us to the conclusion that they also had a designer. Paley wrote this before Darwin's *The Origin of Species*. Dawkins, who uses the passage as the source of the title of his book *The Blind Watchmaker*, argues that Darwin has shown how evolution can produce the living things we see about us without any need for a designer.

The process of evolution is, in principle, a straightforward one. Living creatures reproduce and pass on some of their characteristics to their offspring. Reproduction, however, is a competitive business and not all creatures manage it. The characteristics that are passed down from one generation to the next come from those organisms that are successful in the competition to reproduce. Thus, inheritable characteristics that, either directly or indirectly, assist an organism in its competitive environment are more likely to be passed on than are characteristics that are neutral or harmful.

Since offspring are not exactly like their parents, new characteristics can arise. If a new inheritable characteristic provides the organism with a competitive advantage, then, in time, it will spread throughout the species. This is because those organisms that possess the characteristic are more likely to reproduce than those organisms that do not possess the characteristic – this is what is meant by saying that the characteristic provides the organism with a competitive advantage. Hence, there will be a higher proportion of organisms with the characteristic in the next generation. In very broad terms: what has worked is passed on, what did not work disappears.

Evolution provides the mechanism by which species can become better adapted to their environment, the so-called survival of the fittest. It also provides the mechanism by which organs, such as the eye, the liver, the thumb, the brain, etc., which bestow a competitive advantage, can develop. This mechanism does not depend on a designer, nor is it a process of converging on a particular end point. Dennett, using vivid imagery, suggests that the Darwinian theory of evolution shows how organisms can be built using 'cranes', without the need for 'skyhooks'. A crane is something that stands upon the ground and is built from the bottom up. A skyhook is some mysterious contrivance that descends from the heavens.

Clearly the account that evolution can give as to how human beings have evolved from other species has profound implications for how we view ourselves and how we see our place in the universe. The Copernican revolution removed the earth from the centre of the universe to its present position, orbiting a 'small unregarded yellow sun' far out 'in the uncharted backwaters of the unfashionable end of the Western Spiral arm of the Galaxy' (Adams, *Hitch Hiker's Guide to the Galaxy*, 6). The Darwinian revolution removed mankind from a position somewhere below God and the angels but somewhere above the animal kingdom to a position on all fours with the rest of the animals. However, our present concern is not how we view ourselves but how we should view the supposed need for a supernatural, intelligent designer.

Showing how organs, which appear to have been designed for a purpose, can result from the operation of 'blind' forces of nature undermines the argument from design. The truth of evolution is disputed by some religious fundamentalists, despite the considerable body of evidence in support of evolution, but this is not the place to review the evidence or adjudicate between evolution and creationism (although I, personally, have no doubts as to which theory provides the correct account). The important point is that evolution only has to provide a *possible* account of how life developed on earth in order to show that the argument from design fails to *prove* the existence of God. If the forces of natural selection can produce an eye, then there is no need for a designer of eyes. This does not show that God the designer does not exist, but it does show that the above version of the teleological argument fails to offer any support, even non-deductive support, for the existence of God.

Cosmic coincidences
The starting point for Paley's version of the argument from design is the set of organic forms that exhibit complexity, structure and function. It is undermined by suggesting a mechanism, to account for the existence of such forms, which does not need a design process. The starting point of the second version of the argument from design is the fundamental physical constants and the laws of physics that are necessary for the very possibility of life and the subsequent evolutionary

process. The argument now is not that certain objects within nature are designed but that the universe as a whole must have been designed, its purpose being to give rise to intelligent life.

To give a flavour of the basis of the argument, consider the following examples, starting with the dimensionality of space. Space, as we know, has three dimensions. It is a direct consequence of the three-dimensionality of space that the law governing the gravitational force between two masses is an inverse *square* law, since the dimensionality of the law of gravity is one less than the dimensionality of space. (An inverse square law states that, if the distance increases by a certain amount, the force will decrease in proportion to the square of that amount.) If there were more dimensions of space, gravity would conform to a different law. Only an inverse square law will result in stable planetary orbits. Hence it is only in three-dimensional space that there will be stable planetary systems like our own solar system. Further, the equations of electromagnetism (of which light is a form) have workable solutions only in a spacetime of four dimensions. Both of these were necessary to enable human life to develop on earth.

Further, in order for life to have evolved on earth, conditions had to have been right in the earlier stages of the universe for carbon and the heavier elements to form. This in turn depends on a number of the 'starting conditions' for the universe: the size of the 'strong' force which binds the nucleus of an atom together; the proportion of hydrogen converted into helium during the big bang, which is dependent on the 'weak' force; the gravitational constant; the so-called resonance energies of the atomic nuclei of helium, beryllium, carbon and oxygen, which allows carbon to be produced inside a star but prevents too much of it being converted into oxygen; and so on. Detailed investigations of these cosmic coincidences suggest that relatively small changes in fundamental physical constants would have meant that the universe would have been very different, with the result that human life, and probably any intelligent life, would not have evolved. The argument from design maintains that this fine-tuning of physical laws and constants is so improbable that there must have been a designer at work.

Two anthropic principles
One way of expressing the fact that the universe appears to be fine-tuned for the existence of human life is to say that there is an anthropic cosmological principle at work. The argument from design then says, in effect, that the existence of such an anthropic principle is evidence

for a designer. However, such claims have to be treated with caution. First, there are two different versions of the anthropic principle, a weak version and a strong version.

The weak anthropic principle (WAP) is simply an explicit acknowledgement of the fact that, in order for us to make any observations of the universe, the position in time and space from which we do so must be one at which intelligent life is possible. Thus the following statement describes the WAP: any observed physical laws or values of physical constants must be consistent with conditions that allow intelligent life. The weak anthropic principle does nothing more than draw attention to the background conditions under which our observation of the universe must be made, that is, the conditions for the universe to be able to observe itself. The observations we make must be in accordance with the weak anthropic principle, and so the fact that observations are in line with this principle does not support claims that the universe has been designed. It is simply not possible for intelligent beings to observe that the gravitational force follows an inverse cube law or that the resonance energies of certain elements are different from the values they are observed to have.

The strong anthropic principle, on the other hand, does support the claim that the universe has been designed: the physical laws or the values of physical constants are as they are in order to allow (or perhaps, to ensure) the development of intelligent life. The strong anthropic principle imposes restrictions on what the laws and constants must be, whereas the weak version imposes restrictions only on what laws and constants must be for them to be observable by us (or by similar life forms). The purpose of the weak anthropic principle is to explain why we observe the structure that we do. The purpose of the strong anthropic principle is to explain why the universe is as it is.

To find evidence in support of the strong anthropic principle, it is necessary to determine the probability of a universe being able to support life. Assuming the laws of physics and the values taken by physical constants are contingent, there are other possible universes based on different laws and different values for the physical constants. Given the precise requirements for producing the conditions necessary for life, the majority of these other possible worlds would not be capable of supporting intelligent life. The question is which is more plausible: that the universe was designed for intelligent life or that it arose by chance against the odds?

There is no easy way of assessing the strength of the two alternatives. It appears an impossible task to quantify the chances of the universe having the laws and constants that it does. This is partly because we have no way of knowing whether other universes, with different laws and constants, that are logically possible are also physically possible and, if they are, whether they are all equally likely. Even if we did arrive at a figure, we would still be left with the task of assessing the probability of there being a designer of the universe. No matter how low the probability of the existence of the present universe, if the existence of a designer and creator is impossible, then the more likely of the two is the chance existence of the present universe.

Even supposing a version of the argument from design were to prove the existence of a designer and creator, this is a long way from proving the existence of God, with all the properties ascribed to him. For example, the idea that this creator is also a person finds no basis in the supposed proof of the existence of such a creator.

The problem of evil

The problem of evil arises because a world that contains misery and suffering seems at odds with its having a creator who is omnipotent, omniscient and perfectly good. We can demonstrate this inconsistency in a more formal way. What we have are four propositions: 1) The world contains unnecessary misery and suffering; 2) God is omnipotent; 3) God is omniscient; and 4) God is perfectly good. We now take the proposition that makes a claim about the state of the world (that is, proposition 1) together with two of the propositions about God's nature in order to arrive at a conclusion that is the negation of the third proposition about God's nature. First we allow that God is omnipotent and omniscient and that he exercised these powers knowingly to create the world in its entirety. This, we show, is inconsistent with God being good.

Premise 1	The world contains unnecessary misery and suffering.
Premise 2	If God knowingly created the world in its entirety, then God knowingly created all misery and suffering.
Premise 3	God created the world in its entirety.
Conclusion 1	God created unnecessary misery and suffering.
Premise 4	A being who is good does not create unnecessary misery and suffering.
Conclusion 2	God is not good.

The above demonstration, of an inconsistency between the first premise and God being perfectly good, depends on other premises being true. The truth of premise 2 depends on what it means to create something in its entirety (and would remain true even if there were no misery and suffering in the world). The truth of premise 4 is less clear-cut, but it does seem difficult to see how a good being could create *unnecessary* misery and suffering.

A different approach is to assume that God is good and show an inconsistency between God's omnipotence or his omniscience and the presence of unnecessary misery and suffering. The demonstration proceeds as follows:

Premise 1   The world contains unnecessary misery and suffering.
Premise 4   A being who is good does not create unnecessary misery and suffering.
Premise 5   God is good.
Conclusion 3   God did not create unnecessary misery and suffering.
Conclusion 4   God did not create the world in its entirety.
Premise 6   If God did not create the world in its entirety, then either God lacked the power to do so or God chose not to do so.

If we take the first alternative, we get:

Premise 7   God lacked the power to create the world in its entirety.
Conclusion 5   God cannot be all-powerful.

On the other hand, if we take the second alternative, we get:

Premise 8   God chose not to create the world in its entirety.
Conclusion 6   God chose to allow unnecessary misery and suffering.
Premise 9   A being who is good does not intentionally choose to allow unnecessary misery and suffering.
Conclusion 7   God did not intentionally choose to allow unnecessary misery and suffering.
Conclusion 8   God did not know that unnecessary misery and suffering would result.
Conclusion 9   God is not all-knowing.

As with the first argument, these demonstrations of inconsistency depend on the truth of the supporting premises. However, although there is scope for further work here, there are more obvious responses to the problem of evil. One is, of course, to rethink the nature of God and accept that he is, in some ways, limited. This route takes us into theology and is not one that will be followed here. The second, and perhaps the more obvious, is to deny that the world does contain unnecessary misery and suffering. Since it is difficult to claim plausibly that there is no misery and suffering, the defence against the problem of evil will try to show that the suffering is not unnecessary, because the misery and suffering is unavoidable or because it serves a purpose.

The best of all possible worlds

To reconcile the existence of evil, such as misery and suffering, with a God who is omnipotent, omniscient and perfectly good, we start with the claim that the world in which we live is the best of all possible worlds and that, therefore, the elimination of evil would require an impossible world. God's inability to create an impossible world does not show that God is less than omnipotent, since being omnipotent does not entail being able to do the impossible. Thus to neuter the threat of the problem of evil it is not necessary to show that evil does not exist, only that the evil that does exist is unavoidable and that any attempt to reduce evil will inevitably result in something worse.

The claim that this is the best of all possible worlds was one made by Leibniz (1646–1716), and for this Voltaire (1694–1778) mocked him mercilessly in his satirical novel *Candide*. However, if we start from the assumption that there is a God, then the conclusion that this is the best of all possible worlds is a rational one. What would then remain is the task of trying to understand the reason for the evil that exists, a task construed by Leibniz as that of explaining God's purposes. The problem is that, since the existence of evil is cited as a reason for believing that God does not exist, we cannot counter this simply by assuming that God exists. What is needed is to show that this world is the best of all worlds without assuming that God exists. This is a pretty daunting task.

Pain

Let us focus on pain, or what is commonly, and mistakenly, referred to as physical pain – mistakenly because, of course, either pain is a mental phenomenon or all phenomena are physical. What is meant is pain where there is, apparently, an obvious physical cause, such as injury to the body or an infection. We can begin by asking two questions: why is there pain at all and why is there so much pain? Pain fulfils a biological function; people who do not feel pain do not have early warnings of disease and have to take great care not to damage themselves inadvertently. Thus we can explain the existence of pain in terms of the evolutionary advantage it confers. The existence of pain is clearly not a problem for evolution since no one is trying to claim that nature is benevolent. However, if we are created by a benevolent being, one might suppose that a better mechanism could have been found to do the same biological job as pain.

Now turn to the second question concerning the quantity of pain. Schopenhauer (1788–1860) wrote: 'If the immediate and direct purpose of our life is not suffering then our existence is the most ill-adapted to its purpose in the world ... misfortune in general is the rule' (*Essays and Aphorisms*, trans. R. J. Hollingdale, Penguin Books, Harmondsworth, 1970). Leaving human beings out of the equation for a moment, there are good reasons for thinking that there is an unnecessary amount of pain in the animal kingdom. Should the existence of this amount of pain be of concern to a benevolent being? To say that it should is not to take a sentimental or anthropomorphic view of animals. It is in the nature of benevolence to wish to eliminate pain wherever it occurs. Bentham considered that the capacity animals have to suffer provides us with sufficient reason to consider their interests. Why should God's concern to prevent suffering be limited to just one species? The amount of suffering in the animal kingdom seems gratuitous; it is difficult to see what purpose could be served by it. Turning to humans, we have, through our own efforts, discovered ways of reducing pain, but modern pain killers and anaesthetics cannot prevent the pain of those born in earlier times or in poorer parts of the world. One conclusion to draw is that the excessive amount of pain does not serve a purpose and that the condition of mankind and other animals was not created by a benevolent God but arose through the operation of chance and evolutionary pressure.

The value of free will

Some of the pain in the world arises through the free choice of human beings, assuming, that is, that we have free choice. Sometimes this pain is inflicted as means to ends that are good; sometimes the ends are bad. In short, some of the pain in this world is the result of the evil actions of human beings, and this pain is surely avoidable – why does a benevolent God allow us to behave in this way? Presumably, if there is an answer it is that it is more important we have free will than that the evil, which results from free will, does not exist. Why might it be important that we have free will?

One of the reasons *we* value free will is because free will gives us the power to pursue our own interests. We each assume that it is to our advantage to look after our own interests rather than to entrust them to someone else. However, when the someone else is God, this assumption may be false. God, one way or the other, should be able to ensure a perfect match between what we want and what we get. Suppose the alternatives were, on the one hand, having free will but not always being able to get what is in our best interests, and, on the other hand, not being free but none the less always getting what was in our best interests. The latter alternative is in our best interests and it is this alternative that we should expect from a benevolent God.

The inscrutability of God

At some point in the discussion, the following objection is likely to surface: God, because he is infinite, is beyond our comprehension, and we cannot judge, from our perspective, what will appear right from the perspective of an infinite being. The problem with accepting such a claim is that it means that any rational debate about God is impossible. The arguments for the existence of God relied upon such things as the intelligibility of the universe and of us being able to have a conception of God. If the ways of God are held to be essentially mysterious, then the only resort is faith, which for the rational person can be no resort at all. It also goes against the idea of one of the fundamental properties of God, that God is a person. If this claim is accepted, then God cannot be totally inscrutable. God's purposes must, at least in part, be comprehensible to us.

Free will and responsibility

In our discussion of free will in connection with determinism (chapter 5) we pointed to the link between free will and responsibility: we are responsible for those acts that we perform freely. In other words, free will is a condition for being a moral agent. Therefore, if God is to create moral agents, he must create free will and, hence, must give us the possibility of choosing evil rather than good. However, we also noted that our free choices stem from our character. In order for a person's choice to be a free one, it must be that he or she could have chosen otherwise; a person whose character was different would have chosen otherwise. It does not make sense to say that one could have chosen otherwise no matter what the prior circumstances (which include a person's character). One cannot be responsible for purely chance events.

From our perspective the sense we make of the claim that a person could have chosen otherwise is that a different person in a similar situation would have chosen otherwise. This is the basis for distinguishing actions for which responsibility is assigned and actions for which it is not. However, the situation from God's perspective is completely different. In creating someone with a particular character, who will encounter particular situations, God is making the choice whether evil will result, since the person's character will determine the choices made in those situations. If evil does result, the responsibility is God's. If a free action that produces evil is one performed by a person who could have chosen otherwise, then it was in God's power to have created the person who did choose otherwise. That God did not do this implies that God is not perfectly benevolent.

The problem of evil does, therefore, pose genuine difficulties for the claim that God, an omnipotent, omniscient and perfectly benevolent being, exists. The need to find some purpose that will justify the presence of evil remains. Were there to be life after death, for example, the position would be altered, but, in the same way that we cannot counter the problem of evil by arguing from the assumption that God exists, so we cannot counter it by arguing from an assumption that there is life after death. Such claims need to be independently established before they can be used in this context.

God as a person

The problem of evil exploits a conflict between some of the qualities attributed to God and the existence of evil. When considering the attempts to prove God's existence, we assumed that at least the concept of God does not contain a contradiction. If the concept of God does contain such a contradiction, then it follows that there is no God.

Whether or not it is possible to produce a rigorous demonstration that the concept is coherent, it is certainly possible to identify potential sources of tension within the concept.

What is a person?

Locke defines a person as a 'thinking intelligent being that has reason and reflection and can consider itself as itself, the same thinking thing in different times and places' (*An Essay Concerning Human Understanding*, II, xxvii, 9). This idea of self-consciousness or the awareness of oneself as a continuing subject of experience has become generally accepted as central to the concept of a person. This makes being a person dependent only on being a certain sort of thing. Personhood is thus attributed to self-conscious beings without regard to the nature of any relationships the being has with other things within the universe, including other persons. There is nothing in Locke's definition, or in definitions based on it, that suggests it is possible for two such persons to enter into any form of relationship, let alone one that was mutually rewarding and fulfilling. This, it seems to me, is a serious defect, since what we value in other persons is not (or, at least, not simply) that they are continuing subjects of experience but that we are able to relate to them. As an alternative, I want to explore the idea that personhood is attributed through being able to enter into relationships with others. The claim that God is a person is surely a way of trying to say that it is possible for us to have a certain sort of relationship with God and not that God has self-awareness.

Interpersonal relationships
With this in mind, let us consider what will promote and what will hinder the development of personal relationships. In practice, interpersonal relationships cover a broad range, and we can think of relationships that are unsatisfactory or impoverished in various different ways. Thus we could devise minimal requirements for an interpersonal relationship. Yet surely the properties we ascribe to God cannot be such as to rule out all but the most unsatisfactory sort of interpersonal relationship. On the contrary, God's properties must be consistent with those needed for entering into the fullest, most satisfying of interpersonal relationships.

One requirement of a satisfying personal relationship is intimacy. For many people, among their most intimate relationships are the ones they have with their lovers, that is, relationships of a physical, sexual nature. Our concept of God precludes the possibility that a relationship with God can be of this sort. None the less, claims that physical relationships are poor substitutes for spiritual relationships should be treated with scepticism in the absence of supporting arguments. As well as sexual relationships, there are also intimate, non-sexual relationships, for example, between friends and between parent and child. Is intimacy with God possible?

Embodiment

One of the most important features of a relationship between lovers is that each is embodied. Being embodied locates one in space, it provides a particular point from which the world is viewed and it means that one acts on the world in a particular sort of way, through one's body. These features underpin the possibility of personal relationships. God, on the other hand, is immaterial and omnipresent and so lacks a personal view of the world. God is omniscient and so lacks a particular perspective on what is known; God cannot have knowledge that is personal. God is omnipotent and so can act on any part of the world directly; God has no personal sphere of action. God is not merely disembodied; his disembodiment is *radical*.

Swinburne argues that one can be disembodied and yet still be a person. He invites the reader to imagine gradually becoming less and less affected by things that normally affect our mental state, such as drugs, and ceasing to feel bodily sensations. Imagine also becoming aware of events going on elsewhere, being able to adopt different viewpoints at will and bringing about other changes in the world at will. While acquiring these powers, Swinburne supposes that you remain able to reason and to want, hope and fear. Surely, he concludes, 'anyone can thus conceive of himself becoming an omnipresent spirit' (*The Coherence of Theism*, 105).

Swinburne assumes that being able to imagine something shows it is possible. This may not be the case. While imagining something might lead to the belief it is possible, this does not show it is possible. However, let us set aside this point and, rather than trying to imagine what one's experiences would be like, consider, instead, the effect that becoming omnipresent would have on interpersonal relationships. What if, for example, your lover developed such a tendency? It is difficult to see how the relationship could do anything other than deteriorate. He or she would become less involved in the relationship, more remote, less able to share your concerns. The new powers, such as the ability to move things at will and to read your thoughts, would appear frightening. At the very least, *you* would want to put up barriers. Thus, even if an omnipresent being is able to enter into a personal relationship, becoming omnipresent must tend to diminish rather than enhance the quality of the relationship. But would an omnipresent being really be able to enter into a personal relationship? To answer this, we need to consider more closely what is involved in what I have called the phenomenology of embodiment in order to see what is lost with radical disembodiment.

Descartes, we have seen, concluded that, in essence, he is a mind. He assumes that it is possible for a person to be disembodied even if, as a matter of fact, he finds himself embodied. Being joined to a body is only a contingent fact. However, the disembodied mind that Descartes imagines himself to be is no different, at least in terms of the types of *experiences* it has, from an embodied mind. Phenomenologically, Descartes' mind disembodied and Descartes' mind embodied are the same. Is this a plausible claim?

The phenomenology of embodiment

A list of what would have to be taken away in order to remove the phenomenology of embodiment is much longer than the one implied by Swinburne. It would include the input from the senses – sights, sounds, smells, tastes, feels – and also bodily sensations such as pains, tickles and aches, and kinaesthetic sensations such as moving one's arm or twitching one's nose. Perhaps we also need to take away emotions. Feelings of anger typically have bodily sensations, such as a tension in the face, neck and shoulders, a pressure in the chest, etc. A feeling of shame is often accompanied by sensations of flushing and of hunching one's shoulders to make oneself smaller. Pride is accompanied by feeling oneself expand; happiness by the sensations of laughing or grinning. Fear is accompanied by prickling feelings at the back of the neck, an inability to breathe, the feeling of blood draining from one's face; and so on.

Without these bodily sensations, even if we had emotions they would certainly have a different phenomenological quality. The God of the Old Testament was a God capable of anger, but philosophers have tended to see God as being without emotions, perhaps because emotions, or passions, were seen as examples of a person being taken over, being passive rather than active. A passive role is not deemed suitable for God.

As noted above, we would also have to take away a viewpoint on the world. It is our perceptions that locate us in the world. There are many recorded instances of people having out-of-body experiences; typically they describe themselves looking down and seeing their own body (say, on an operating table), hearing voices talking about them, and so on. However, although these out-of-body experiences are experiences as if from a point outside of the body, they still contain many of the aspects of embodied experience, for example, perceptions from a certain location in space. In other words, it is as if the person does have a spatial location even if the spatial location is at some place other than the location of their body.

Embodiment carries with it the distinction between me and not-me, a distinction that has no meaning for an omnipresent being. As a result, an embodied being has an interest in what happens in the way that a disembodied, omnipresent being cannot. Much of what makes relationships between persons *personal* are shared and conflicting interests. Persons are not disinterested observers of the world, even if, at certain times and for certain purposes, they try to be. An inter-personal relationship that lacked a concern for shared and conflicting interests would be impoverished as a result.

Persons are not only observers of the world, they also perform actions. What is the difference between, on the one hand, acting to bring it about that X happens and, on the other hand, intending X to happen and it happening? Actions are intentional, but the fact that what happens is what I intended to happen does not seem enough. Acting certainly involves moving things that are part of me, rather than part of not-me, but this is not enough either, since there is a difference between the action of moving my arm and the event of it moving. Imagine staring at a vase of flowers on the table, formulating the wish for it to slide sideways (one might describe this as willing it to move sideways) and it moving. Again, there is a difference between my moving it and it moving. The phenomenology of acting seems to involve being connected to one bit of the world in one way and to the rest of the world in a different way. Without the phenomenology, there are no actions, only events, even though these events may be intended or willed.

Actions of persons are also, by and large, intelligible. They serve a purpose, since there are links between a person's interests and the actions that the person performs. When actions do not appear to further a person's interests, there is room for wondering whether something went wrong with the action, or even whether an action was intended. The more powerful a person, the less reason to suppose some failure of execution and the more obvious should be the connection between the person's interests and the person's actions. Yet God is supposed to be responsible for everything that happens. How can one see any connection with interests? These supposed 'actions', being unintelligible and unconnected with any set of interests, cannot be seen as actions at all. This failure to be able to discern interests behind the 'actions' of an omnipresent being is a further bar to having a personal relationship with such a being.

The different attempts to prove God's existence focus on different aspects of our concept of God: perfection, necessary existence, self-caused, creator, and so on. Even if a proof were successful, it would not provide a comprehensive list of properties to be included in the concept of God. Showing that one aspect of the concept of God is instantiated does not show that the other aspects are also instantiated. Proving the existence of an omnipotent, omniscient, omnipresent, perfectly benevolent being (even assuming this were possible) would not be enough for most people who believe in and worship God. The need of many believers is for a personal God to whom they, as individuals, can relate and not for some distant, awesome figure. That a need exists does not, of course, entail the existence of what will satisfy that need, and just because people need a personal God neither means that such a God exists nor that this property is consistent with the other properties attributed to God. The foregoing discussions suggest it might not be. How individuals respond to this (whether they are believers or not) is a matter for each to decide for him or herself.

Summary

■ When we ask whether God exists, we are asking whether the concept of an immaterial, omnipotent, omniscient, omnipresent, perfectly benevolent personal being who created the universe and all that exists in it is instantiated.
■ The ontological argument concludes that a being such that no greater being can be conceived must exist. Kant criticized it for treating existence as a predicate. According to this criticism, saying that God exists does not add anything to God's qualities; neither can existence be treated as a perfection.

- The cosmological and teleological arguments for God's existence take the existence of the universe or the nature of the universe as calling for some further explanation, either in terms of a first cause or in terms of a goal. However, I have found no compelling reasons for thinking that either of these roles needs to be filled, or for thinking that, if they are filled, they are filled by a being that has all the other attributes of God.
- That the world contains suffering which appears to be unnecessary is undeniable. Yet it is difficult to reconcile this suffering with the existence of a benevolent and omnipotent, omniscient being other than by taking refuge in the notion of the inscrutability of God's purpose.
- The qualities attributed to God, in particular those of omnipresence and of being immaterial, seem inconsistent with the notion of God as a person. We can make sense of the notion of a disembodied person but not that of a person that lacks the phenomenology of embodiment.
- The qualities of omnipotence, omniscience and perfect benevolence attributed to God also seem to be incompatible with human free will – it is difficult to see how God could allow us to do wrong; the value of free will does not seem sufficient to compensate.

Questions raised

- Although (it is generally agreed) existence is not a predicate, can it be claimed that necessary existence is? Is attributing necessary existence to something bestowing on it an important property?
- Are the cosmic coincidences that make life possible just too improbable to be explained by the weak anthropic principle? Are we forced to accept some version of the strong anthropic principle that holds that the universe must have been designed for living things?
- Can we conceive of persons that do not have the phenomenology of embodiment? Or, if not, can we conceive of persons that lack many of our experiences that result (or appear to result) from being embodied?
- Is it possible to give reasons as to why free will might be a quality that a creator would value in his/her creations? Would we need free will in an ideal world?

8 Morality

Introduction

In this and the next chapter, we turn to look at the third of the three main areas into which we have divided philosophy. Although the discussions will still be abstract, the issues are of much more immediate concern, and the reasoning, because it is aimed at action, is practical reasoning. It is convenient to distinguish between actions at a personal level and actions at the public level, although, as with most distinctions in philosophy, it is not a hard and fast one. Personal actions may have public consequences, and it is individuals who carry out public actions. Actions in the private sphere fall within the scope of moral philosophy, the topic of this chapter. Actions in the public arena take us into political philosophy, the topic of the next chapter.

We are all able to recognize moral issues and can generally distinguish moral reasons from those that are not, but this does not mean that we are able to produce a clear criterion for distinguishing the moral from the non-moral. Some argue that the clear criterion does not exist because morality is subjective. There are various versions that this subjectivism can take.

Moral considerations are usually seen as opposed to self-interest and the egoist as someone who rejects morality. However, it can be argued that we always act out of self-interest and so immorally. Morality becomes pointless if it is impossible for us, as egoists, to act morally. Even if this subjective egoism can be countered, acting to promote self-interest can be presented as a moral principle. The question then becomes whether we can lay down tests that will allow us to reject this *ethical* egoism.

Though we are generally able to tell good from bad, it is not so easy, any more than it was for 'moral', to say exactly what is meant by 'good'. It is not even clear that we can attach an objective meaning to the word. Considering this will lead into a more general consideration as to whether we can say how things ought to be on the basis of the way things are – that is, whether we can derive values from facts.

The evaluations we make about both the morality of actions and the moral character of agents should be capable of being supported with reasons. This still leaves open the question as to the exact role of reason in morality and whether reason alone is sufficient to determine the answers to moral questions. Reasoning can tell us the means needed to achieve a certain end, but can it also determine what the end should be?

Some have argued that the ends are human happiness and that the morally right action is one that maximizes happiness. This moral theory, known as utilitarianism, results in prescriptions that are different from those arrived at by the Kantian theory based on duty and reason. Even where there is agreement as to what one ought to do, different reasons are given in support. The problem is in deciding which, if either, gives the right account. A third way of approaching morality focuses on what it is to be a good person rather than on which action is right. Virtue ethics aims to set out the character traits we should develop.

What is distinctive about moral considerations?

Most people are familiar with moral issues in a way that they are not familiar with the issues that have been discussed under the headings of metaphysics and epistemology. In general, people are able to give examples of moral issues and moral judgements, but it does not mean that they can say what is distinctive about a moral issue or what makes a judgement a moral judgement, or even why moral judgements are important.

The examples people give of contemporary moral issues are likely to include abortion, euthanasia, discrimination, punishment and so on. The debates on these issues take place at several levels. Take abortion: there is the discussion as to whether, and the circumstances under which, abortion should be legally available; there is the discussion as to the resources to be allocated to making abortion available in those cases; there is also, and perhaps most importantly, the discussions a woman has, perhaps with herself, perhaps with her partner, perhaps with other people with whom she can discuss these things, about whether or not to have an abortion. At each of these different levels there is interplay of moral and non-moral considerations.

For the moment, let us concentrate on the decisions affecting the individual. The following sorts of questions may go through the woman's mind: what are the consequences for me, and those closest to me, of having and of not having an abortion? Do I have the right to remove this clump of cells growing inside me? Does this unborn baby inside me have the right to live? Do I want the baby? What sort of life would the baby have? Will I be able to support it? What sacrifices will I have to make? Will I lose my job or miss out on promotion? Will it spoil my figure? Will I be able to cope with having a baby? Will I make a good mother? And so on.

The answers the woman gives to each question may suggest different courses of action. For example, she may fear that if she has the baby she will lose her job or miss the chance of promotion or fail to regain her figure or damage the relationship she has with her partner. These considerations provide her with reasons for having an abortion. On the other hand, she may feel that she is being selfish in worrying about the effect on herself, or she may feel that, although she will mind losing her figure or not being promoted, she wants to have the baby and would regret not having it. These considerations provide her with reasons for not having an abortion. She may feel that it would be unjust to the unborn baby to have an abortion, or she may feel she has the right to decide what she does with her body and that this overrules any right to life the baby may have.

Perhaps, if she were to think just of herself, she would do one thing, but if she were to take others into account, she would do something else, although this may depend on whom she takes into account. She may describe abortion to herself in one way, say as removing an unwanted clump of cells, and come to one conclusion; but then she may describe it to herself in another way, say as taking an innocent life, and come to a different conclusion. She may think that, if things turn out one way, then having an abortion would have been a good thing, but if they turn out a different way, then it would have been a bad thing; but she is not sure how things will turn out.

What can moral philosophy offer to people who are faced with making such difficult decisions? In the above situation, can it provide the woman with a clear recommendation? Can it tell her what she ought to do, while leaving her to decide whether or not to do it? Can it do no more than help her think clearly about the issues, analyse the concepts being used and separate out the different sorts of reasons? One indication that philosophy might have something relevant to say is that she is looking for reasons for doing one thing rather than another, reasons for actions. She is engaged in what Aristotle called practical reasoning. Practical reasoning may be used to arrive at decisions having no moral implications, but many philosophers think there is a strong link between practical reason and morality. Some have suggested that moral judgements, somewhat like mathematical truths, can be arrived at by reason alone.

Ethical subjectivism

Morality is about choosing the right action or about being a good person, yet different people have different ideas about what is right and what is good. One person will come to one conclusion; another person will come to a different conclusion. Each thinks he or she is right and the other wrong. Moral issues arise because people disagree in this way.

One way of accounting for such widespread disagreements is to say that they show moral judgements to be subjective and that it follows that one person's view is as good, or as bad, as another's. This is a view commonly expressed, although often the implications are not appreciated; perhaps the view would not be embraced so enthusiastically if they were. People who think all moral judgements are subjective are, in effect, subscribing to a particular theory about the nature of moral judgements. This theory is called ethical subjectivism. Its simplest expression is this: when people make moral judgements they are really saying what they approve or disapprove of. Someone who says 'Eating meat is wrong' is, according to the theory, really saying 'I disapprove of eating meat'; someone who says 'Homosexuality is not wrong' is saying 'I do not disapprove of homosexuality'.

Objections to ethical subjectivism

There are two immediate objections to this version of ethical subjectivism. The first is that it implies we are infallible when making moral judgements, in the way we are infallible when we express our likes and dislikes. If I say, sincerely, 'I like ice cream' then, since I am the only one who can really know what I like, I must be right. If moral judgements are subjective in this way, then what applies to 'I like ice cream' also applies to 'Taking money from people is wrong', 'Giving to charity is good', 'Homosexual behaviour is wrong'. When these statements are sincerely expressed, each is simply a statement about how I feel, and I am the only one who can really know what I feel. The problem is that we do not think we are infallible when it comes to making moral judgements.

The second objection is that people never actually disagree even though they appear to make contradictory moral judgements. If you say 'Homosexuality is wrong' and I say 'Homosexuality is not wrong' we are not really disagreeing, because what you are saying is that you disapprove of homosexuality and what I am saying is that I do not disapprove of homosexuality. Since we are talking about different things – I am talking about what I approve or disapprove of and you are talking about what you approve or disapprove of – we do not contradict each other. To contradict each other, we would have to make opposite claims about the same thing.

How damaging are these criticisms? Some philosophers have thought them to be fatal to this simple version of ethical subjectivism. It is certainly the case that ethical subjectivism has strange consequences, consequences that, were it not for the theory, we would take to be false. However, it may be that it is because we fail to realize that morality is subjective that we fail to realize that each of us is infallible in our moral judgements and that there is no moral disagreement between people. The question comes down to whether or not, once we see the consequences of taking moral judgements to be subjective, we are prepared to accept them.

There is, however, a more subtle criticism of ethical subjectivism, one that threatens to undermine its claim to be a coherent theory at all. Its basic tenet is that judgements of the form 'X is wrong' should be translated as 'I disapprove of X'. Now saying that I disapprove of something is not saying that I dislike it. It is possible to dislike something without disapproving of it and, equally, one can like the things one disapproves of. Is the ethical subjectivist able to give an account of what it is to disapprove of something? If not, then moral judgements have not been explained. Why should there be a problem here? There will be a problem if the only way to understand disapproval is in terms of wrongness. Disliking something is not thinking that it is wrong, whereas disapproving of something does involve thinking it is wrong. This becomes circular: disapproval was used to explain what was meant by calling something wrong, but now wrongness must be used to explain disapproval. What this means is that ethical subjectivism has not managed to give an account of moral judgements after all.

Emotivism

A version of ethical subjectivism that has been proposed to avoid the awkward consequences noted above is known as emotivism. It holds that making a moral judgement is not making a statement at all. Thus 'Homosexuality is wrong' should not be seen as making a claim, not even the claim 'I disapprove of homosexuality'. What the person who says this is really saying is something like 'Down with homosexuality!'. In other words, a moral judgement is the expression of an attitude.

Expressing an attitude, unlike reporting an attitude, is not something that is true or false.

Emotivism escapes the first two criticisms made above. Since my moral judgements are not stating anything, even some fact about myself, they are neither true nor false, and so they are not the sorts of thing about which I can be infallible (or fallible, for that matter). Secondly, although moral judgements that appear contradictory are not actually making contradictory statements, they are expressing attitudes that are contrary. When I say that something is wrong and you say it is not, we are certainly disagreeing, since we have different attitudes.

Finally, emotivism is not drawn into the same problem of circularity as ethical subjectivism. If saying 'X is wrong' is used to express an attitude, we do not need to explain what attitude is expressed; the expression of the attitude is the means by which we understand the attitude. Thus 'homosexuality, yuk!' and 'down with homosexuality' express different attitudes to homosexuality, and we do not need a concept of disapproval that is distinct from dislike to explain the attitude. We might want to say that the attitude expressed by 'homosexuality is wrong' is closer to that expressed by 'down with homosexuality' than to 'homosexuality, yuk!' but such an explanation is not necessary. The question as to how we understand the attitude expressed by others is an interesting one, but it does not need to be answered in order to accept the account of morality given by emotivism.

Can emotivism allow for rational discussion? You and I may not be making statements when you say 'Homosexuality is wrong' and I say 'Homosexuality is not wrong', but this neither means that we cannot discuss homosexuality nor that there is no point in our discussing it. The point of the discussion would be for each to persuade the other to adopt a different attitude, and attitudes can be changed through reason. However, not all discussion aimed at persuasion is rational, and moral discussions might turn out to be similar, in form if not content, to a discussion between two people with different attitudes towards a new pop song. One person might enthuse about the lyrics or the guitar playing or the particular quality of the singer's voice. The result might be that the other comes to see (or rather hear) the song differently and so change his or her mind about it. There is also the possibility that the qualities that one person singles out as reasons for liking the song are the very qualities that the other person dislikes. There can now be no further recourse. The different attitudes are irreconcilable.

Emotivism allows a role for moral discussion but, it is objected, it is the wrong sort of role. The aim of such discussion is that of changing attitudes rather than arriving at truth. A moral argument should be about putting forward good reasons for a moral judgement. This should involve showing that arguments are sound by showing that the premises are true and that the conclusion can be validly drawn from the premises. If, however, one's aim is to change another person's attitude, then this may be more easily achieved not by genuine argument but by persuasion masquerading as argument or by rhetoric. People can be led to believe false premises and can be fooled into accepting invalid arguments. If false premises and invalid arguments change an attitude, then, according to emotivism, the premises and arguments are good enough. If the result aimed for is not objectivity, then validity and truth are not directly relevant.

Limiting the scope of moral judgements

It may be that, when people say that moral judgements are subjective, they are thinking of particular sorts of judgements and then assuming that what applies to these applies to all moral judgements. At root is a mistake over the nature of a disagreement regarding judgements relating to certain types of activity. A disagreement that seems to oppose two conflicting ethical statements is actually a disagreement that opposes an ethical statement and a meta-ethical statement. We can illustrate this with regard to sexual behaviour. Some people believe it is morally wrong to have sex outside marriage or to use contraception or to have a homosexual relationship, whereas others believe that, provided consenting adults are involved, it is for individuals to decide for themselves. (Other people being deceived or hurt as a result of the sexual activity may make it a matter of morality, but this is only indirectly because of the sex.) To say that it is wrong to have sex outside marriage is to make an ethical claim. To say that it is up to the individual may look as if an ethical claim is being made – namely, it is not wrong to have sex outside marriage – but this is actually a meta-ethical claim – namely, whether or not one has sex outside marriage is not a matter of morality. In other words, claiming that sex is a matter of personal choice may be wrongly interpreted as claiming that judgements people make about sex are subjective moral judgements. From which it is a small step to think that moral judgements are subjective. When someone claims that moral judgements are subjective, we need to see whether he or she is prepared to accept that this applies to all moral judgements and not simply a particular type of moral judgement. It would mean, for example, that they would simply be expressing a personal preference when they say that torturing small children is wrong.

An objective meaning of 'good'

We might wonder whether it is possible to produce independent reasons for maintaining that morality is objective rather than subjective. One possible line of enquiry is to ask what we mean when we say something is good. The simplest sort of moral judgement we can make is to commend something or someone as good, although not all such commendations are moral judgements.

A thing is good if it performs its function well

Aristotle argues that, when we apply the word 'good' to something, the meaning of 'good' is to be understood in terms of the thing's function. Thus, when we describe a knife as good, we mean that it cuts well, since cutting is its function. Likewise, a good pen writes well, a good dancer dances well, a good hearing aid enables its wearer to hear well and so on. If Xs have a certain function, then describing a particular X as a good X does two things. First, it commends this particular X to anyone who wants the relevant function performed (the perfectly reasonable assumption being that anyone who wants a function performed would prefer to have it performed well rather than performed badly). Second, it tells us something about this particular X since, in order to perform a certain function, it must have certain characteristics. For example, a good knife will be sharp; a good pen will have a certain balance, its nib will be smooth, it will allow ink to flow freely and so on.

It is possible for two people to commend things that have exactly opposite properties – such commendation, being a reflection of the speaker's own preferences and attitudes. However, to commend a functional object as a good example of its kind is to be constrained by the objective properties needed for the thing to carry out that function. I can commend a blade for being blunt (when, for example, I would have seriously injured myself if it had been sharp) but I cannot commend it as a good blade.

The function of man

What about commending another person as good? Aristotle thought that *man* (that is, any human being) has a function and that this function is based on the defining characteristics of human beings that distinguish them from other biological species. The proper function of human beings, according to Aristotle, is to carry out the activity specific to human beings, the activity of reason or the intellect.

This does not seem to offer a very promising account of what it is to be morally good. We can find many activities that are distinctive of human beings – telling jokes, for example – but it does not follow that man's function is to carry out such activities or that someone (morally) good is someone performing such activities well. Aristotle also talks in terms of the function people have by virtue of their position in society, for example, as a flautist or a potter. A good teacher, a good musician, a good manager are all people who perform particular roles well but they may not be morally good.

'Good' as an attributive adjective

Before continuing the discussion, let us first consider a logical distinction made by Geach (1919–). Basing his distinction on the grammatical distinction between attributive adjectives and predicative adjectives, he described the logical distinction as follows. Consider first the adjective 'red'. From the proposition 'This is a red book' follow two further proposition: 'This is a book' and 'This is red'. Adjectives that function in the same way that 'red' functions here he calls predicative adjectives. However, an adjective such as 'small' does not function in the same way. From the proposition 'The sun is a small star' we cannot infer 'The sun is small'. 'Small' he calls an attributive adjective.

Geach then claims that 'good' is an attributive adjective. From a proposition such as 'X is a good potter' or 'X is a good comedian' we cannot infer 'X is good'. This, Geach claims, is true no matter what noun follows 'good'. Even when, grammatically, 'good' appears by itself and seems to function as a predicative adjective it is really an attributive adjective. Although we might say 'X is good', there is always the understanding that X is a good instance of some kind of thing rather than just simply good. The question is, a good example of what kind of thing? Do we mean someone who is a good example of a human being? Even assuming that this is what we mean, there are two further problems: first, can we say what makes for a good example of a human being and, second, if we can, is this really what we mean when we say that someone is morally good?

Take the first problem. We can certainly talk about something being a good example of its kind in the case of species other than humans – a good example of an oak tree, a good example of a puma and so on. Moreover, what counts as being a good example of one's kind can be determined objectively. Judges at a dog show, by and large, use objective criteria to determine who is top dog. When we pick out cats, dogs, trees, etc. as good examples of their kind, we are, at the very least, picking out those individuals who are flourishing. Can we suggest that a good person is someone who is flourishing as a human being?

Is a good person one who is flourishing?

Again, there are problems with this suggestion. First, although we may agree on what counts as flourishing in the case of cats or oak trees, agreement is not so easy in the case of human beings. There are many different ways in which human beings can live, and this means that there are many different ways in which they can flourish. The second problem is the one mentioned before: there seems to be no necessary connection between flourishing and moral goodness. Consider how we can judge people to be flourishing – for example, by the extent of their material possessions, the number of their offspring, etc.; these do not seem to connect with being morally good.

Facts and values

The very enterprise of trying to discover characteristics of goodness has been criticized on the grounds that there is a crucial distinction between fact and value, which it ignores. A fact is a state of affairs that makes a proposition true. If the proposition that John is kissing Mary is true, then there is a fact, a certain state of affairs, that makes it true. This fact involves John and Mary and a relation between them, namely the relation of one kissing the other. A proposition such as that John is married to Mary is made true by a much more complicated state of affairs, since the relation of being married involves more than just John and Mary. In order for John to be married to Mary there must be the institution of marriage, there must have been a ceremony and so on, all of which involve other people. None the less, if, say, there is a dispute as to whether John is married to Mary, that is, a dispute over the truth of a proposition, this dispute will be settled by the facts.

However, if there is a dispute over whether marriage is a good thing, this is a dispute over values and, or so it is claimed, it cannot be settled by the facts. In other words, we cannot decide whether marriage is a good thing simply by looking at the world, in the way we can to decide whether John is married to Mary. What then is a value? Values, it has been suggested, are to do with our attitude to the facts – roughly speaking, whether we approve or disapprove of them. Thus it is possible for two people to agree on the facts but disagree on the values to be placed on them.

It has been said that facts are objective whereas values are subjective, that we discover facts but create values. Values are not determined by the facts – different people may have different attitudes to the same facts, and this means that we cannot derive values from facts. Now the discussion in the preceding section has shown that this view is too black and white: we can infer whether or not a knife is a good knife, which is to infer a value, from the facts about its sharpness. However, here we are dealing with something that has a function. Where there is no agreed function, it is not clear whether we can infer values from facts. In the case of moral values, there is a problem when it comes to deciding whether or not someone is a good person, since there is no agreement as to the function of a human being.

Does evolution provide moral values?

One argument for countering the claim that it is not possible to derive moral values from facts about human beings is based on the claim that patterns of behaviour, including moral behaviour, have been determined largely by evolution. The conclusion is that evolutionary success determines moral values. To give an example, there is a theory that, for a male human to maximize the chances of his genetic material being passed on, his best strategy is to assist in the rearing of his offspring but also to be on the lookout for opportunities for casual sex outside this family arrangement. Whether or not this theory is correct is not the issue here; the issue is what follows if it is correct. If it really is the best strategy, then genes that programme this sort of behaviour will be passed on more often than genes that do not. This sort of behaviour will then tend to spread throughout the species. In other words, if it is the best strategy for human males then, in time, human males will be genetically programmed to be philanderers. Does it follow from this that the males who behave as philanderers are good?

The process of evolution has been described as the survival of the fittest. If the philandering male is the one who survives, then the philandering male is the 'fittest'. There is the need for caution here, however, regarding the use of 'fittest'. It can be used descriptively (as above) to mean something like 'the best able to survive', although, in fact, it is not the philandering male who survives – his philandering may result in a short, if exciting, life – but philandering male behaviour. So 'fittest', in its descriptive sense, should be read as 'best able to reproduce successfully'. The second sense in which 'fittest' can be used is to commend. To say 'She is the fittest person on the running track' is not merely to describe but to express approval. Hence 'survival of the fittest' is sometimes used to commend those who survive as the most deserving. It is the failure to distinguish this sort of equivocation between the two uses of 'fittest' that lends plausibility to the suggestion that evolution provides moral values.

Evolutionary psychology (previously known as sociobiology) aims to describe and explain observed behavioural patterns in terms of inherited genes. Although organisms, such as human beings, have been described as 'gigantic lumbering robots' and as 'survival machines' for genes, this is clearly not how we see our purpose in life. Indeed the notion of the 'selfish gene' using us for its own end, although a powerful metaphor, is still only a metaphor. Ensuring the survival of genes is not something that we do intentionally; it is not even, for example, a reason for our having sex, let alone a reason for all the other things we do. Since, as we have said, morality is to do with reasons, furthering the 'interests' of our genes cannot underpin morality. Evolution cannot supply us with ready-made moral values.

A broader view of objectivity

Caution needs to be exercised when using the terms 'subjective' and 'objective'. These terms can be used to draw different distinctions, and it is important to be clear just what contrast is being made. Consider the following three statements:

a)   Sylvia weighs 9 stone.
b)   Sylvia is generous.
c)   Sylvia is my favourite teacher.

We can classify these statements as subjective or objective in different ways and give different reasons for our classification. First, that a) is objective and b) and c) subjective, since Sylvia's weight can be measured whereas we cannot measure generosity or whether she is my favourite teacher. A second classification has it that a) and b) are objective and c) subjective, because the first two say something about Sylvia whereas the third says something about me and what I think of her. The third classification has it that all three are objective, since in each case there is a fact or state of affairs that will make the claim true. The facts relating to the second and third statements are more complex than might appear to be the case for the first, but the difference may not be so great. The state of affairs that makes it the case that Sylvia is generous involves Sylvia and the way she behaves but also a society in which there is agreement as to what counts as generous behaviour. The state of affairs that makes it the case that Sylvia weighs 9 stone also relies upon agreements as to standards of measurement.

What we can say is that, if there is an objectivity to be found in moral judgements, it is not the same as the objectivity we find in judgements such as 'Paris is the capital of France' or 'Gold is a metal'. A moral judgement, such as that Sylvia is generous, cannot simply be dismissed as a subjective expression of the preferences or feelings of the person making the judgement. The fact that there is disagreement over moral judgements such as that abortion is wrong and abortion is permissible need not be because it is not possible to make objective moral judgements, but because both statements are too simplistic or too general to capture the truth. The questions as to whether moral judgements are objective and in what way they might be objective are central questions of moral philosophy.

Psychological egoism

Psychological egoism is the theory that we do everything out of self-interest and are incapable of acting in any other way. People might discuss what they ought to do and how they ought to take account of other people's interests but, it is claimed, they do not act on this basis; in the end, people do what they want to do. People might give money to charity or help an old person with his or her shopping, but, even here, they are doing it not for the other person but for their own advantage.

This sort of cynical view is often adopted by someone who wishes to impress or to excuse his or her own conduct. None the less, it is possible that it correctly describes the hidden motives that drive all our actions. We must therefore consider the evidence for such a theory of human nature and, given that there are many apparent counter-examples, see how it allows these. A counter-example is provided whenever someone acts against his or her interests. First consider all the small acts of kindness people perform, day in and day out – giving money to charity, helping a friend in need, helping a blind person across the road, etc. No doubt many such cases are not really counter-examples. Acts of kindness are often repaid in kind, as are acts of unpleasantness, and so one may do things for others out of self-interest. There are further instances (perhaps, helping a blind person across the road) in which the kind deed is done not in the expectation that it will be reciprocated, but to impress some third party who, as a result, will be more favourably disposed towards us.

Even so, cases remain that cannot be made to fit the theory in either of these ways. In order to explain these away, the theory introduces the idea that people get pleasure from being kind and that this is why they are kind. People help others even when there is no apparent payback simply because they get a pleasurable feeling from doing so. The pay-back, in other words, is the pleasure it gives a person to act in this way.

What are we to make of this theory? It cannot be denied that many of the things people do, which at first blush appear selfless, turn out not to be so. An action does not count as selfless if it is carried out with the intention of being repaid by the recipient, of being repaid indirectly by some other person or of giving oneself pleasure. However, this does not mean that there are no selfless acts. Whether or not there are selfless acts seems to be an empirical matter and one that can be settled only after widespread research into the motives behind human action. A further development of the theory, which purports to give an account of the causes of human actions, suggests that such an empirical enquiry is unnecessary.

Beliefs and desires are the causes of actions

The aim of the following argument is to establish that there can be no selfless acts. To appreciate the argument we need to consider the form taken by the explanation of any action. The following are examples of actions and their possible explanations. I put my savings into a particular building society because I believe it has the highest rate of interest. I buy a CD because I like one of the tracks that has been released as a single. I start to learn a foreign language because I think it will be useful. The first thing to notice is that these explanations are incomplete. Believing that a building society provides a high rate of interest is not enough; I must also want a high rate of interest. Liking one of the tracks on a CD is not enough; I must also believe that many of the other tracks will be similar. Generalizing, we can say that any explanation of an action must have two components: a belief and a desire. My performing action A is explained if (a) I believe A will result in X and (b) I desire X.

The next step is to say that the relevant belief/desire combination not only explains the action, it is also the cause of the action; it explains the action precisely because it causes the action. We encountered such explanations of actions in chapter 6, where they were seen as part of a causal theory of behaviour, the theory being dubbed (by its critics) 'folk psychology'.

An objection is that it is not only desires that combine with beliefs to cause actions. When I visit a relative in hospital it may not be because I want to, that is, have a particular desire, but because I think I ought to. In this case, I act contrary to my desires. A response to this objection is to say that thinking I ought to do something will not cause me to do it: I must also want to do what I think I ought to do! In other words, in order for a reason to be a reason for *me*, it must, in some way, relate to what I want or need or desire. Davidson (1917–) has expressed this by saying that it is something towards which I have a pro attitude. The theory of psychological egoism can be stated as follows: any action I perform, for which there is a reason, must have resulted from a pro attitude I had. Where there was a choice of actions, the one I actually performed must have been the one for which I had the strongest pro attitude. In other words, I do what I most want to do.

Objections to psychological egoism

There are several points to note at this stage. First, this claim, that we always do what we most want to do, is no longer an empirical hypothesis which might be true or false. It should be seen as a necessary truth, because what we most want to do cannot be determined independently of what we actually do. I might *think* that what I most want to do is X, but if I do Y then Y was really what I most wanted to do. Second, this logical claim, that we always do what we most want to do, does not mean that we always act selfishly or that we can never act morally. Such a conclusion follows only if we assume that we act selfishly when we do what we most want to do. Sometimes, in this broader sense of 'want', our wants are selfish, but at other times they are not. Wanting to give away all my money to help those more in need is not a selfish want, and the fact that giving away my money is what I want to do does not, in itself, make giving away my money selfish. In this broader sense of want, doing what one most wants to do is not the same as acting selfishly. It is also important to draw a distinction between performing an action that has good consequences for oneself and performing an action *because* it has good consequences for oneself. I may well benefit from being kind to others, but this does not mean that I am kind to others in order to get these benefits. I may even want these benefits, but this particular want may not have been my reason for action.

To sum up, the claim that we always act out of self-interest can be taken either as an empirical claim, as to what sorts of desires actually motivate people, or as a logical claim. If the latter, what is in a person's self-interest is, by definition, what that person actually does. The empirical claim has certainly not been established, and the fact that there are cases of what appear to be unselfish action may show it to be false. The logical claim, although true, is trivial. It can tell us nothing about whether or not an action is selfish. Hence we can dismiss the threat that psychological egoism seemed to pose to the possibility of morality.

Ethical egoism

Whereas psychological egoism suggests that morality is not possible because, as a matter of fact, everyone acts in his or her own self-interest and this precludes their ever acting in the interests of others, ethical egoism recommends self-interest as a principle on which to act. Ethical egoism claims not that it is impossible to act other than out of self-interest but that it is a mistake to do so. It does not imply that morality is impossible, in the way that psychological egoism does, since it presents itself as a moral system. An important point to note is that the ethical egoist is not simply saying, 'I should act in accordance with my own self-interest', but is putting forward acting out of self-interest as a moral principle that applies to everyone. This means, among other things, that the ethical egoist is recommending that others act according to *their* interests. However, ethical egoism is so different from most people's idea of morality that to accept it as a moral theory is to make the notion of morality seem empty – the least we might expect of any criterion of morality is that it disqualifies something based purely on self-interest.

The possibility that has suggested itself to some philosophers is that the *logic* of moral judgements will ensure that ethical egoism fails to qualify as a moral principle. Kant, for example, argues that the moral principles derived from self-interest will involve logical inconsistencies or be such that no rational person could accept them. Other philosophers have thought that what is needed is not a formal or logical restriction but a restriction on the content of moral judgements.

Kant's categorical imperative

In chapter 5 we looked at the connection between free will and responsibility. The will is the faculty for doing one thing rather than another and, for Kant, it can either be autonomous (that is, self-determined) or be determined by something outside itself (a situation that Kant referred to as 'heteronomy of the will'). The idea of the will being self-determined seems similar to the idea of being able to choose otherwise, although the condition, suggested by Kant, for the will being autonomous is very different from the condition, suggested in chapter 5, for being able to choose otherwise. Kant argued that, as we are essentially rational beings, we act autonomously when our will is determined by reason. When, however, feelings and emotions determine it, we are not autonomous. It is reason that tells us what we ought to do and, for Kant, an action has moral worth only if it is determined by reason.

Kant thinks that, if reason is to determine our actions, then we must follow principles that have themselves been determined by reason. The immoral person may act rationally, in the sense that she or he acts according to principles, but does not act in accordance with the dictates of pure reason, that is, of reason alone, since the principles have been determined by feelings and emotions, which means that rationality is in the service of the non-rational.

It can be noted that, contrary to what we might expect, Kant does not think that there is a conflict between acting in accordance with reason and acting out of self-interest. However, this is because he believes that the self is essentially rational and hence true self-interest lies in following the dictates of reason. Actions that we would normally see as being determined by self-interest, Kant would describe as actions in which the person is not autonomous. When one behaves selfishly, emotions and feelings have determined one's will. Such actions, according to Kant, do not serve a person's true self-interest.

Categorical and hypothetical imperatives

Let us see how through the use of reason we may arrive at moral principles. Principles or, as Kant refers to them, maxims guide conduct. These principles can therefore be thought of as 'imperatives' or commands. Kant divides imperatives into two sorts. Hypothetical imperatives are ones that tell you what to do on the assumption that you want some other end. In effect, the hypothetical imperative says that if you want X, do Y. For example, if you want to do well in your exams, study hard. A hypothetical imperative cannot command everyone but only those who want to achieve the end for which the action is a means. Not everyone is commanded to study hard, only those who want to do well in their exams. In Kant's view, moral principles could not be hypothetical imperatives since moral principles have to be universal; they must apply to everyone. A moral principle is a categorical, not a hypothetical, imperative.

This might suggest that there are many categorical imperatives, corresponding to various different moral principles. However, Kant seems to imply that there is just one, although with several different but supposedly equivalent formulations. In one of its formulations, at least, the categorical imperative is not so much a direct guide to action as an indirect one. It is a guide as to which principles to accept as guides to action. In other words, it provides a test for whether or not a principle is a moral principle.

Kant's test is in two parts and the principle has to pass both parts. The test is this. First we have to suppose the principle in question were to become a universal law of nature so that everyone, including oneself, would have to act in accordance with it. Thus we have to suppose that the principle becomes a law, like the law of gravity, for which obeying is not an option since there is no alternative. Now it may not be possible for the principle to become a universal law in this way. By 'not possible' we do not mean not physically possible but not *logically* possible. It will not be logically possible if a contradiction results from trying to make the principle universal. If it is not possible for the principle to become a universal law, then the principle fails the test. We shall see an example of a principle that fails the first part of the test below. The second part of the test is whether a rational person would agree to the principle becoming a universal law. In other words, the second question is: would it be rational to bind other people with such a law, given that one would also be binding oneself?

The universality requirement

Let us see how ethical egoism might produce a principle that fails the first test. It can often serve one's own interests to make a promise to someone else. Perhaps one wants to borrow money but, in order to do so, has to promise to pay it back. Perhaps it is simply a matter of avoiding an unpleasant scene by promising to make amends. It can also serve one's own interests not to keep that promise: not to pay back the money, not to make amends because some other favourable opportunity has arisen. Someone who acts out of self-interest can explain why he or she broke the promise by pointing to the advantage gained. Thus the principle being followed is 'I will break a promise whenever it is to my advantage'. This, however, is not general enough, since it makes an implicit reference to the person putting forward the principle. Thus, the general principle that is being recommended by the ethical egoist for everyone to follow will be something like: everyone should break promises when it is in their interest to do so.

Such a principle could not become a universal law. When one makes a promise, one gives a commitment to keep that promise. Thus the principle that is to be a universal law both makes a commitment and takes away that commitment. In effect it would be saying: people should both commit themselves to doing something (by making a promise) and not commit themselves to doing it (by being free to break their promise). If breaking promises became widespread then nothing could count as making a promise. The action that purported to be one of making a promise (which, typically, involves uttering the words 'I promise') would not count as doing so since no one would believe that any commitment had been made. Hence the principle could not become a universal law since it involves a contradiction.

The requirement of rational endorsement

Not all the principles that the ethical egoist proposes will fail the first part of Kant's test. Some, at least, do not result in a contradiction when taken to be universal laws of nature. We therefore need to apply the second test to see whether any rational person would endorse the principle becoming a universal law. We can see that endorsement might not be rational since, in general, the benefits of acting out of self-interest arise when others do not act out of self-interest. Were everyone to act out of self-interest, the result might be beneficial to no one. In which case it would not be rational to endorse a universal law requiring everyone to act out of self-interest.

A formulation of such a rule is this: act so as to look after one's own interests and disregard the interests of others. If I am the only one following such a rule then I am going to benefit because I will not be burdened by helping others, but I will still receive help, should I need it, from those with a more caring attitude. However, if everyone is following the same rule then the benefits are less assured. Given that misfortune can fall at any time, I would be constantly in danger of needing help without the prospect of assistance. Given that this is the case, it would not, or so Kant argues, be rational for me to agree to everyone following such a principle. Hence the principle fails the second part of Kant's test and so is not a moral principle.

There seem to be two points that need further consideration here. The first is whether the argument that it would be irrational to agree to the principle of self-help becoming a universal law of nature really stands up. The second, a more general one, is whether this reliance on rationality really gets to the roots of morality and whether it provides the right sort of objections against ethical egoism.

What ends can reason endorse?

Let us start with the first point. What are the grounds for saying that it is irrational to agree to the principle of self-help becoming a universal law? If everyone lives by the principle of helping only himself or herself then I may find myself in trouble. But is it irrational to take this risk? Would not the rational person assess the benefits and risks of each of the possible outcomes and base decisions on this? Perhaps each of us would come up with different analyses (each taking his or her own character and circumstances into consideration) and hence arrive at a different decision. This would mean that reason does not give a simple answer applicable to everyone.

Kant, I suspect, would not agree that this is the way the rational person comes to a decision. For him, this would be reason in the service of self-interest, or, rather (given what we have said of Kant's idea of self-interest), of reason being determined heteronomously. Kant requires that it is reason unaided that must determine whether or not to accept the principle as a universal law. Yet it is difficult to see the grounds reason would have for either accepting or not accepting the principle of self-help as a universal law. Reason balks at a contradiction, but were the principle of self-help to become a universal law of nature this would not produce a contradiction. It might be imprudent to agree to such a principle becoming a universal law, but this, for Kant, is not a strong enough objection.

The way that Kant sets up the test, it is not clear what counts as rational. He will not accept doing something as a means to an end as rational, unless the end is one a purely rational being would be bound to have. Yet many of the ends that a normal human being has are not ones that a purely rational being is bound to have. Emotions and feelings, etc., are denied an influence since a purely rational being does not have emotions and feelings. A rational being may have no reason for accepting a principle as a universal law but equally has no reason for rejecting a principle as a universal law, other than if a contradiction results. It is difficult, therefore, to see how the second test can do anything other than echo the first test. The second test becomes distinctive only if we can call upon some further notion, such as prudence, but this takes us away from pure reason. Thus, as at least some of the rules derived from ethical egoism pass the first test, they will also pass the second test.

This leads to the more general point that reason alone fails to show that ethical egoism is not a moral theory, since morality is not a matter of pure reason. A purely rational person, who was not swayed by feelings but made decisions solely on grounds of duty, would not be an exemplar of a perfectly good person. Warmth of personality and a natural inclination to be kind and considerate would feature quite high on most lists of what it takes to be morally good.

Utilitarianism

Do we have alternative ways of characterizing moral judgements, ways that put some restriction on their content directly rather than indirectly via logic? The Kantian approach to moral philosophy is termed 'deontological', meaning that it is based on duty. An important alternative to a deontological approach is termed 'consequentialist'. Instead of looking at whether one has a duty or obligation to perform a certain type of action (telling the truth, keeping a promise, etc.), a consequentialist approach considers what results from the action. More precisely, a consequentialist theory is one in which the criterion of an action being right or wrong lies only in the consequences of the action. Utilitarianism is the best-known and most important example of a consequentialist approach. While it did not originate with Jeremy Bentham (1748–1832), it was Bentham who first set out utilitarianism as a workable moral theory. Underpinning utilitarianism is the so-called principle of utility, and Bentham devotes the first chapter of his *An Introduction to the Principles of Morals and Legislation* to this principle. The chapter opens with the following sentences: 'Nature has placed mankind under the governance of two sovereign masters, *pain* and *pleasure*. It is for them alone to point out what we ought to do, as well as to determine what we shall do.'

There are two quite distinct claims made here, claims that mirror those of the two versions of egoism. One is that pleasure and pain determine what we do and the other is that pleasure and pain determine what we should do. The first claim is a psychological claim about human motivation. The second is a claim of normative ethics. It is important to note that the two claims are independent. One can hold that one *should* act so as to increase pleasure and decrease pain without also holding that, as a matter of fact, this is the basis on which people do act and vice versa.

The psychological claim (if it is to be even plausible) is referring to the (prospective) pleasure and pain to be experienced by the *individual* about to act. The ethical claim, on the other hand, is referring to the sum total of pleasure and pain that will result from the action. Although Bentham's utilitarianism deals with pleasure and pain, it is impartial between those who experience this pleasure or pain. One's own pleasure and pain should count for no more than, but also no less than, anyone else's pleasure and pain. Mill (1806–1873) expresses this point when he writes: 'the happiness which forms the utilitarian standard of what is right in conduct, is not the agent's own happiness, but that of all concerned. As between his own happiness and that of others, utilitarianism requires him to be as strictly impartial as a disinterested and benevolent spectator' (*Utilitarianism*, 268).

The ethical egoist recommends that everyone should be trying to maximize his or her own pleasure and minimize his or her own pain. The utilitarian does not have to appeal to logical inconsistency to show that this is not a satisfactory moral basis for action. The utilitarian's objection is that acting on such a principle does not maximize the sum total of pleasure or minimize the sum total of pain. This seems to get closer to the root of the matter: most of us will feel that what is wrong with ethical egoism is that it does not take account of anyone else and how they might be affected.

Difficulties for utilitarianism

However, there are problems for utilitarianism, and these we should now explore. The first is the radical nature of the conclusions that the utilitarian is liable to arrive at. We saw above that Kant was able to give a reason for keeping promises, by showing that a principle of breaking promises whenever it suited could not qualify as a moral principle. Similar arguments could be put forward for telling the truth, sticking to agreements and so on. A utilitarian, on the other hand, concludes that the right thing to do is to break a promise, tell a lie or cancel an agreement when doing so maximizes pleasure and minimizes pain. The reasoning of the utilitarian would not be the same as that of the ethical egoist, since the utilitarian would take into account how everyone is affected. Thus, some account is taken of the inconvenience caused to the person to whom the promise had been made. None the less, there will be circumstances in which the loss to this person is more than offset by the gains of other people. The net gain would, for the utilitarian, justify breaking the promise.

Indirect consequences
Can the utilitarian justify this sort of conclusion? One option is to say that here utilitarianism has the right answer and traditional ethics has the wrong answer. This draws upon the underlying assumption that the amount of pleasure and pain produced is the sole criterion for determining the morally right action. This response will be examined in more detail later, but for the moment consider an alternative option

for the utilitarian, which is to review the evidence in case any consequences have been overlooked. A more sophisticated utilitarianism
takes account of the indirect as well as the direct consequences of
breaking a promise. A particular effect is that the person to whom
I make the promise will not trust me in the future, which leads to
further consequences. More generally, the practice of promising itself
will be undermined, which will also have consequences. The difficulty
with these indirect consequences (consequences of consequences)
becomes apparent when we try to assess their affect on the total
happiness. Even if indirect consequences result in an increase of pain
(of some sort), and so decrease overall happiness, we cannot know
whether this will be sufficient to reverse the former judgement. None
the less, indirect consequences cannot be ignored, and in many sorts
of cases they seem to offer the promise of reconciling utilitarianism
with conventional morality.

Appeal to indirect consequences, however, is not going to satisfy
a Kantian. The objection to utilitarianism levelled by the Kantian
is that, even when utilitarianism yields the 'right' answers (as judged
by the Kantian), it is for the wrong reason. It may be that, by drawing on (possible) indirect consequences of breaking a promise, the
utilitarian can show that the balance of consequences is in favour
of keeping rather than breaking the promise. But, for the Kantian,
favourable consequences are not the reason for keeping a promise. The Kantian's point is that one should keep a promise because a
promise is a commitment and one should honour a commitment
whatever the consequences. Suppose you have arranged to meet
someone at a particular time but, while *en route* to this appointment,
witness a road accident. Should you keep your appointment and
leave the accident victim bleeding to death or should you break your
promise and use your first-aid skills to save the victim's life? If you
save the victim, you are treating the person to whom you made
your promise as a means to an end, whereas if you keep your promise
you are not treating the victim as a means to an end. Hence the
Kantian response is to keep the promise. Most of us would, I suspect,
consider this to be a callous attitude. However, even the deontologist
who concedes that there are some situations where the consequences
cannot be disregarded will treat such cases as exceptions, whereas
the utilitarian will routinely consider the pros and cons of keeping a
promise.

The argument is not all one-sided. The utilitarian may counter
with examples where, even taking into account possible indirect

consequences, it is clear that the balance of pleasure over pain lies in the direction of breaking rather than keeping a promise. To insist that the promise be kept in such cases, the utilitarian may suggest, is pedantic and smacks of 'jobsworth'. Surely increasing happiness or reducing suffering is more important than sticking to the rules.

Justice

An area in which utilitarianism has come in for a great deal of criticism is that of justice. It is a feature of utilitarianism (or, rather, of act utilitarianism, to distinguish it from an alternative known as 'rule utilitarianism') that we cannot say of a type of action that it is right or wrong. Some instances of a particular type of action may maximize happiness while other instances may not. Each separate action must therefore be considered on its merits. We may adopt certain rules of thumb (for example, that murder and theft will decrease rather than increase happiness) but there will always be exceptions. For the utilitarian, an appeal to justice carries no weight. The utilitarian will accept that, where possible, justice should be seen to be done since, were the state to appear unjust, this might provoke disquiet and concern. However, whether or not justice should actually be done is a matter determined solely by consequences.

Imagine a racially motivated murder that results in unrest and the threat of civil disorder in a community. Suppose that the police arrest a person, found in suspicious circumstances, who is innocent of the murder. Suppose that, despite his innocence, the result of convicting this person will be an easing of racial tension and a removal of the threat of civil disorder. Suppose, on the other hand, that if the person is not convicted then, given that the police have no further leads, violence will erupt and many people will be hurt or even killed. In this sort of situation, the utilitarian view is that the person should be framed and convicted, even though this is unjust. Indirect consequences, such as loss of faith in the police should this perversion of justice be discovered, may be sufficient to alter the conclusion but, where the threat of social disorder is serious enough, the right thing to do (according to the utilitarian) will be to ensure that the cover-up is effective. Here utilitarianism is certainly at odds with conventional morality, which considers justice to be a right and, moreover, one that is inalienable – meaning that it cannot be negotiated away to secure better consequences.

The meaning of 'happiness'

In these conflicts between utilitarianism and conventional morality, we sooner or later come to the question: how important is it that pleasure is increased and pain decreased? Should this be the sole standard against which we measure whether an action is right or not? Do we value having more pleasure and less pain above all other things? Is increasing the amount of pleasure and decreasing the amount of pain the primary aim of morality? There are certainly objections to saying 'yes' to such questions. First let us examine the utilitarian position more closely.

To date in this account of utilitarianism, I have tried to stick, as far as possible, to the terms 'pleasure' and 'pain'. This is partly because these are the terms Bentham uses but also because their meaning is clear. In the passage quoted from Mill, however, the more general term 'happiness' was introduced. Indeed, if utilitarianism has a slogan it is 'the greatest happiness for the greatest number'. One reason for using 'happiness' is to replace the clumsy expression 'increasing pleasure and decreasing pain' with 'increasing happiness'. The person who ceases to be in pain may not experience pleasure but is happier now than formerly.

Preference utilitarianism

More importantly, the claim that we all want happiness is more plausible than the claim that we all want pleasure. Sometimes we are prepared to accept pain as a means to gaining something else, something that makes us more happy (although it does not necessarily involve more pleasure). It may be that people who sacrifice pleasure for other ends, say curtailing their social life in order to pass exams or to get on at work or to save money, are merely sacrificing short-term pleasure for long-term pleasure. Yet it is not obvious that this is so in all cases. Pleasure, like pain, is a sensation, and people often do things with no regard to the sensations that will result. It is more plausible to talk of happiness rather than pleasure and to say, for example, of the person who gives up going to the theatre and eating out in order to pass an exam, that passing the exam will make him or her happier.

None the less we need to be cautious and not assume that, because we all want happiness, this means we all want the same thing. Whereas the causes of pleasure and pain are similar for everyone, the things that make people happy can be very different. If one thing makes one person happy but a different thing makes another person happy, how do we know what to do to maximize happiness? We certainly cannot assume that providing a particular sort of experience for people will achieve this, since there is no experience that is guaranteed to make everyone happy.

It is in response to these sorts of concerns that the classical utilitarianism of Bentham and Mill has given way to what can be referred to as 'preference utilitarianism'. Preference utilitarianism has the same aim as classical utilitarianism, namely to maximize happiness, but differs in its conception of happiness. Happiness is now construed as the satisfaction of desires. Sometimes what I desire is a particular (pleasurable) sensation or the cessation of a particular (painful) sensation. Sometimes what I desire is to achieve a certain result – get into a team, get a job, win the lottery – or to do something – climb a mountain, run the marathon, study quantum mechanics, play a game of tennis, make love to someone and so on. Achieving or doing certain things may or may not be associated with sensations of pleasure. Sometimes, I may have to put up with sensations of pain to achieve what I want. Happiness, in these cases, is not having the sensation but experiencing, achieving, doing whatever it is I want. Getting what I want counts as an increase in happiness, even though, sometimes, it leaves me *feeling* disappointed and unhappy.

This notion of happiness, as the satisfaction of preferences, reflects a richer conception of life. It also treats people as autonomous and capable of determining for themselves what they want out of life. Classical utilitarianism, on the other hand, assumes it knows what people want and tries to give it to them irrespective of their wishes. What is not so clear, however, is whether this conception of happiness, as satisfied wants, can be used to underpin morality. Even if pleasure does not seem an essential requirement for a good life, if faced with the simple choice of increasing pleasure or increasing pain, morally it would seem right to increase pleasure. However, where the choice is between satisfying and not satisfying desires, what is morally right depends on the nature of those desires. Satisfying a strong desire would, on utilitarian calculus, count in favour of a certain action, but is it not possible for some desires to be morally repugnant? Now it might turn out that the satisfaction of desires that the majority of us find morally repugnant results in a net decrease in happiness. There may even be evolutionary explanations of why this is so. None the less, it seems unsatisfactory to leave it to chance or evolution to decide the matter.

Suppose that the paedophile has a strong desire just to stroke a child's cheek and that the child does not mind or even wants him to do so. Such considerations seem irrelevant to whether it would be morally right for the paedophile to do this or for us to promote his doing it. Moreover, our concerns here are surely not that there may be other, indirect consequences that will alter the balance, making it wrong for the paedophile to satisfy his desire. We just do not feel that the paedophile's desires have to be taken into account at all when deciding the morality of the action. The fact that they might be strong desires does not increase the pressure on us to place them in the scale pan; if anything, the opposite is true.

Kantianism versus utilitarianism

To illustrate the difference in approach of Kantianism and utilitarianism to morality, let us consider how they would tackle the same moral issues. This will involve looking at the aspects each considers relevant and the arguments each employs as well as the conclusions that each reaches. The first issue to be considered is that of punishment. To many, the important debate about punishment is about the appropriate levels of punishment for different crimes, that is, about the appropriate degree of severity or leniency. However, more fundamental is whether punishment in any form is morally right and, if so, how it can be justified.

Punishment

First consider why Kantianism and utilitarianism might, for different reasons, each consider punishment wrong. Punishment can take many forms, including fines, beatings, imprisonment and death. For the utilitarian, what these different forms have in common is that they impose on the person being punished something that he or she does not wish to have imposed; the effect of punishment, and sometimes the intention of punishment, is to make the criminal suffer. This can be justified only by a compensatory increase in happiness somewhere else. Thus a utilitarian justifies punishment by saying that it will deter others from committing similar crimes in future and so prevent the suffering of would-be future victims. For the utilitarian the justification of punishment depends on its deterrent effect.

The Kantian may be concerned because punishment involves treating the criminals in ways that, ordinarily, would violate his or her rights. Were this the case it would show a lack of respect for another human being. Any appeal to the deterrence effect of the punishment, far from providing a justification, would compound the problem, since the criminal is being used as a means rather than being treated as an end in him- or herself. If the Kantian is to justify punishment, it must be by showing that punishment does not violate the criminal's rights and does not degrade the criminal but, in fact, treats the criminal with respect by treating him or her as a moral agent. For the Kantian, taking responsibility for one's actions involves accepting that one deserves to be treated according to how one behaves. In particular, if one breaks a moral law then one deserves the appropriate punishment. Thus, in fact, punishment does not show a lack of respect for the criminal; although this may seem strange, it is the withholding of punishment that would show a lack of respect. To fail to punish a criminal is, in effect, to say that the criminal was not responsible for his or her actions. In other words, it is to say that the criminal was not a moral agent.

From these two different justifications for punishment, different attitudes and approaches to punishment follow. For the Kantian, punishment should always be exacted, no matter what the consequences of doing so. For the utilitarian, punishment should be exacted only if it will bring about a net increase of happiness. For the Kantian, it is essential that the guilt of the criminal is determined – punishing the innocent and failing to punish the guilty are equally wrong. For the utilitarian, actual guilt or innocence is secondary to the perception of guilt or innocence, since it is the perception that will largely determine the effectiveness of the deterrent and hence the resulting balance of happiness. Punishing an innocent person who is thought to be guilty may have a greater deterrent effect than punishing a guilty person who is thought to be innocent. Even allowing for the unhappiness of the innocent person who is unjustly punished, the overall result may be greater happiness. For the utilitarian, this would be sufficient justification.

Abortion

I began this chapter by suggesting that moral debates were conducted at several levels. The debate we have just considered was clearly at the level of social policy. The debate on abortion may be conducted at the level of determining the social policy, but there are also important debates at the level of the individual making a choice as to whether or not to have an abortion. Clearly this is not an issue for every woman who becomes pregnant, but we can suggest two sorts of situations in which it might be. In the first, a couple has intercourse and, despite taking reasonable steps to prevent conception, the woman becomes pregnant. The woman does not want to have a baby but nor does she want to do anything that is morally wrong. (We shall assume, to avoid further complications, that the man does not offer a different viewpoint but is in agreement with her.) Her question is then: is it morally permissible to have an abortion to prevent an unwanted baby? She is looking for moral reasons that will allow her to do what, moral considerations apart, she wants to do.

In the second, a couple, in a stable relationship, decide to have a baby, but when the woman becomes pregnant a medical problem is discovered. This may be a threat to the mother's life if she continues with her pregnancy or it may be some defect in the foetus that will seriously impair the quality of life of the resulting child. Here the debate arises not as the result of a conflict (or potential conflict) between morality and self-interest but between different moral considerations.

Although there is space to explore the issues only very briefly, I want to examine the guidance that might be provided, in these two cases, by our two moral theories. Take the first case. What does utilitarianism have to say? The course of action that is morally right is the course of action that maximizes happiness. Thus, the woman can take account of her own wishes – perhaps she is still studying at university, perhaps she has a promising career, perhaps she has children and does not want any more – but she has also to consider how others are affected. What will be the consequences for the man who fathered the child, her parents, her friends, her other children (if she has any), her colleagues at work, and, of course, the unborn baby?

The issue with regard to the unborn child turns on whether merely being alive is a positive benefit, irrespective of what life is like, or whether the only benefit in being alive is that it provides the opportunity for happiness. Even if the latter is the case, then assuming the financial and social situation of the woman is near to the mean for the Western world, her extra child can be expected to add to the sum total of happiness. Against this can be set the idea that, if happiness is the satisfaction of preferences, then, since the baby has no preferences (other than, perhaps, the avoidance of pain), abortion is neutral from the baby's point of view. Just how helpful it will be to the woman to consider the question in utilitarian terms, I will leave to the reader to judge. It is certainly not possible to say, without knowing the particular circumstances, the conclusion that will be arrived at. It is possible that the woman will not be able to arrive at any conclusions as to what is morally right since she will be unable to assess the consequences.

Will she be any better off appealing to deontological ethics? There is the potential for a much sharper contrast between what she might want to do and what she ought to do. The potential existed with utilitarianism, but there, what she wanted was at least a factor in determining what she should do. Here, what she wants carries no weight at all. She must not consider the consequences at all but only the sort of action she is proposing to carry out and whether this sort of action is morally permissible.

It has been suggested that, in having an abortion, a woman is committing murder. Since murder is wrong, having an abortion must also be wrong. Several aspects of this argument can be questioned. If abortion really is committing murder then abortion is wrong, but this is because 'murder' does not simply describe an action; it also condemns it as wrong. 'Murder' has an evaluative as well as a descriptive meaning. In order to know that abortion is murder, we must already have judged that abortion is wrong. Thus we have begged the question we were trying to answer by comparing abortion with murder. If we are not to beg the question, we should compare abortion with killing an adult human being. The conclusion that having an abortion is wrong does not now follow automatically, since it has not been established that killing an adult human being is always wrong. There are cases, such as killing in self-defence, which most would think were not wrong, and others, such as euthanasia, capital punishment and acts of war, where the morality of killing is disputed. Thus we see two gaps in the argument to show that abortion is wrong. The first is the gap between terminating a pregnancy and killing an adult human being. The second is between killing an adult human being and doing something wrong.

Again, there is not space to deal with these issues fully, and all we can do is point to some of the further moves that can be made. One move is to argue that terminating a pregnancy is not like killing an adult human being, since, whereas an adult human being is a person, a foetus or embryo is not. A person, it is claimed, is self-conscious and, although a foetus may be conscious, it is not self-conscious. The problem with this move is that, if it permits abortion, it also permits the killing of a newborn baby, since this is not self-conscious either.

A different sort of move focuses on the second gap. It looks at when killing an adult human being is permissible and also at the distinction between killing and letting die. Although, in general, we are under an obligation not to kill people, we are not under a similar obligation to save the life of anyone who will die without our intervention. Where we do have this obligation, it is because of some special relationship – say, it is a friend or member of the family or someone to whom we have given a special commitment. By taking steps to prevent getting pregnant, the woman is saying that she does not want a baby and so does not take on any special commitment to support it. In which case if, despite these precautions, she becomes pregnant, she is not obliged to carry the baby to term. Since the foetus is using the woman's body against her wishes, she is justified in having it removed. The consequences of removing the foetus are, of course, that it dies, but the death of the foetus is not what is intended and is therefore not relevant to whether or not the abortion is permissible. An example that is in some ways similar is that in which another person dies for want of bone marrow that only you can supply. Although you do not intend the person to die, you do not wish to undergo the operation to remove some of your bone marrow and, even though this decision will lead to the person's death, you are not obliged to do so.

Clearly there are different views that can be taken on these claims and counter-claims. It may be that one or other of these positions will strike a chord with the woman and lead her to the conclusion that the abortion is permissible or to the conclusion that it is not. She will then have a reason for what she takes to be the morally correct view. What seems equally clear, however, is that, while deontological considerations might enrich her moral reasoning, there is no guarantee it will provide an unequivocal answer, any more than there was with utilitarianism.

The problems are similar when we look at the second situation, where there are medical complications in the pregnancy. Seeking guidance from utilitarianism brings the same practical problem as before: how to assess the consequences of the two alternative actions? Where there is a high probability that the woman will die if pregnancy is continued or a high probability that the baby's life will be one of unrelieved pain, the utilitarian answer may be clear: she should have an abortion. Whether this is the correct answer is, of course, another matter.

In this situation, perhaps Kantianism has greater problems. Where it is the woman's life that is in danger, the choice may be between saving the baby by letting the woman die and saving the woman by killing the baby. If killing is judged worse than letting die then abortion is wrong. Where it is the baby's condition that is the problem, it may be that the sanctity of life means that abortion will be considered wrong for the same reason that euthanasia will be considered wrong. Against this it may be that the child's best interests are served by pregnancy being terminated and that a parent must act in the best interests of the child.

Virtue ethics

Deontological and consequentialist theories, of which Kantianism and utilitarianism are representatives, might appear to exhaust the possibilities when it comes to moral theories: either we consider the action itself, and the obligations that we have to perform or refrain from performing it, or we consider the consequences of the action. However, there is an important moral theory that does not directly consider actions or their consequences at all. This theory is virtue ethics, and it focuses on the character of the moral agent, with actions and consequences entering the scene only indirectly. Earlier in this chapter we considered the meaning of 'good' and, in particular, its meaning when applied to things with functions. To be of a certain kind, capable of carrying out a certain function, is to have certain characteristics, which means there are criteria for being a good example of this function-performing kind. If we suppose that to be morally good is to be a good example of a human being, then we have the basis for criteria for moral goodness. Something like this seems to have been behind Aristotle's moral philosophy: what we should strive to be (and hence, by implication, what is morally good) is a good example of a human being. We should aim to flourish. Now if it is hoped that this will lead, through agreement as to what counts as a flourishing individual, to agreement as to what is morally good, then this hope is liable to be short-lived, for reasons discussed earlier. None the less, this does not invalidate the Aristotelian ethics that developed from this starting point, and it is to this that we shall now turn.

What is a virtue?

For Aristotle, to be a good person is to have a good character, that is, to be generous, brave, just, honest and so on. These different character traits involve predispositions to act in certain ways. However, they involve more than predispositions to act, and this is what has to be captured by the concept of a virtue. Take the virtue of generosity and see how the character of someone possessing this virtue might be different from another person who, although not possessing the virtue, none the less has a similar predisposition to action. A deontologist might decide that generous actions are morally right and that he or she has an obligation to act generously. The recognition of this obligation will produce a similar predisposition to that of a person who possesses the virtue of generosity. When asked for money by someone in need, both respond positively. However, one will respond out of duty, the other out of the goodness of his or her character. Thus the manner of giving will be different; the virtuous person will act spontaneously and warmly whereas the deontologist may deliberate (since there may be other obligations to fulfil) and may give without any warmth (since, in acting out of duty, the person may be acting contrary to what he or she would otherwise want to do). Having the virtue of generosity will also involve having certain emotions. The generous person will take pleasure in giving and will be distressed if they cannot give someone what he or she wants; they may be shocked or angered by ungenerous acts. The deontologist, on the other hand, may take no pleasure in giving – indeed, for Kant, experiencing pleasure in doing the right thing casts doubt on the moral worth of the action. For the deontologist, emotions are simply not relevant.

There is also an important difference between possessing the virtue of generosity and being generous out of habit. Although the generous person may act spontaneously, he or she does not act unthinkingly. To possess the virtue of generosity is to possess the ability to make correct judgements. The person who is habitually generous may give his or her children too much money, so that they do not appreciate its value, or may give when he or she cannot afford to do so. We are inclined to see character traits as having opposites. Thus we see the opposite of being generous is being mean, the opposite of being brave is being cowardly. Aristotle, however, saw a virtue as the mean between two extremes, one extreme being the extreme of deficiency, the other the extreme of excess. Thus, generosity lies between meanness or stinginess (deficiency), on the one hand, and profligacy (excess), on the other. Bravery, or courage, lies between cowardice (deficiency), on the one hand, and foolhardiness or recklessness (excess), on the other. To be virtuous is to possess the ability to make the judgement, in different circumstances, as to where this mean lies. For Aristotle, it was to act rationally, although this is not a matter of applying certain general principles, as it might be for the deontologist.

How do I acquire the virtues?
If courage is a virtue, then cowardice and foolhardiness are both vices. To become good, we must acquire the virtues and shun the vices. Two questions arise in response to this injunction: first, how do I acquire the virtues and second, which character traits are virtuous? Let us consider how we might acquire character traits. This is an important question, since it is commonly supposed that character is the result either of one's genetic make-up or of what takes place in one's formative years, though more likely a combination of both. Whichever, one would not be capable of determining one's own character, although one might be capable of determining another person's character. Aristotle certainly thinks that children should be brought up to be virtuous, that their characters should be moulded by their upbringing. He concedes it is possible that anyone not brought up in the proper way may become irredeemably vicious ('vicious', in this case, being the adjective derived from 'vice'). Assuming, however, that an individual possesses some virtues, or is virtuous to some degree, he or she can acquire virtues or become more virtuous through practice. If one acts generously even when it does not come naturally, then gradually it will become second nature. Of course if, as a psychological theory, this turns out to be false, and if it is the case that we are unable to alter our character, then 'become virtuous' is an empty injunction. Further, since we would not be responsible for our character, we could not be blamed or praised for actions arising out of it. This is a similar problem to that faced by deontological or consequentialist moral theories by the suggestion that people are not able to act freely. However, a person's character may seem less likely to be something the person can control than individual actions. Having raised this problem, let us turn to the one that holds a greater philosophical interest, namely, what are the virtues?

Determining the virtues

Aristotle produced and argued for a list of virtues. When, in the thirteenth century, Aristotle's moral philosophy became integrated into Christian thought, a different list of virtues was produced. The Christian virtues, for example, include humility, whereas Aristotle would no doubt think that the virtue lies between the deficiency of humility and the excess of arrogance. He extols the virtue of munificence, which, although not the opposite of humility, is inconsistent with it. Anyone asked nowadays to list virtuous traits would probably produce a further set of characteristics. This should not surprise us; the request to produce a list of moral principles would result in a similar diversity. Moreover, the response to the diversity will be the same: give reasons as to why a particular candidate should be included in the list. Let us look at the sorts of reasons that could be given.

True happiness
First, we return to Aristotle and to a concept that plays a particularly important role in his ethics, that of *eudaimonia*. There are several possible translations of this Greek word: happiness, well-being, flourishing, none of which captures the meaning of the original. First, it is something that is possible only for rational beings and so, although plants and animals can flourish, they cannot achieve *eudaimonia*. 'Happiness' captures some of the meaning but carries with it an association of pleasure that is not in *eudaimonia*. A closer translation might be 'true happiness', which carries with it the idea that one can feel happy and think one is happy without having achieved true happiness. The problem, however (apart from the clumsiness), is that we may still feel that, in the way that different things make different people happy, we each find true happiness in a different way, particular to our interests and personality. If this is so, and if being virtuous is seen as the way to achieve *eudaimonia*, then there will not be a single set of virtues that will suit everyone. One possibility is to try to refine our concepts of virtues and *eudaimonia*, or true happiness, in tandem.

Another strategy is to say that the virtues are the character traits of a good person. We may be able to recognize, in an immediate, non-analytical way, that certain individuals are good and from this produce a list of virtues. Thus we may hold up, as exemplars, Christ or Ghandi or Mother Theresa. However, we might think that no human being (with the possible exception of the son of God, were there to be such a person) is perfect and that we still have to judge which character traits of, say Ghandi, are virtues and which are human failings.

A virtue benefits its possessor
So let us turn, finally, to the sort of discussion we might enter into when determining the virtues. First, we have to deal with a problem as to what sorts of reasons we can accept. If our goal in life is

eudaimonia or true happiness, and if the virtues are the route to this goal, then a virtue would seem to be something that benefits its possessor. In which case, saying that it benefits a person to possess the character trait X would be a reason for saying that X is a virtue. This would seem to be in the spirit of Aristotle's ethics. However, it runs counter to our contemporary view, which is that, if moral goodness benefits its possessor, it does so only incidentally. In trying to determine *moral* virtues we are trying to determine morally good character traits and not character traits that are good for the person concerned. Despite this, many of the Aristotelian virtues strike us today as morally worth having. This may not be a coincidence. Morality can be seen as a set of rules that enables us to live together in society. If, as Aristotle suggests, we are essentially social animals, then we are more likely to flourish and find true happiness within a society that runs smoothly. It is, of course, possible to get the benefits of society through other people following the rules and get additional benefits by breaking them oneself. However, while this may work in the short-term and for some individuals, it can be argued that it is not the best long-term strategy: one cannot rely on bucking the trend. Some individuals may not suffer from smoking heavily all their lives, but this does not alter the fact that the best way to avoid lung cancer is not to smoke. Let us go along with the claim that virtues benefit their possessor, that virtues make their possessor a good human being and that the two features are interrelated.

Consider the arguments that might be advanced for the claim that generosity is a virtue. First, we can see how being generous will be an advantage to the possessor: a generous person will be popular and well liked. Further, being generous to other people will probably result in their reciprocating when you need help from them. As a drawback, there is the possibility that others will take advantage of the generous person, but, remembering that a virtue is the mean between deficiency and excess, if others are exploiting what purports to be generosity, it probably is not. Likewise if one's generosity leaves one impoverished. Second, we can also see how being generous makes one a good human being: those in need benefit from another's generosity. Third, we can see how the two are interlinked.

It might, at this stage, be felt that the above argument is just a little too glib. By introducing this idea of correct judgement, of getting just the right degree of generosity, we ensure that there cannot be an argument against generosity being a virtue. If an apparently generous person does not benefit from his or her generosity, then we can say that he or she was not really generous because they did not judge situations quite right; what may look like generosity was really profligacy or meanness. It might seem, then, that we can argue for any character trait being a virtue just so long as we can find other traits that represent a greater degree and a lesser degree of that character. Thus we might say that greed is a virtue; indeed it is one of the virtues that drives our society. It is possible to be too greedy just as it is possible to be not greedy enough. Someone who is not greedy enough will not push themselves to get more, whereas someone who is too greedy will push themselves too much.

It could be that this shows the vacuity of virtue ethics, but, before rushing to this conclusion, let us exercise the virtue of judiciousness. First, we might note that the concept of greed already carries with it the suggestion of excessiveness, of wanting more than one's share. We can, of course, conceive of something that is more excessive, that is, excessive greed, but this seems no more than a device. Thus it may be that our language already incorporates the Aristotelian idea of a virtue being a mean between excess and deficiency. Second, we may note that, when circumstances change, the mean position between the two extremes may also change. What, in a period of scarcity, may seem like greed, may, in a period of abundance, be overly parsimonious or frugal. Claiming that greed is a virtue may be no more than a dramatic way of expressing the need for a different response to changed circumstances.

Before leaving virtue ethics, let us consider the contribution it might make to the debate between the Kantian and the utilitarian on punishment and abortion. In the case of punishment, the relevant virtue is that of justice, of treating people fairly in the way that they deserve. Thus, virtue ethics appears to side with the Kantian. However, justice is not the only virtue that might be involved. There is the virtue of being generous, which might lead one to give an offender another chance, of compassion, which might lead one to take account of the offender's upbringing and social circumstances, of tolerance and so on. Of course, all these virtues must be exercised to the right degree: being compassionate is fine, but one must not be over-sentimental; it is right to be tolerant but not too easy-going. Thus, the argument as to whether to punish someone and to what degree is enriched by the considerations of virtue ethics, but it is difficult to see how it can arrive at a general answer to the question of punishment. This should not be surprising since, as we have said, the focus of virtue ethics is not actions but character. Similar considerations apply to the discussion on abortion.

Choosing between theories

Having looked at these attempts to provide a theoretical underpinning for our moral reasoning, we need to take a step back to see where that leaves us. None of the theories, Kantianism, utilitarianism or virtue ethics, is a complete, fully worked-out theory. These are not theories that can be taken off the shelf and used as instruction manuals. Each theory provides no more than a framework within which to discuss a moral issue, along with some exemplar arguments; a framework that may or may not be appropriate. There are various suggestions as to how to make the choice between moral theories, but none is very promising.

First, there is the suggestion that the theory whose results most closely accord with our moral intuitions, that is, with our views of right and wrong that we have prior to any theorizing, should be the one that is accepted. This suggestion has a number of drawbacks. Our moral intuitions are the product of all sorts of influences: religious beliefs, cultural traditions, local customs – not to mention the indirect effect of the theories themselves. There is nothing to say that our moral intuitions are a touchstone of moral truth and hence that they can provide the basis for choosing between different theories. It may seem that we can derive moral rules from our intuitive moral judgements in the way that we can derive rules of grammar from our intuitive linguistic utterances, but the analogy is a tenuous one. There is, for example, a much greater agreement as to which linguistic utterances are grammatically correct than as to which moral judgements are correct. Disputes over whether an utterance is grammatical can be settled arbitrarily in the way that moral disputes cannot. Part of the motivation for a moral theory, but not for a grammatical theory, is the unreliability of individual judgements. A moral theory aims to put morality on a sounder basis in order to be able to adjudicate between conflicting intuitions. There is the danger of circularity if we try to use our moral intuitions to distinguish between theories, although this circularity should not be seen as 'vicious'. Goodman describes the process of justification as 'the delicate one of making mutual adjustments' between general rules and accepted particular instances (*Fact, Fiction and Forecast*, 64). (A similar idea arises in the next chapter with Rawls's notion of 'reflective equilibrium'.)

Second, we could choose a theory according to the grounds on which it bases moral judgements. Thus, Kantianism assumes that morality is based on the actions of a perfectly rational being, the choice of such actions being unaffected by feelings or emotions and carried out regardless of consequences. Utilitarianism assumes that morality is based on bringing about the right consequences, namely, ones in which happiness is maximized. Virtue ethics assumes that we should each try to become a good person, able to exercise rational judgement in different situations. Although this seems like a straight-forward choice, it is one that cannot be made without seeing the logical consequences of these assumptions. In other words, we need to exam-ine the particular moral judgements that flow from the assumptions before choosing between assumptions. What we find is that, for some issues, in some types of circumstances, one set of the assumptions seems better, but for other issues, in other circumstances, the other set of assumptions seems better. We also find cases of moral dilemma in which the dilemma arises precisely because of the opposing pull of con-sequences, duties and virtues.

The next proposal is to develop a theory that combines the theories. Unfortunately, if we take the idea of a moral theory seriously, it is not a matter of having theories available so that we can pick and choose between them as it suits us. A moral theory was meant to remove arbitrary choices or choices based on subjective considerations. Hence, if we are to combine the theories, we need some procedure for deciding which one to use and when. This faces us with a familiar problem, that of trying to choose which theory is better. As before, the only available criterion seems to be our intuitions, and these do not provide a good basis for choice.

If morality is simply a matter of reasoning, and if reasoning is a process that can be emulated by computers, then it will be possible to produce some formal procedure, some terminating algorithm, to arrive at moral answers. For some, only a formal procedure for arriving at a decision can guarantee objectivity, and the inability to find such a procedure would be confirmation of the subjectivity of morality. Instead, moral theories can be seen as partial models based on different simplifying assumptions. Sometimes these models will give a good fit, sometimes they will not, sometimes it will not be clear.

What does moral reasoning consist in? What do we do when faced with a moral dilemma? We think about the problem and try to weigh all the different considerations. If we are fortunate to know such a person, we may seek advice from someone whose understanding, wisdom and moral integrity are greater than our own. Most of us talk about the problem with other people, who are not necessarily our moral superiors, in order to find out how they *feel* about it and what they *think* about it. Sometimes talking about it is a matter of externalizing one's internal thought processes and clarifying them in the process. Sometimes it is a matter of finding out how other people see the situation, in order to get it into perspective and see whether we are giving undue weight to certain aspects.

It would be wrong for philosophy to oversimplify the complexities of the human situation. Equally, though, we need some way of exploring and managing these complexities. The sorts of considerations discussed above certainly enrich the moral debate even if they do not produce definitive answers.

Summary

- Moral judgements have been seen as no more than statements of personal preference. On this view, there are no real moral disagreements between people. Emotivism offers a more sophisticated view, that moral judgements express attitudes. Moral debate, however, becomes an exercise in rhetoric aimed at changing attitudes, and reasons are not viewed as good or bad but merely as effective or not effective.
- Although the descriptive meaning of 'good' can often be read off from the function of what is being commended, this does not seem to help when applied to people. People, as such, do not have a function. Nor does the notion of flourishing seem to provide an independent way of determining moral goodness.
- There are two versions of egoism that have the potential to undermine morality in two different ways. Psychological egoism claims that we act only out of self-interest and so it is impossible for us to act morally.
- Ethical egoism claims that we ought to act out of self-interest. Kant argues that it can be disqualified as a moral theory on logical grounds, but it is not clear that he is successful.
- For Kant, the perfect moral agent is a purely rational being who acts in accordance with reason alone and who is not influenced by feelings and emotions. However, doubts can be raised as to whether a purely rational being has any interests and hence whether a purely rational being has any reason to act.

- Utilitarianism is a consequentialist moral theory that judges actions according to whether they maximize happiness. Unless indirect consequences are taken into account, the moral judgements generated by utilitarianism can differ significantly from our moral intuitions. Although actions have indirect consequences, these are more difficult to determine than direct consequences.

- Virtue ethics considers neither actions themselves nor their consequences directly. It starts with the moral agent, who is rational, like Kant's moral agent, but not purely rational. The possession of a virtue involves acting rationally, but it also involves acting in a certain way and having certain feelings and emotions. However, it is difficult to determine virtuous characteristics and even more difficult to give a general account of how someone in possession of a particular virtue will behave.

- Moral theories are attempts to systematize the moral decision-making process. Kantianism, utilitarianism and virtue ethics use examples of different forms of moral arguments and emphasize different elements in moral issues. Their strength, and weakness, is that they concentrate on one type of feature of the moral landscape, such as consequences or duties, and so oversimplify.

Questions raised

- Reasons and emotions play a part in making moral judgements, but can we say what should be the balance between the two? Can morality take account of feelings and emotions and yet still be sufficiently objective?

- How do we characterize the nature of a moral judgement? Can we do this on purely logical or grammatical grounds or do we need to specify a particular sort of content?

- How do we resolve moral dilemmas? Are there some moral dilemmas for which there is no right answer? If we are unable to formalize the procedure for arriving at an answer, does this mean that our judgements are not backed up by reason?

- Philosophy can enrich moral debate, for example, by sharpening the reasoning employed, but can it hope to make a more telling contribution? Can philosophy tell us what is right?

9 Political Issues

Introduction

We begin by examining the questions as to whether any government is justified in carrying out the measures it does and what such justification could be based on. Governments, of course, claim different powers, and we can draw the distinction between actions that are justified and actions that are not. Anarchism, however, claims that no action of government is justified.

It is thought that a government is not justified in exercising absolute power. One limitation on the power which it is entitled to exercise is the obligation it owes to the citizens. One set of obligations arises out of rights the citizens have. We will examine further the concept of a right and the extent to which government may be permitted to overrule these rights.

Two writers who have written recently on the role of the state and the principles on which it should run are Rawls and Nozick. Examining the broad thrust of their arguments will involve discussion of a number of key issues in political philosophy and show some of the areas of current debate.

The legitimacy of government

When an organization such as the Mafia sends around its 'officials' to demand money from the businesses in its patch, this is called a protection racket. Local businesses are coerced into paying money and suffer the consequences if they fail to cough up. On the other hand, when government officials demand money from businesses, this is called taxation. As with protection rackets, businesses are coerced into paying the money and suffer consequences for not doing so. Admittedly, in the Western democracies at least, the consequences of non-payment do not include being beaten up, but they can wreck a person's life just as effectively and deprive him or her of freedom.

A number of suggestions can be made to counter the idea that there is no essential difference between the two cases. First, there is the use to which the money is put. In the case of taxation, the money is put to the service of the community as a whole, whereas protection money just lines the pockets of the local hoods, and those paying the money receive no benefit. No doubt in many cases this suggestion points to a genuine difference, but not necessarily. The gang may provide protection from other gangs; it may look after its own people. The money itself may stay within the local economy and its recirculation may therefore indirectly benefit those from whom it was extorted. Some of it (if only a small proportion) may even be used for supporting worthy causes. In the case of government taxation, on the other hand, the money can be put to uses with which taxpayers disagree, such as funding a nuclear deterrent. It can move out of the local community, perhaps even going in the form of grants to support rival producers elsewhere. Some of it will certainly go in salaries to those working in a bureaucratic structure whose main function is the collecting of more taxes. Taxpayers' money may enable some members of the bureaucracy to enjoy a better life style than many of the taxpayers themselves. Furthermore, despite paying taxes, the taxpayer may not receive the services she or he requires from government. For example, the forces of law and order may not be able to control the local Mafia who are running a protection racket!

A second suggestion is that, when the Mafia demand protection money, the 'small man' has no choice in the matter. A moment's reflection will show that the average taxpayer is in a similar situation. Although there are appeals procedures for those who think they are being taxed unfairly and there are published guidelines that set out tax liabilities, it is the government that dictates these liabilities, and appealing may be to no avail. Further, not all governments are elected democracies and not all governments set much store on even the appearance of fairness.

Third, it may be suggested that, when the government collects taxes this is legitimate, because government has authority, whereas the activities of the Mafia are not backed by the necessary authority and so are not legitimate. If true, this would be an essential difference between the activities of government and the activities of the Mafia, but, before being able to accept that it is true, we need to be able to answer the important question: from what does the authority of government (or, if we do not wish to beg an important question, the authority claimed by and attributed to government) derive? If government does have this authority, and the Mafia does not, then what authorizes government? Is it only certain sorts of government (e.g., democracies rather than totalitarian regimes, governments of one political flavour rather than another, etc.) that are so authorized?

Authority and power

Power

First we must distinguish authority and power, which are separate if overlapping concepts. Power is a causal concept. Having power is having the ability to change things, to get things done. Typically, people who have authority also have power. An officer in the army has authority over the men and women in his or her command and the power to make them risk their lives to capture an enemy position. The judge has authority in the courtroom and the power to send the condemned criminal to gaol. The employer has authority within his or her company and the power to hire and fire workers. The teacher has authority in the classroom and the power to make his or her pupils study.

It is, however, possible to retain the authority but lose some or all of the power vested in this authority. The person might still have the semblance of power but not the power itself. An officer may fear mutiny and so not be able to ask for sacrifices. A judge, blackmailed by the Mafia, may be powerless to prevent a miscarriage of justice. The employer may not dare to sack a worker for fear of the unions. The teacher may be unable to control the pupils. Conversely, it is possible to have power without authority. The ringleader of the mutiny, the Mafia boss who pulls the strings, the shop steward who decides whom the company can hire and fire, the pupils who disrupt the lessons, all exercise power but lack the authority of those whose power they usurp or undermine.

Authority

The situation is complicated by the fact that, although the above figures do not have the authority of those they are replacing, they do have some sort of authority. The ringleader of the mutineers does not have the authority of the commanding officer; the Mafia boss does not have the authority of the judge; the shop steward does not have the authority of the employer; the disruptive pupil does not have the authority of the teacher. Yet the Mafia boss and the shop steward do have authority within their respective organizations. The leader of the mutineers has the authority to speak for the others. Even the disruptive pupil operates with the tacit consent of the other pupils; he or she possesses some form of 'street cred'. This illustrates the point that authority can come about in different ways and the result can be a conflict of authority. When we look more closely at the concept of authority, a distinction must be made between *de facto* and *de jure* authority. Literally, *de facto* authority is actual authority whereas *de jure* authority is rightful or legitimate authority.

De facto authority
When a person has *de facto* authority, the authority has not been invested in him or her. The authority has come with power, yet it is more than power. The Mafia boss may have power over the judge and, through this, power over the legal system, but this does not give him the same authority that the judge has. However, we can imagine a situation in which there is a breakdown of (so-called) legitimate government and where, because of the power he wields, people come

to bring their grievances to the 'godfather'. Through this process, the Mafia boss may acquire a similar authority to that which the judge held previously.

Similarly, the shop steward may have the power to dictate how a firm is run but does not have the authority to run the firm. However, were there to be a successful workers' revolution, which overthrew the (so-called) legitimate government, then the union leader might acquire *de facto* authority to run the company. The leader of a successful coup not only takes over the levers of power but may also rule with *de facto* authority. Although he or she may not, in the eyes of many of the citizens or in the eyes of foreign powers, have any right to govern, it is with this person that others must negotiate.

De jure authority

Legitimate governments, assuming that any exist, are governments having the right to govern; they have *de jure* authority. The question that arises is: in what ways, if any, do governments acquire *de jure* authority? In Europe, in the Middle Ages, kings claimed that their authority to rule came from God. It was believed that the king had authority because he had been appointed by God to carry out God's will. From God came both the right and the duty to rule the state. Obedience was owed to the king not because of his personal characteristics but because of his position. The authority of the king was taken to be supreme, with the obedience of the king's subjects not being provisional on what the king did or refrained from doing.

The suggestion that rightful authority comes from God is clearly not something that nowadays is universally accepted. Even those believing in God may not think that God is the source of *de jure* authority. Hobbes (1588–1679), an important figure in political philosophy, argued that the authority of the king rested upon his ability to provide security to his people. A state of nature, claimed Hobbes, is a state in which every man is an enemy to every man and hence one in which the life of man is 'solitary, poore, nasty, brutish and short' (*Leviathan*, 186). The only way to avoid such a state is for a group of people to grant to a single person, the king, the authority and the power to rule absolutely. Thus, unlike in the previous case, the king's authority comes from his subjects who raise him up above themselves, not from God, and his obligation is to his subjects, not to God. To our way of thinking, however, Hobbes grants too much authority to the king. He supposes that the citizens of a state have no rights, since their rights have been freely given up in return for security.

Anarchism

Before considering more modern alternatives to these views as to how authority is acquired by the ruler of a state, let us consider a more radical alternative, namely that the sort of authority we are considering cannot be acquired at all. Clearly rulers and governments do exist with the authority to rule, but the suggestion to be considered is that this authority is, in every case, a *de facto* authority; people acquiesce in being governed, but this acquiescence does not provide those who govern with the right to govern. Their authority is not *de jure* because no one *could* be given the right to carry out the actions that governments invariably do carry out. Such a view is termed 'anarchism'.

There are various objections to anarchism that proceed along the lines that it is impractical and idealistic and that it would not work because it assumes human beings are (morally) better than they actually are. Something like this is behind Hobbes's position: unless the king is given supreme authority, and the power that goes with it, he will not be able to impose a condition of peace. Whether or not these criticisms are sound is not the point here. Our concern here is not to advocate the dismantling of nation states, nor are we considering proposals as to whether and, if so, how anarchic arrangements would work. What we are considering is whether any political arrangements other than anarchy can be *justified* and, if so, the justification that can be given. If it is possible to justify a non-anarchic political structure, the form of the justifications will indicate the sorts of governments that are legitimate. We will restrict ourselves to considering two accounts that have had a significant impact on political philosophy, namely the accounts given by Rawls (1921–) and Nozick (1938–2002). Before doing this, however, we need to look more closely at the notion of rights and obligations. We shall also consider, briefly, the idea of a contract theory.

Rights

Natural and legal rights

The notion of a right is important in both moral and political philosophy. Being a British subject is thought to confer on me a number of rights. I have the right to vote in general and local elections. I have the right of redress should goods I purchase be faulty. If arrested I have the right to phone a solicitor and the right of legal representation should it come to a trial. These are rights that I might not have were I a citizen of some other state; they are legal rights. I have these rights first because I qualify as a citizen of a particular state and second because the government of that state has passed certain laws relating to its citizens. In this sense, the rights mentioned above are contingent; I have them through an accident of birth and the vagaries of parliamentary votes. Whether I really am entitled to such rights will depend on the legitimacy of the government and its entitlement to operate a legal system that grants these rights.

In addition to these legal rights, many people would claim that there are other rights, rights that are not dependent on living under a certain legal system or being a member of a particular state. These other rights are termed 'natural rights'. My natural rights might be thought to include such rights as the right to life and the right to be treated justly. The American Declaration of Independence of 1776, which was strongly influenced by Locke's account of natural rights, contains the following statement: 'We hold these truths to be self-evident, that all men are created equal, that they are endowed by their Creator with certain unalienable Rights, that among these are Life, Liberty and the pursuit of Happiness.' Locke, as one might expect from someone living in his time, sees natural rights as God-given. Of more relevance is that he also sees it as *self-evident* that all human beings have these rights.

Not all philosophers would agree with Locke, even to the extent of saying that we have such natural rights, let alone that it is self-evident what our natural rights are. Bentham described as nonsense the claim, made by the French Revolutionary Declaration of the Rights of Man and the Citizen, that there were natural rights. What can be said in support of there being natural rights? Even if we accept that there are natural rights, can we determine just what natural rights we have? The list given by Locke contains the rights to life, liberty and the pursuit of happiness. The list of human rights laid down by the United Nations is much longer and includes the rights to food, shelter, education and so on. Is it possible to justify all these as rights?

The claim that human beings have natural rights is a normative rather than a descriptive claim. That is, it lays down a standard to be complied with rather than describing the situation as it is. If we consider the circumstances in which people find themselves, there are many whose lives are threatened, who do not enjoy liberty and who are not able to pursue happiness. If it is the case that everyone has the rights to life, liberty and happiness, it is clear that having the right to something does not guarantee that one will have it. On the other hand, the fact that a right is not respected does not mean that the right is not possessed. How does having a right make a difference? Although the right to liberty does not guarantee liberty, it does provide a claim against those depriving someone of liberty. At the very least it justifies a claim for reparation. More importantly, it provides grounds for seeking that person's release. If a person has the right to liberty it means that others have an obligation with respect to ensuring that person's liberty.

Rights and obligations

Rights always entail obligations. This does not mean, as many people appear to believe, that if one has a right one must also have an obligation. In general, the rights that a person has impose obligations on *other* people. Although rights generate obligations, this does not mean that all obligations arise out of rights. Friendship, for example, imposes certain obligations. I have an obligation to help a friend when he or she is in need, and if I did not do so, I would not be much of a friend. None the less, my friend has no right to such help from me. On the other hand, if I go into business with a friend, for which purposes a contract is drawn up requiring that I provide assistance should certain events occur, then the friend has a right to this assistance and I have obligations over and above any obligations of friendship.

In cases where an obligation involves a right, failure to fulfil the obligation constitutes unjust treatment. In cases where no right is involved, there is no injustice in failing to carry out the obligation, whatever else is wrong with this. Failing to help a friend is not, in itself, acting unjustly, although it may well be acting meanly, selfishly or callously.

Thus rights are entailed by obligations of justice. When someone has a right, others are obliged by considerations of justice to treat that person in a certain way. Further, justice is not simply a matter of what is required by law. If it were, then it would make no sense to try to determine whether or not the law was just. The claim that there are natural rights amounts to saying that there are obligations of justice that are independent of the laws of any particular society. This does not seem an extravagant claim, although the extent of such obligations is a matter for further discussions.

The state of nature

Legal rights are conferred on a person by the state of which he or she is a member. Natural rights, should they exist, are not dependent on being a member of any particular state. It is a useful theoretical device to suppose that natural rights are the rights a person possesses living in what has been termed a state of nature. Sometimes philosophers have referred to a state of nature in such a way as to suggest that they are talking about an actual state of affairs, existing in prehistorical times. However, the importance of the concept of a state of nature does not depend on its being a factual account of some period in the past but on whether it enables us to reach a clear understanding of the different ways in which rights can arise.

Locke envisaged a state of nature as one in which people are governed by the laws of nature. However, he thought that the law of nature placed obligations on people and that these obligations are discovered by reason. On the other hand, Hobbes's view, as we have seen, is that nature is 'red in tooth and claw', and that in a state of nature everyone is at war with everyone else. Without the constraints of society, we would all be driven by greed and fear. Not only does this mean that life would, generally, be unpleasant, it also means that there would be no natural rights. For Hobbes, the only obligation a person has is to himself or herself. Rights, such as the right to life, arise only when we voluntarily renounce individual power.

Rousseau (1712–1778) describes the state of nature in terms reminiscent of a romantic idyll, a state in which men were noble savages, a state to which, if only it were possible, we should return. A significant feature of his account is that, in this state of nature, human beings do not possess the full range of what we think of as human emotions. He suggests that the primitive savage is motivated by two things, self-preservation and also compassion, which should not be seen as something moral or virtuous but just a brute fact about humans. A human being in a state of nature can show compassion towards another human being just as an animal will show 'compassion' for another animal by licking its wound or sharing food with it. The compassion of the savage should be seen, like self-preservation, as a cause of a certain type of behaviour and not as a reason for behaving in a certain way.

Although Rousseau is inclined to describe the state of nature in romantic terms, in other ways his account is more perceptive than that of Hobbes. Hobbesian man in a state of nature is vicious, that is, has vices, but lacks virtue. Rousseau, on the other hand, suggests that we cannot describe the 'noble savage' in moral terms at all, any more than it would be appropriate in the case of animals. The implication is that a whole range of emotions must be in place before moral judgements are applicable. These emotions can arise only within society. The state of nature does not provide scope for them to arise. There is, therefore, a sense in which human beings in a state of nature are not fully human.

Humans are essentially social animals

A similar conclusion was reached by Aristotle, although by a very different process. Aristotle maintained that a human being was essentially a social animal and that it was only within society that it was possible for humans to realize their full potential. One conclusion to draw from these discussions about the state of nature is that natural rights, if they exist, are independent of the laws of any particular society, although they can operate only within the context provided by society. The claim that there are natural rights is the claim that we have certain obligations of justice towards other people no matter what legal requirements society places on us. Obligations arising from natural rights are a feature of *any* human society.

Social contract theory

One way in which social obligations can be set up is through a social contract. Thus Locke imagines the situation in which 'any number of men, in the state of nature, enter into society to make one people' (*Second Treatise on Civil Government*, VIII.89). They do this by resigning what Locke calls their 'executive power of the law of nature', that is, their entitlement to defend their natural rights. The function of the contract is to authorize those who are to run society, that is, the government, to carry out measures that will both preserve the natural rights a person has and also improve his or her condition, compared with being in a state of nature. Thus Locke envisages a social contract granting authority to the government through putting obligations on the citizen but also imposing obligations on the government towards the citizens. The laws framed by the government must build on and develop the natural rights each citizen already has.

As with the idea of a state of nature, the drawing up of a social contract should not be taken as a historical event. What we have here is another device to help us reach an understanding of the nature of our social obligations. The idea behind the social contract theory is that the obligations imposed on us by society are those to which we would freely assent were we to participate in the drawing up of a social contract. Locke sees people born into a society as *in effect* signing up to a contract; they give implicit consent to the pre-existing arrangements of that society. The authority of government stems from a hypothetical contract that is endorsed by the individuals who constitute society. The assumption is that a hypothetical contract that receives implicit support can have the same effect as an actual contract that grants authority and is equally binding on those who are party to it.

Rawls

The veil of ignorance

Rawls, in his influential book *A Theory of Justice*, takes the idea of a social contract as a starting point for developing a conception of justice. He acknowledges that society exists for the mutual benefit of its members (they should be better off living in a society than not) but also that there is inevitably a conflict of interests between the different members of the society, with each trying to increase her or his share of those benefits. The solution to this conflict of interests, according to Rawls, is a set of principles, the principles of social justice, which will regulate the society by determining how the benefits and burdens are to be shared out fairly.

Can we assume that society will automatically regulate itself in such a way that the principles followed are just? For Rawls, the answer must be 'no', because some members of a society will have more power than others and will use this power to skew the principles to their own advantage. The only way that a person will agree to a set of just principles is by ensuring that considerations of his or her own particular interests are not allowed to affect the choice made. The theoretical device that Rawls uses he calls a 'veil of ignorance'. Once behind this veil of ignorance, a person no longer knows his or her interests and so is not able to choose principles that will advance those interests. Rawls sets out to describe the set of principles that he thinks would result from rational beings making their choice from behind a veil of ignorance.

Now, in order to make this metaphor of a veil of ignorance do some work, it is necessary to spell out exactly the nature of the ignorance and how it prevents a distortion of the choice of principles. Rawls argues that the veil of ignorance must conceal from the person what natural aptitudes he or she might have, together with his or her place in society. More than this, it must conceal from a person his or her conception of the good, how prone he or she is to taking risks and how liable to being optimistic or pessimistic. It must conceal from him or her the particular nature of his or her own society and the generation to which he or she belongs. What can be known, however, are general facts about human society and human psychology.

Game theory

Rawls draws heavily on game theory and, in particular, on the concept of a maxi-min strategy to arrive at the principles that a rational being would choose from behind the veil of ignorance. Some of the relevant principles of game theory can be illustrated by considering one version of the prisoner's dilemma. It involves two people who are being interrogated separately on suspicion of having committed a crime, the punishment for which is eight years in prison. Each has to decide whether to say nothing or to give evidence against the other. If both say nothing, the lack of evidence is such that they will be convicted for a lesser offence with, say, one year in prison. If, on the other hand, both give evidence against the other, then they will receive five years in prison. If one gives evidence and the other keeps quiet, then the one who gave evidence will get off scot-free while the other will get the full eight years.

This is represented by table 1, which shows the punishment that prisoner A will receive depending on what both prisoners A and B do. (A similar table can be drawn up to show the length of sentence B would receive.) What is the rational thing to do in such circumstances? If we consider the prisoners as constituting a team that has the aim of minimizing the total time spent in prison, then this will be achieved if they both keep quiet. However, looking at it from A's point of view, A is always better off giving evidence. If B keeps quiet, A will get off

Table 1

Length of sentence A receives		A	
		Stays quiet	Gives evidence
B	Stays quiet	1 year	0 years
	Gives evidence	8 years	5 years

free rather than serve eight years, whereas, if B gives evidence, A will get five years instead of eight years. The rational strategy for A is to minimize the harm that B can do by making the worst outcome as good as possible. If A stays quiet, his worst outcome is eight years in prison, but if A gives evidence, his worst outcome is only five years in prison. This strategy, of maximizing the minimum outcome, is the so-called maxi-min strategy. The maxi-min strategy is to give evidence. Of course, the problem is that, if both A and B reason like this, then both will give evidence and so both will serve five years. This outcome is worse for both of them than if they had both kept quiet.

We might try to extrapolate such a result to society as a whole where, instead of prisoners trying to avoid long sentences, we have individuals trying to maximize the benefits they obtain from society. Such extrapolation is not without problems, but one conclusion that might be drawn is that people should not be left to make free choices, since individuals will try to make their worst outcome as good as possible and so society as a whole will be worse off. Instead we should have institutions that force people to co-operate. This conclusion goes counter to what a liberal such as Nozick would claim, which is that people should be left to act in their own interests and that the results of doing this are as if there were an invisible hand at work ensuring that society as a whole benefits.

Two principles of justice

Rawls argues that there are two functions for the principles of justice. The first function is to assign basic rights and duties, the second to determine the distribution of benefits and burdens. He assumes that these two functions can be kept separate and that the principle relating to the first function takes priority over the principle relating to the second. In other words, there should be no pay-off between basic rights and the distribution of benefits. The first principle states that each person has an equal right to the basic liberties. These basic liberties include the freedom to vote and to hold political office, freedom of speech, freedom of conscience, freedom from arbitrary arrest, freedom to own personal property. The second principle, which Rawls terms the 'difference principle', introduces a different conception of equality. It does not guarantee equality of wealth but holds that, if there is to be any deviation from an equal distribution of wealth, it must be to everyone's advantage.

Rawls does not object to inequalities as such. Inequalities can exist so long as the poorest are better off than they would be if everyone were equal. Imagine starting from a position of economic equality, that is, one where everyone has equal wealth. A process that results in some people being better off and others worse off than before would not be socially just, even if the gains were greater than the losses. On the other hand, a process that makes some people better off than others will be justified if the effect is also to improve the position of the worst-off section of society. In other words, increasing the inequality between different sections of society is permitted if in doing so we also increase the minimum level. This is the maxi-min strategy at work. Rawls acknowledges that people need incentives and that entrepreneurs and risk-takers not only give themselves a relative advantage over other people, they may also create wealth and so benefit society as a whole. He suggests that it would be rational for a person choosing from behind the veil of ignorance to promote institutions that allow such wealth creators to operate, providing that their activities resulted in the poorest also being better off. Such a society, he is saying, would be a just one, even though it might contain gross inequalities of wealth.

Of course, if economic theories which advocate the beneficial effects of such wealth creators turn out to be false (that is, inequalities always make someone worse off compared with the state where everyone is equal) then a society with inequalities in wealth would be an unjust one. Whether or not this is the case could, in principle, be determined from behind the veil of ignorance, since the facts of individual and social psychology are not obscured by it. In other words, those choosing from behind it should be in a position to judge which inequalities would, and which would not, benefit everyone.

Objections

Are the principles that Rawls arrives at really the principles of a just society, as he claims? And, if they are, is a society operating with such principles justified in imposing constraints on its citizens in order to achieve such ends? There are a number of objections that can be raised to Rawls's arguments. First, take the process by means of which Rawls thinks he can arrive at principles of justice. Different people might well start with different ideas about the original condition, that is, the condition of rational beings trapped behind the veil of ignorance. As a result, they could end up with different principles. Rawls disputes this because he thinks that these initial differences would not matter, since, by reflecting on the principles that result from the initial assumptions and testing them against our convictions as to what is just, there will be a convergence of views. Where there is a discrepancy between principles arising from different accounts of the original condition and different convictions of what is just, we 'can either modify our accounts of the initial situation or we can revise our existing judgements' (*A Theory of Justice*, 20). A change in one, Rawls argues, will feed back to produce a change in the other. By reflecting, in this way, on the original condition and our convictions of justice, we will eventually reach a state of what Rawls calls 'reflective equilibrium'. But what guarantee do we have that, when each person reaches such a reflective equilibrium, there will be widespread agreement?

Rawls's assumption is similar to Kant's: that the set of principles arrived at through the exercise of reason will always be the same. There is a difference, in that those in the original condition are not *purely* rational, in Kant's sense, but we can ask of them the same question that we asked of Kant's purely rational beings, namely: do they have any real basis for making choices? We know that our interests influence our choices and that people with different interests may not be able to agree, but, equally, people with no interests (or, what amounts to the same thing, people who do not know what their interests are) might agree on nothing. If, for example, people are in ignorance of their conception of the good, then how do they decide that basic freedoms are more important than happiness? If inequalities of wealth can be justified by the poorest being better off, why cannot the same justification be used for inequalities of basic rights?

Those in the original position are supposed to have access to 'the general facts about human society', 'the principles of economic theory', 'the basis of social organisation and the laws of human psychology' (*A Theory of Justice*, 137). Yet many of these 'facts' and theories are disputed by those whose political views differ. We may hypothesize that, if those in the original position were provided with the relevant facts and theories, they would arrive at just principles, but this does not enable *us* to arrive at just principles. We are not actually in the original position but are trying simply to specify what it would be like. As such, we do not have these facts and theories, and so each of us (including Rawls and other political philosophers) has to reason from what each thinks are the relevant facts and theories. It is difficult to see how, with different economic theories, different people are going to converge on the same principles of justice. We are not simply talking about different starting materials being fed into the same piece of machinery which is designed to iron out such difference, but of different starting materials being fed into different pieces of machinery, each being biased towards different outcomes.

Nozick

Historical versus end-result principles

Rawls's conception of justice is not the only possible one, as we see when we consider Nozick's criticisms of Rawls. According to Nozick, when Rawls derives his principles of distributive justice, one of the assumptions he makes is that no one has any prior claim on the benefits to be distributed. Rawls assumes, or so Nozick suggests, that the benefits to be distributed are like manna from heaven. Nozick describes Rawls's principles of justice as 'end-result' principles, meaning they are principles that aim at achieving a certain end result. In deeming a certain distribution of benefits to be just, Rawls takes no account of the distribution of benefits that previously existed. Those from whom benefits are removed, in pursuit of a more just distribution, are treated as having no claim on the benefits, since the distribution as a whole was unjust. Nozick's view is that there are differential entitlements and that therefore Rawls's end-result principles of justice are inappropriate. Nozick contrasts end-result principles of justice with what he calls historical principles of justice. A historical principle determines the justice of a distribution in relation to past circumstances that might create different entitlements to the goods being distributed.

At this point we need to introduce the idea of the structure of a distribution. One distribution of benefits differs from another if at least one person receives different benefits in the two distributions. It is possible, however, for different distributions to have the same pattern of distribution, in which case the different distributions are structurally identical. Suppose that, in distribution A, Peter gets £6 and Paul gets £4, whereas in distribution B, Paul gets £6 and Peter gets £4. Since each receives different amounts in the two distributions, A and B are different distributions. None the less, the pattern is the same: £6 to one person, £4 to the other. This means that distribution B is structurally identical to distribution A.

According to Nozick, end-result principles determine only the structure of distributions so that different distributions that are structurally identical appear as equally just. However, Nozick argues, different distributions may not be equally just even though they are structurally identical. Using a historical principle, it is not only the pattern of the distribution which is important but also *who* receives *what*. Thus, if I owe £6 to Paul and £4 to Peter, then distribution B will produce a just distribution of my £10, whereas distribution A, although structurally identical, will not. The reason for one distribution being just and the other unjust is that the two recipients have different entitlements. This difference in entitlements is dependent on past events, in this case, say, Peter and Paul lending me different sums of money.

Nozick appeals to another example to make the same point, namely a set of exam results received by a group of students. There is no structural difference between awarding grades according to the marks actually scored and awarding the same set of grades in the reverse order, with the top student receiving the grade previously awarded to the bottom student and so on. An end-result principle would not distinguish between these two distributions and both would be deemed equally just. However, despite the structural identity, Nozick argues that the second distribution is unjust, since students are entitled to a grade that represents how well they performed in the exam.

The nature of the veil of ignorance, behind which Rawls places those in the original position, ensures that entitlement considerations cannot enter into the principles of distributive justice. Now it may be that, when it comes to the distribution of the benefits and burdens of society, there are no entitlements, in which case Rawls's procedure escapes Nozick's criticism. For example, it could be argued that there is a sense in which no one *deserves* a better exam grade than anyone else. Inequalities in ability and diligence are distributed at random and so to award benefits on the basis of this random distribution is unjust.

Property

What is the case that Nozick makes for historical principles of distribution being more just than end-result principles? The crucial concept Nozick relies upon is that of property or, the more general expression used by Nozick, holdings to which a person is entitled. Some of the goods of a society, he claims, already belong to members of that society, and it would be unjust to take these goods away even if redistribution resulted in what would otherwise, from the point of view of the structure of the distribution, be a preferable state of affairs.

Even if a distribution of goods is achieved that, in accordance with end-result principles, is just, there is the problem of maintaining this distribution. In particular, what is to stop people giving away what they have? If this is not prevented, then the distribution may be replaced with one that, again according to end-result principles, is unjust. It has been said that if you gave everyone in the country £100 this afternoon, 10 per cent of the population would have it all by teatime tomorrow. Even if this is an exaggeration, we are certainly familiar with the creation of gross inequalities through the free actions of individuals. Football players and pop stars, for example, become very rich because a large number of people freely give them money. Admittedly, those making donations receive something in return, but there is no guarantee, and little likelihood, that the new distribution will satisfy end-result requirements for a just distribution. Hence, to maintain a just distribution, the state must constantly interfere to prevent people giving away their benefits. We might ask by what authority the state can stop people freely giving away that to which they are entitled. Such authority would imply that individuals were not entitled to dispose of their benefits as they wish, which is to say that there would be no such thing as property. If something is not mine to give away then it is not really mine.

Entitlement
For Nozick, a distribution of holdings is just if the holdings a person has are the ones to which he or she is entitled. To underpin this claim, Nozick has to provide satisfactory criteria for determining entitlement.

His suggestion is that a person is entitled to a holding in one of two ways. In the first, the holding previously belonged to no one and has been acquired through a just process. In the second it has been freely transferred to the person by someone else who was entitled to the holding. A further suggestion is that someone might acquire a holding as compensation for an injustice. This leaves Nozick with the task of establishing what is to count as a just process for an original acquisition and what is to count as a free transference.

In the course of the discussion, Nozick makes two assumptions. These are, first, that inequalities in natural abilities are not in themselves unjust and, second, that inequalities resulting from voluntary exchanges, in which those with more abilities make use of them, are also not unjust. Whereas Rawls sees natural abilities as a collective asset, Nozick does not. It is not that Rawls thinks a person should not benefit from his or her natural abilities but that she or he should benefit only if the net result is that everyone else also benefits. Nozick, on the other hand, can see no reason why an equality of assets should be the favoured situation and so does not see why deviations from a situation where there is an equality of assets require some special justification.

The role of the state

A fundamental issue between Nozick and Rawls is that of inequality and the requirements of justice to remove inequality. According to Rawls, inequalities in natural assets and abilities constitute an injustice and so give rise to an obligation to compensate those who lack these benefits. This, if correct, provides the state with the justification to interfere in the lives of its citizens.

Nozick's view, however, is that inequalities in natural assets and abilities do not constitute an injustice and hence do not provide the state with an entitlement (let alone an obligation) to redistribute wealth. In fact, not only does Nozick think that Rawls has failed to demonstrate such an entitlement, he thinks that any such demonstration is impossible since there is no such entitlement. This is an important claim. If he is correct, then many of the activities carried out by all modern-day states, including Western democracies, involve violations of the rights of the individuals who constitute that state. For example, taxation for the purpose of supporting the welfare state is a redistribution that, Nozick claims, involves a violation of rights.

Nozick's criticisms of Rawls fall short of justifying anarchism, since he argues that it is possible to justify the activities of a minimal state but nothing more than this. What he means by a minimal state will be explained shortly, but it is worth noting that, although Nozick thinks that the redistribution of wealth is not a legitimate activity of the state, he does not think we have no reason for helping those less well off than ourselves. Considerations of benevolence suggest there are good reasons for helping others, but moral obligations to help others are obligations that the individual should fulfil voluntarily and not be made to fulfil by the state. Nozick offers no objection to voluntary organizations being set up to counteract these inequalities, nor does he try to suggest that such voluntary organizations will be ineffective. In other words, Nozick is neither advocating nor defending a form of moral egoism in which everyone has to fend for him- or herself. His arguments concern the role of the state and the legitimacy of its actions.

The minimal state

Despite thinking that many of the functions that the state carries out are unjustified and involve violations of basic rights, Nozick none the less argues for a minimal state rather than anarchy. The role of this minimal state is 'limited to the narrow functions of protection against force, theft, fraud, enforcement of contracts, and so on'. This means that, among other things, it 'may not use its coercive apparatus for the purpose of getting some citizens to aid others, or in order to prohibit activities to people for their *own* good or protection' (*Anarchy, State and Utopia*, ix). Yet even this minimal state is, to a degree, redistributive, or at least appears to be redistributive, as some people have to pay for the protection of others. A state that is not redistributive, even to this degree, Nozick calls an ultra-minimal state. Such a state, although it has a monopoly over the use of force, offers protection only to those who are willing to pay for it. Since Nozick argues that, in general, the state does not have the right to redistribute goods (doing so violates rights), he has to provide a justification for the apparently redistributive role of the minimal state.

Nozick's argument to justify the legitimacy of the minimal state is complex, and we cannot go into the details. The starting point for the argument is an account of a set of individuals living in a state of nature, which, as we have previously noted, is not intended as a historical description of a state of affairs that necessarily existed. The aim is to show how, starting from a situation in which individuals are assumed to have no obligations, it is possible to proceed, through a series of stages, each one justified, to the point where we have arrived at a minimal state. The main stages will be outlined, although without attempting to provide full justifications.

First we suppose individuals in a state of nature come together and co-operate for mutual defence. A specialization of roles may develop so that out of this co-operation comes the formation of agencies that protect the rest of the group. The protection offered to other members of the group, who become, in effect, clients of the protective agencies, will obviously include preventing individuals from outside the group committing theft, assault and so on. In addition it must also provide protection from other members within the group. Thus it will be involved in procedures for sorting out disputes between the different members signed up to the agency and will need to enforce its decisions. Although there might, initially, be several protective agencies operating in a particular region, Nozick outlines a plausible scenario whereby these eventually agree a procedure for sorting out disputes between their respective clients (or carve up the geographical area into separate regions), since the alternative is more costly. The result will be a dominant protective agency within a geographical region.

Such a dominant agency would still be viewed as a purely commercial venture and not yet a state. It may offer different degrees of protection to those living within the geographical region where it is dominant, according to how much they wish to pay. More importantly, there may be some people who choose not to pay and who do not receive any protection from the agency. A state, on the other hand, must offer protection to all who live within its geographical boundaries. However, although there appears to be this clear difference between a dominant protective agency and a state, Nozick argues that this appearance is deceptive. To see why, consider two sorts of protection policy that might be offered by the protection agency. The first is an 'economy package', which will protect against theft, assault, etc. The second is a 'fully comprehensive' policy that will include protection against others trying to enforce claims of justice. Since we are supposing that this protective agency has become dominant, only *its* procedures for deciding claims will be acted on and so it will exercise a *de facto* monopoly on the exercise of force within a region. However, the effect of this will be that someone who has a 'fully comprehensive' cover deprives others who are not signed up with the protection agency (referred to as independents) of their right to enforce justice privately as they see fit. Such an infringement of rights, Nozick suggests, should be compensated for. One form this compensation can take is for the protective agency to extend to these independents protection against unjust claims by its members. This might appear to be a redistribution of resources (from those who pay for the fully comprehensive policy to those who pay nothing) but it is in fact an example of compensation and so does not stand in need of justification in the way that genuinely redistributive policies do. By offering some sort of protection to all those within its sphere of influence, the dominant protection agency becomes a minimal state.

Free riders

A problem faced by voluntary organizations that try to provide a certain type of service is being taken for a ride by individuals who receive the benefits without contributing to the costs. For example, the residents of a street may form a voluntary organization to provide street lighting. If all the residents become members, then all will benefit and all will share in the costs. However, if residents are not forced to join the organization, some may avoid the costs yet still benefit from the street being lit. How do the other residents react to such free riders? Some may be prepared to bear the extra costs rather than not receive the benefit at all. Some may themselves opt to become free riders, thus threatening to bring about a complete collapse of the organization. Some may try to exert pressure on the free rider. To force someone to contribute to the costs would, says Nozick, be a violation of rights. Although the term 'free rider' carries a pejorative connotation, everyone has a right to decide how to dispose of his or her own holdings and so whether or not to contribute to the scheme.

The free rider problem might be seen as posing a threat to Nozick's minimal state. Why would anyone pay for protection if he or she can get these services free? Nozick argues that this prospect of free protection as compensation for the loss of rights would not lead people to quit the agency. His reason is that the compensation is limited. He goes on to suggest that, since the agency protects independents only against its own clients, the 'more free riders there are, the more desirable it is to be a client always protected by the agency'. (*Anarchy, State and Utopia*, 113). Thus, Nozick thinks, almost universal participation will be achieved.

The upshot, according to Nozick, is that not only does the dominant protective association fulfil the criteria for being a state (we have passed over the other criterion, which is that of having a monopoly of force), but also the 'moral objections of the individualist anarchist to the minimal state are overcome. It is not an unjust imposition of a monopoly; the *de facto* monopoly grows by an invisible-hand process and *by morally permissible means*, without anyone's rights being violated' (*Anarchy, State and Utopia*, 114–15).

Objections

Objections to Nozick can come from two directions. From one side, those sceptical of the legitimacy of any form of government could argue that Nozick has not succeeded in justifying even a minimal state. From the opposite direction could come the criticism that, without a more convincing account of property entitlement, Nozick has not established his claim that the state violates rights when it attempts to redistribute wealth to obtain greater equality.

Anarchist objections
Nozick has indicated a process whereby the minimal state could arise by morally permissible means. However, he has not shown that any minimal state has to arise in this way, and he certainly has not shown that any existing state arose in this way. Given the emphasis he places on historical processes, even if an example of his minimal state existed, he could not justify the exercise of authority by such a state if it had not actually arisen by morally permissible means. Saying that it could have arisen in this way does not seem to be enough. Thus even a minimal state, were one to exist, might not be justified.

The minimal state may sound attractive to those inclined towards liberalism, but, even if it were possible to bring such a state about, it is doubtful that it would survive. Nozick's invisible-hand processes rely upon people acting rationally out of self-interest. Since this does not call for people to act morally, it might be thought to represent a fairly modest expectation for human decency, but it ignores the fact that people often do not act either rationally or in their own best interests. Indeed, selfishness should perhaps be seen as a fairly harmless vice compared with spitefulness, sloth, greed, envy, vindictiveness, sadism, self-loathing, pride, sexism, racism and so on. The fact that many such vices thrive on irrational behaviour does not seem to lessen their occurrence.

How damaging is this criticism? Even though all states, other than Nozick's minimal state, will violate the rights of their citizens, certain types of governments are preferable to the alternatives that would otherwise exist. Thus, although it may not be possible to justify the power exercised by Western democracies, it is plausible to claim that the alternatives to such democracies would, in practice, involve (and have been seen to involve) far worse violations of rights.

Objections to Nozick's account of property
One of the key concepts in Nozick's argument is that of entitlement to property. Consider the two legitimate ways Nozick gives for acquiring property. The first way is relevant only if no one previously held the property. However, there are few examples of original acquisition. Most property is acquired in the second way, by being transferred from someone else, with present holders of property being a long way down the line from the original act of acquisition. It is, therefore, difficult to determine either that the original acquisition was just or that all subsequent transactions involving the property have been just. Absence of the requisite historical knowledge must cast doubt on entitlement claims that are based on a historical process. To assume that the present distribution of property is historically just runs the risk of legitimizing gross injustices. If we take as our baseline a state of affairs that is grossly unjust, then any future entitlement claims are invalidated. Can a person be entitled to an apartment, even though purchased on the open market by a legitimate legal procedure, if, a century or more ago, the land on which it is built was seized and the original inhabitants dispossessed?

Yet, although there are problems with Nozick's account of property, the notion of property is an important one. Many individuals place a high value on the right of ownership, and a society in which there was no private ownership would be very different from the societies in which the majority of people live today.

Ideologies and arguments

It was suggested at the very beginning of this book that philosophy can be described as conceptual analysis. The debate between Nozick and Rawls has illustrated that significant differences can occur in the analyses of key concepts, for example, the concept of justice. This serves to illustrate the point, often made, that political concepts are 'essentially contested', that is, that there is no agreed understanding of concepts such as *justice*, *rights*, *equality*, *liberty*, *authority*, etc. Many key philosophical, as well as political, concepts might be thought of as 'essentially contested', and this might go some way towards explaining the common perception of philosophy as never providing answers. In the case of political concepts and perhaps, although to a lesser extent, moral concepts, the contests take place outside of, as well as within, philosophical debate. The contests over political concepts occur not just between philosophers, who offer different analyses, but also between any two people who subscribe to different political ideologies.

At the beginning of *Anarchy, State and Utopia*, Nozick makes the following confession: it was with reluctance that 'I found myself becoming convinced of (as they are now often called) libertarian views' (*Anarchy, State and Utopia*, ix). This was because 'many of the people who take a similar position are narrow and rigid, and filled, paradoxically, with resentment at other freer ways of being' and 'most of the people I know and respect disagree with me' (*Anarchy, State and Utopia*, x). In general, many of the political views that people have are not the product of rational argument but are the result of subscribing to a political ideology. What determines the ideology? Marx and Engels argue that different ideologies are associated with different classes and the ideology of a particular class serves the interest of that class. Particular ways of thinking may be more deep-rooted than this. For example, some feminists have argued that the very reasoning that philosophers employ, and which they take to be 'neutral', is actually rooted in masculine ways of thinking and is one of the means used to subjugate women.

If different views on property or justice or the distribution of assets and abilities are put down to differences in class membership, how is political debate possible? If the very structure of an argument is put down to gender bias, how is any discussion possible? Is disagreement a symptom of belonging to the 'enemy camp'? Must we accept that political debate is not possible, unless it is about the finer points of a shared ideology? Must we accept the more radical feminist claims and concede that the possibility of rational debate does not exist?

The claim that a political writer can be dismissed on the grounds that she or he is writing from within an ideology clothes itself in the guise of a contribution to political debate but, in fact, removes the possibility of conducting any such debate. Such claims are peculiarly self-defeating. If the criticism that having a particular ideological grounding vitiates what a person has to say, then this same criticism may also apply to the person making the criticism. Likewise the suggestion that the concepts of a subject vary systematically with the ideological commitments of those employing them applies as much to the concept of 'ideology' as to any other concept, and so the very language in which the criticism is expressed is itself 'contested'. In other words, the criticism deprives itself of the context and structure needed for it to be an effective criticism. This is not so much an argument against the claims of the ideologue (perhaps there can be no such argument) as a warning against accepting them.

Summary

- Governments have *de facto* authority to govern; anarchism claims that they do not, and cannot, have *de jure* authority to carry out the actions they do. This claim needs to be examined carefully, irrespective of whether anarchism offers a practical alternative to our present forms of government.
- It is often claimed that there are two sorts of rights: legal rights, that is, rights enshrined in the laws of a state, and natural rights. Natural rights are those rights (if any) possessed by all human beings, no matter what society they live in.
- The rights of one person entail obligations for other people. These obligations are obligations of justice. There are, however, obligations other than those entailed by rights.
- According to Rawls, the principles of a just society are those that would be chosen by rational people operating from behind a veil of ignorance which concealed from them details such as their social circumstances, their natural abilities, their conception of the good and so on. In practice, Rawls suggests, the procedure for arriving at these principles involves a reflexive equilibrium between our conception of the 'original position' (that is, the position of those operating from behind the veil of ignorance) and our pre-existing convictions of justice.
- Nozick criticizes Rawls for using end-result principles of justice and failing to acknowledge the importance of historical principles of justice, which take account of prior claims. Of two structurally similar distributions of wealth, one may be unjust because it ignores the entitlements of individuals or of sections of society. However, the problem with historical principles is precisely that of determining entitlement.

■ Nozick claims that we can justify a 'minimal state', which offers protection to all those living within its geographical area and provides compensation for infringements of rights by other members of the state, but that it is not possible to justify anything more than this minimal state.

Questions raised

■ Anarchism may not be a very practical political philosophy, but is it the only morally acceptable one? Has Nozick succeeded in justifying at least a minimal role for the state? If so, is a more extensive role also justified, or does this amount to unjustly imposing forced labour on its citizens?

■ Human beings, in general, appear to have a strong urge to own things. Can entitlement to property be given a foundation in historical processes or must we accept that, in principle, these can be overruled by end-result considerations?

■ Can issues about such things as the levels of taxation and spending by governments be settled by arguments and reasoning, or do they, in the end, come down to the particular ideology which a person embraces?

Guide to Further Reading

Authors of works quoted from or referred to in the text appear in capitals.

Chapter 1   The Nature of Philosophy

There are a number of other introductions to philosophy. The following texts are interesting introductions that will complement the present work.

Hollis, M., *An Invitation to Philosophy*, Blackwell Publishers, Oxford, 1985.
This is called an invitation rather than an introduction to philosophy. It does not attempt comprehensive coverage and the approach is an unusual one. It is, however, stimulating and raises issues in an interesting way.

Russell, Bertrand, *The Problems of Philosophy*, Oxford University Press, Oxford, 1980.
This is still a classic introduction to philosophy, although the scope is limited largely to the theory of knowledge and, to a lesser extent, metaphysics.

Scruton, R., *Modern Philosophy: an introduction and survey*, Sinclair-Stevenson, London, 1994.
This is rather long to be considered an introduction, but it deals with a large range of issues in an interesting and often provocative way. The writing is lively and the style engaging.

Chapter 2   The Start of Modern Philosophy:
Descartes' *Meditations*

DESCARTES, R., *Meditations on First Philosophy*, with *Selections from the Objections and Replies*, trans. J. Cottingham, Cambridge University Press, Cambridge, 1986.
The quotations are taken from this translation of the *Meditations*. The book includes an abridged version of the *Objections and Replies*, Descartes' responses to his critics, which were published along with the *Meditations*. It also contains an introduction by Bernard Williams.

DESCARTES, R., *A Discourse on Method*, together with *Meditations* and *Principles*, trans. J. Veitch, J. M. Dent, London, 1994.
This is an alternative translation of the *Meditations* and includes two other works of Descartes and an introduction by Tom Sorrell.
There are a number of books published on Descartes. The following two will give further insight into Descartes' life and work:

Kenny, A., *Descartes: a study of his philosophy*, Random House, New York, 1968.

Williams, B., *Descartes: the Project of Pure Enquiry*, Penguin Books, Harmondsworth, 1978.

Chapter 3   Perception and Reality

AYER, A. J., *The Problem of Knowledge*, Penguin Books, Harmondsworth, 1956.
Although this is now over forty years old, it still provides a good account of the issues discussed in this chapter. In particular, refer to chapter 3 on perception.

BERKELEY, G., *A Treatise Concerning the Principles of Human Knowledge*, in *Philosophical Works*, J. M. Dent, London, 1975.
There are many editions of this, often accompanied by other works. Berkeley's style of writing is lively and concise.

HUME, D., *Enquiries Concerning Human Understanding*, Oxford University Press, Oxford, 1975.
This volume also has Hume's *Enquiries Concerning the Principles of Morals.*

HUME, D., *A Treatise of Human Nature, Book I*, Fontana, Glasgow, 1962.

Again, there are many editions of Hume's *Treatise*. The above consists of just the first book, which deals with the topics considered in the present chapter.

LOCKE, J., *An Essay Concerning Human Understanding*, ed. John W. Yolton, J. M. Dent, London, 1976.
As with Berkeley and Hume, there are many editions. Locke, unlike Berkeley, writes at length and is often repetitive. I would not recommend the beginner trying to read the *Essay* in its entirety but to concentrate on Book II, especially the first few chapters.

Bennett, J., *Locke, Berkeley, Hume: central themes*, Clarendon Press, Oxford, 1971.
There are many books on these three authors. This one concentrates on how they treat the themes of meaning, causality and objectivity.

Chapter 4   Knowledge, Belief and Logic

GOODMAN, N., *Fact, Fiction and Forecast*, Harvard University Press, Cambridge, MA, 1979.
This work contains Goodman's new riddle of induction.

Hodges, W., *Logic*, Penguin Books, Harmondsworth, 1977.
There are a number of introductions to logic. This assumes no previous knowledge and provides many examples.

KANT, E., *Critique of Pure Reason*, trans. Norman Kemp Smith, Macmillan, London, 1963.
There are many different editions. This is not recommended for the beginner.

Kripke, Saul, *Naming and Necessity*, 2nd edn, Blackwell Publishers, Oxford, 1981.
This is not an easy book, but the style is approachable and the content challenging. It is a little off the point of the discussion in this chapter, but it does clarify a number of important distinctions.

KUHN, T. S., *The Structure of Scientific Revolutions*, 2nd edn, University of Chicago Press, Chicago and London, 1970.
A fairly specialist work that is probably of more interest to those who have a scientific background.

O'Hear, A., *An Introduction to the Philosophy of Science*, Clarendon Press, Oxford, 1989.
A useful introduction.

QUINE, W. V. O., *From a Logical Point of View*, 2nd edn, Harper Torchbook, New York, 1963.
This contains a number of papers published by Quine, including *Two Dogmas of Empiricism*, in which he attacks the analytic/synthetic distinction.

Chapter 5   Space, Time, Causality and Substance

EINSTEIN, Albert, *Relativity: the special and general theory*, Methuen, London, 1960.
This, as a subtitle suggests, is a popular exposition by Albert Einstein. Despite this, it contains some mathematics (though largely confined to the appendices). It is demanding but also rewarding.

MACKIE, John, 'Causes and Conditions', *Causation and Conditionals*, ed. Ernest Sosa, Oxford University Press, Oxford, 1975.
In this paper, first published in the *American Philosophical Quarterly* (October 1965), Mackie analyses the claim that a cause of an event is a necessary and sufficient preceding condition. The collection of papers, one of the series of Oxford Readings in Philosophy, contains other interesting papers, including a criticism of Mackie by J Kim.

Ray, Christopher, *Time, Space and Philosophy*, Routledge, London, 1991.
This book deals with some of the topics considered above (such as Zeno's paradoxes, whether space and time are absolute, and relativity), although in much greater depth, as well as other topics (such as time travel). A useful introduction to some issues in the philosophy of science.

Scruton, Roger, *Kant*, Oxford University Press, Oxford, 1982.
A slim, readable introduction to one of the most difficult philosophers. Many of the ideas in metaphysics discussed in the preceding chapter are introduced here.

Sklar, Lawrence, *The Philosophy of Physics*, Oxford University Press, Oxford, 1992.
This covers some of the same ground as Ray, but with greater rigour. It also considers probability in physics and the implications of quantum mechanics. This is not an introductory text, but any efforts made to understand it are well rewarded.

Strawson, Peter F., *Individuals: an essay in descriptive metaphysics*, Methuen, London, 1959.
Strawson characterizes descriptive metaphysics as describing the structure of our thoughts about the world, in contrast to what he calls revisionary metaphysics, which tries to improve this structure. Like Kant, he explores the idea that our conceptual structure is objective.

Chapter 6   The Mind

Churchland, Paul M., *Matter and Consciousness*, MIT Press, Cambridge, MA, 1988.
This is specifically written for those who are not philosophers or experts in artificial intelligence or in neuroscience. It provides a comprehensive introduction to the main issues in the philosophical and scientific debate on conscious intelligence.

DENNETT, Daniel C., *Consciousness Explained*, Penguin Books, Harmondsworth, 1993.
Dennett is his usual provocative self. Here he provides a sustained attack on Cartesian dualism, which he follows up with what he refers to as an empirical theory of the mind.

McGinn, Colin, *The Character of Mind*, Oxford University Press, Oxford, 1992.
According to the preface, this is intended as an introduction to the philosophy of mind. It is, however, not a bland survey of the subject but presents some clear and often contentious views on the mind.

NAGEL, Thomas, 'What is it Like to be a Bat?', in *Mortal Questions*, Cambridge University Press, Cambridge, 1979.
This article, first published in *Philosophical Review* in 1974, has been very influential. It attempts to throw light on the nature of consciousness and the reason why consciousness makes the mind–body problem particularly intractable.

SEARLE, John R., *The Rediscovery of Mind*, MIT Press, Cambridge, MA, 1994.
Searle, like Nagel, thinks that consciousness is the important characteristic of the mental and argues that it has been neglected by materialist accounts of the mind.

Chapter 7   God

ADAMS, Douglas, *Hitch Hiker's Guide to the Galaxy*, Pan Books, London, 1979.
This has no real relevance to the present work but it is amusing!

DAWKINS, Richard, *The Blind Watchmaker*, Penguin Books, Harmondsworth, 1986.
This is popular science rather than a philosophy book but stimulating reading none the less.

Flew, Anthony, *God and Philosophy*, Hutchinson, London, 1966.
The aim of the book is to examine arguments for the existence of God and, through this, to provide an introduction to the philosophy of religion. The tone of the book is captured by one of the remarks on the back cover: 'Splendidly pugnacious . . . the cavalry charge of the secular intelligence'.

Gribbin, John, and Rees, Martin, *Cosmic Coincidences*, Black Swan, London, 1992.
A very readable popular science book. Chapter 10 considers the ways in which the universe is 'tailor-made for man'.

Hick, John (ed.), *The Existence of God*, Macmillan, New York, 1964.
A useful collection of readings, from Plato to twentieth-century philosophers, on the various proofs of the existence of God.

Hume, David, 'Of Miracles', in *An Enquiry Concerning Human Understanding*, 3rd edn, rev. P. H. Nidditch, Oxford University Press, Oxford, 1975.
A short but very influential essay, in which Hume argues that the evidence against the occurrence of a miracle will be outweighed by the evidence in favour of it.

KRIPKE, Saul, *Naming and Necessity*, 2nd edn, Blackwell Publishers, Oxford, 1981.
This was listed in the Further Reading Guide to chapter 4. Here its relevance is with regard to the causal chain theory of names.

Mackie, J. L., *The Miracle of Theism*, Clarendon Press, Oxford, 1982.
Mackie examines all the arguments for the existence of God and sets out his reasons as to why they do not succeed.

SWINBURNE, Richard, *The Coherence of Theism*, Clarendon Press, Oxford, 1977.

This is a defence of theism against philosophical criticism in which Swinburne argues that the claims made by religious believers about God are generally coherent.

Chapter 8 Morality

Aristotle, *The Nichomachean Ethics*, Penguin Books, Harmondsworth, 1976.
This is well worth reading for its insights into what is important in life as well as for its philosophical arguments.

BENTHAM, Jeremy, *An Introduction to the Principles of Morals and Legislation*, included in Mill's volume below.
In this, Bentham sets out the principles on which his programme to develop a system of morality and law is founded.

GEACH, Peter, 'Good and Evil', in *Theories of Ethics*, ed. Philippa Foot, Oxford University Press, Oxford, 1967.
This article contains Geach's account of the difference between attributive and predicative adjectives. The volume in which it appears contains a number of other useful articles.

Glover, Jonathan, *Causing Death and Saving Lives*, Penguin Books, Harmondsworth, 1977.
This considers a wide range of moral issues from a largely utilitarian framework. It has been an influential book. Glover suggests ways in which utilitarianism needs to be modified.

Hursthouse, R., *On Virtue Ethics*, Oxford University Press, Oxford, 1999.
This is intended as a textbook to familiarize students with the distinctive approach that virtue ethics provides to a variety of problems and issues in philosophy. It is an interesting introduction to the subject.

KANT, I., *Groundwork of the Metaphysics of Morals*, trans. Mary Gregor, Cambridge University Press, Cambridge, 1998.
Kant's work is notoriously difficult, but, while there are difficult passages in this text, it provides a reasonably approachable introduction to the essential elements of Kant's moral philosophy.

MILL, John Stewart, *Utilitarianism*, ed. Mary Warnock, Collins/ Fontana, Glasgow, 1962.
As well as an article by Bentham (see above), this edition contains Mill's essay 'On Liberty', which has been an influential work in political philosophy.

Nuttall, J., *Moral Questions: an introduction to ethics*, Polity Press, Oxford, 1993.
This provides an introduction to moral philosophy through looking at a number of practical moral issues. Deontological and utilitarian approaches to moral issues are examined.

Mackie, J. L., *Ethics: inventing right and wrong*, Penguin Books, Harmondsworth, 1977.
Mackie argues against there being objective values and claims that, since moral judgements make an implicit, and false, claim to objectivity, they are in error.

Rachels, James, *The Elements of Moral Philosophy*, 2nd edn, McGraw-Hill, New York, 1993.
This is an excellent and wide-ranging introduction to moral philosophy. Rachels argues for what he takes to be a minimum conception of morality that all moral theories must include.

Singer, P. (ed.), *Applied Ethics*, Oxford University Press, Oxford, 1986.
This contains some important articles, in particular by Tooley and Judith Jarvis Thomson, as well as by Singer himself, on a range of moral issues.

Smart, J. J. C., and Williams, Bernard, *Utilitarianism For and Against*, Cambridge University Press, Cambridge, 1973.
This considers utilitarianism, the case for, being presented by Smart, and the case against, being presented by Williams. Williams does not contrast utilitarianism with, say, Kantianism, but spells out the implications of adopting a consequentialism based on happiness.

Williams, Bernard, *Morality: an introduction to ethics*, Cambridge University Press, Cambridge, 1972.
A short but useful introduction to ethics, particularly good on the issue of objectivity.

Chapter 9   Political Issues

HOBBES, Thomas, *Leviathan*, Penguin Books, Harmondsworth, 1985.
There are many editions of this work available. It is Hobbes's most famous work, in which he develops his moral and political philosophy. He gives his account of man in a state of nature and explains why the state has to have absolute power.

LOCKE, John, *Second Treatise on Civil Government*, ed. Peter Laslett, Cambridge University Press, Cambridge, 1988.
Like Hobbes's *Leviathan*, Locke's *Second Treatise* contains an account of man in a state of nature, although the picture painted is different from Hobbes's. Locke develops the idea that political authority is based on consent.

NOZICK, Robert, *Anarchy, State and Utopia*, Blackwell Publishers, Oxford, 1974.
Although there are some quite difficult passages, the book is well written and quite exciting in places. I found myself being convinced against my expectations.

RAWLS, John, *A Theory of Justice*, Harvard University Press, Cambridge, MA, 1971.
Personally I found this much harder going than Nozick. The arguments are very carefully constructed.

ROUSSEAU, Jean-Jacques, *The Social Contract and Discourses*, ed. G. D. H. Cole, J. H. Brumfitt and J. C. Hall, J. M. Dent, London, 1973.
Rousseau's work presents a third account of man in a state of nature. For Rousseau, political authority comes from the general will of the people.

Wolff, Jonathan, *An Introduction to Political Philosophy*, Oxford University Press, Oxford, 1996.
An excellent introduction to the subject.

Index